Teradata 14 SQL

An Authorized Teradata Certified Professional Program Study Guide

Exam TE0-142

First Edition

ISBN 978-0-9894005-0-3
Printed by Cerulium Corporation

Stephen Wilmes
David Glenday

Copyright

Trademarks

Special Acknowledgement

A special thank you to the following individuals that contributed to the Study Guide content: Paul Derouin, Micheal McBride, David Micheletto, James Petruzzelli, Larry Rex, Eric Rivard, Paul Sinclair, and Brett Svenkeson.

About the Author - Steve Wilmes

Steve Wilmes founded Cerulium Corporation in 2007. As Chief Executive Officer, his goal is to establish Cerulium as a premier data warehousing Technology Company. Cerulium's strategic growth is globally focused on six lines of business including education, consulting, BI solutions, productivity tools, application integration and assessment services. These lines of business have been highly successful by utilizing strategic data warehousing solutions provided by Teradata that spans across the consumer, and commercial markets.

Mr. Wilmes has over 20 years of experience in the computer industry and is known to be a detail-oriented, results-focused leader. He is an internationally recognized expert in several aspects of data warehousing including hardware, software, SQL, operating systems, implementation, data integration, database administration, and BI solutions.

Mr. Wilmes earned a bachelor's degree in business administration and economics from Augsburg College and he is also a Teradata Certified Master.

Mr. Wilmes resides just outside of Columbia, South Carolina, with his wife, Becky. He has been involved with numerous civic, educational, and business organizations throughout his career. Some of his more recent associations include working with the Richland County Sheriff's Department – Region 4 Community Member, and volunteer for local organizations where he shares his technical expertise.

About the Author - David Glenday

David Glenday has been consulting on Teradata for the past 13 years. He has significant experience in Entertainment, Semiconductor and Telecommunication industries in the following lines of business: Finance, Strategic Planning, Product Development, Marketing and Sales

Mr. Glenday has leveraged his business experience, formal education and extensive Teradata knowledge to develop numerous reporting solutions. Including developing and optimizing queries, creating ETL processes and reports using Tableau, Microsoft Excel and the major BI tools.

He enjoys teaching and has taught various Teradata classes to both large groups and small across various industries.

David is skilled with Teradata's Aster product as both a SQL and SQL-MR developer and administrator. Using these skills he consults on big data predictive analytics and discovery projects using Teradata, Teradata Aster and Hadoop.

Mr. Glenday graduated with a BA in International Business in 1991 and an MBA in 1997 from California State University Fullerton. He is also a Teradata Certified Master.

Mr. Glenday is based outside Las Vegas, Nevada. He, his wife Kristi and their two children are very active with Cub Scouts, Girl Scouts and his family finds volunteering very rewarding. David enjoys flying. He has had his pilot's license since 1989 and is always looking for more time to devote to his hobby.

Table of Contents

The Teradata Certified Professional Program 1
  Pursue Teradata Certification with Confidence™ 1
  Your Teradata 14 Certification Upgrade Roadmap 2
  Certification... Knowledge Building to Mastery 6
  Path to Teradata 14 Mastery 7
  Exam Registration 7
  Where to Find More Information 8
Chapter 2: SELECT Command 9
  Certification Objectives 9
  Structured Query Language 9
  ORDER BY 13
  DISTINCT Option 17
  WHERE 19
  Compound Comparisons 20
  Comparisons Against Nulls 26
  Using IN and NOT IN 28
  Using the LIKE operator 31
  Chapter 2: Practice Questions 36
Chapter 3: HELP, SHOW, EXPLAIN Commands 39
  Certification Objectives 39
  HELP Commands 39
  SHOW Commands 48
  EXPLAIN 51
  Chapter 3: Practice Questions 55
Chapter 4: Data Conversions 59
  Certification Objectives 59
  Data Types 59
  Data Conversions 66
  CAST 69
  Rounding 70
  FORMAT 72
  Date Formats 75
  User Defined Functions (UDFs) 77
  User Defined Types (UDTs) 78

Formatting for Internationalizations 79
Chapter 4: Practice Questions 81
Chapter 5: Aggregation 85
Certification Objectives 85
Aggregations 85
GROUP BY ROLLUP 91
GROUP BY GROUPING SETS 93
GROUP BY CUBE 95
Chapter 5: Practice Questions 97
Chapter 6: Subquery Processing 103
Certification Objectives 103
Non-Scalar Subquery 104
Non-Scalar Correlated Subquery Processing 107
Scalar Subquery 109
Scalar Correlated Subquery 109
Subquery Processing with Derived tables 110
Chapter 6: Practice Questions 111
Chapter 7: Join Processing 115
Certification Objectives 115
Table Aliasing 115
Join Processing 116
INNER JOIN 117
OUTER JOIN 119
Residual Conditions 123
Evaluation Order 125
Self-Join 126
Cross Join 127
Cross Join - Continued 128
Join Consideration and PPI 128
Chapter 7: Practice Questions 130
Chapter 8: Date and Time Processing 133
Certification Objectives 133
Temporal Data Types 133
Temporal Functions 134
DATEFORM 136

Date Arithmetic ... 137
EXTRACT ... 139
Date and Time Literals ... 141
INTERVAL Processing ... 144
OVERLAPS ... 147
Chapter 8: Practice Questions ... 149
Chapter 9: Character String Processing ... 153
Certification Objectives ... 153
TRIM ... 154
CHARACTER_LENGTH and CHARACTERS Functions ... 158
OCTET Function ... 159
POSITION ... 159
INDEX ... 161
SUBSTRING and SUBSTR ... 162
Imbedded Services Functions ... 164
Chapter 9: Practice Questions ... 168
Chapter 10: OLAP Functions ... 171
Certification Objectives ... 171
Teradata On-Line Analytical Processing Functions ... 172
Cumulative SUM – SUM / OVER ... 177
Ranking Data using the ANSI RANK / OVER ... 179
RESET WHEN ... 186
SAMPLE and SAMPLEID ... 188
TOP [n] [WITH TIES] ... 193
Chapter 10: Practice Questions ... 195
Chapter 11: Set Operators ... 199
Certification Objectives ... 199
UNION ... 200
UNION ALL ... 202
INTERSECT ... 204
EXCEPT/MINUS ... 205
Multiple Set Operators and Precedence Order ... 206
Chapter 11: Practice Questions ... 208
Chapter 12: Data Manipulation ... 211
Certification Objectives ... 211

DELETE 212
INSERT 213
INSERT/SELECT 214
UPSERT 216
MERGE 217
Chapter 12: Practice Questions 220
Chapter 13: Data Interrogation 223
Certification Objectives 223
CASE 224
COALESCE 229
NULLIF 231
Chapter 13: Practice Questions 232
Chapter 14: View and Macro Processing 235
Certification Objectives 235
Views 235
Macro Processing 240
Parameterized Macros 245
Chapter 14: Practice Questions 248
Chapter 15: Transaction Processing 251
Certification Objectives 251
Transactions 251
Transaction Locking 252
Transaction Modes 257
Transaction Semantics – BTET Mode 260
ANSI Mode Transactions 261
Transaction Semantics – ANSI Mode 262
Aborting Transactions 262
Chapter 15: Practice Questions 264
Chapter 16: Data Definition Language 269
Certification Objectives 269
CREATE TABLE 269
Referential Integrity 277
Primary Key vs. Primary Index 283
Index Options 284
No Primary Index (NoPI) 287

Default Primary Index 288
CREATE TABLE AS 289
Altering a Table 290
Dropping Database Objects 291
Renaming Database Objects 292
Partitioned Tables 292
Queue Tables 298
Trigger Processing 299
Using Roles 303
Chapter 16: Practice Questions 306
Chapter 17: Temporary Tables 311
Certification Objectives 311
Before You Begin 311
Derived Tables 312
Volatile and Global Temporary Tables 317
Chapter 17: Practice Questions 326
Chapter 18: Temporal Tables 331
Certification Objectives 331
Period Temporal Data Types 332
EXPAND ON 352
Temporal Tables 354
Transaction Time and Valid Time 355
Transaction-Time 356
Valid-Time 357
Bitemporal Tables 360
AS OF Queries 377
Chapter 18: Practice Questions 380
Chapter 19: Stored Procedures 385
Certification Objectives 385
CREATE PROCEDURE 387
Stored Procedural Language (SPL) Statements 388
BEGIN / END Statements 389
Establishing Variables and Data Values 390
CALL Statement 395
Exception Handling 396

DML Statements....399
DDL Statements....400
External Stored Procedures....401
Macros or Stored Procedures for Tactical Queries....403
Chapter 19: Practice Questions....405
Appendix....407
Answers to the Chapter Practice Questions....407
Index....409

The Teradata Certified Professional Program

Pursue Teradata Certification with Confidence™

The Teradata Certified Professional Program (TCPP), launched in 1999, develops and manages Teradata's premier, and only, certification testing program. Teradata authorized training and proctored exams, available globally to customers, partners, associates, and students, are instrumental in establishing an industry-standard measure of technical competence for IT professionals using Teradata technology. Recognized as a leader in Data Warehouse RDBMS technology and valued by major global companies using Teradata, more than 57,000 Teradata Certifications have been awarded.

The new Teradata 14 Certification Track consists of seven exams that combine for achievement of six certifications and provides a logical progression for specific job roles. Starting with the core Teradata 14 Certified Professional credential, individuals have an opportunity to demonstrate knowledge by achieving Certification as a Technical Specialist, Database Administrator, Solutions Developer, Enterprise Architect, and the most prestigious Teradata Certification – Teradata 14 Certified Master.

The purpose of this Certification Exam Study Guide is to assist you with your goal to become Teradata Certified. This Guide will provide focused content areas, high level explanations around the key areas of focus, and help you to determine areas of further study prior to sitting for the Teradata Certification examination.

Although the Exam Study Guide will assist you in exam preparation, you must be knowledgeable of the subject areas in order to pass the exam. This Guide is intended for individuals who have completed the recommended training and have the recommended amount of Teradata experience. **We do not guarantee that you will pass the exam simply by reading the Exam Study Guide.** Only hard work, hands-on experience, and a positive attitude will help you to achieve exam success. We wish you the very best of luck!

"When hiring, I always look for Teradata Certified Professionals. Not only does it provide me a good understanding of a candidate's knowledge level, it also shows a commitment to continuous learning and self-improvement. That's a great trait to have in every employee and the Teradata Certified Professional Program makes it easy to recognize."
Teradata Certified Master, Insurance Industry

The flowchart and matrix below are designed to help you define a path to the knowledge, skills, and experience needed to achieve Teradata 14 Certifications.

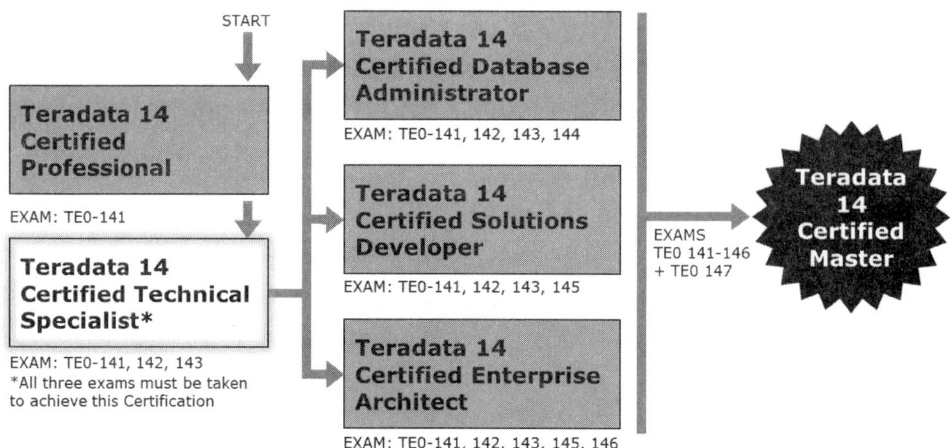

Your Teradata 14 Certification Upgrade Roadmap

Teradata 12 Certified candidates, in good standing, are eligible to take the *Teradata 14 Bridge from Teradata 12 Exam (TE0-14B).* The Bridge exam is a hybrid of all three (3) Teradata baseline Certification exams,

and covers content changes to Teradata Basics, Teradata SQL and Teradata Physical Design & Implementation exams.
A passed exam result on the Bridge exam will yield the *Teradata 14 Certified Technical Specialist* designation. A candidate may then continue on the Teradata 14 track until achieving the desired Certification level.

Teradata 14 Certifications	
Teradata 14 Certified Professional	
Exams Required: • TE0-141 – Teradata 14 Basics Must be passed before continuing on certification path	Recommended Teradata Experience: 6-12 months Recommended Preparation Courses: • Introduction to the Teradata Database
Teradata 14 Certified Technical Specialist	
Exams Required: • TE0-141 – Teradata 14 Basics • TE0-142 – Teradata 14 SQL • TE0-143 – Teradata 14 Physical Design and Implementation 3 Exams to be passed in sequential order	Recommended Teradata Experience: 1-2 years Recommended Preparation Courses: • Introduction to the Teradata Database • Teradata SQL • Advanced Teradata SQL • Physical Database Design • Physical Database Tuning

Teradata 14 Certified Database Administrator

Exams Required:
- TE0-141 – Teradata 14 Basics
- TE0-142 – Teradata 14 SQL
- TE0-143 – Teradata 14 Physical Design and Implementation
- TE0-144 – Teradata 14 Database Administration

4 Exams to be passed in sequential order

Recommended Teradata Experience:
2-3 years

Recommended Preparation Courses:
- Introduction to the Teradata Database
- Teradata SQL
- Advanced Teradata SQL
- Physical Database Design
- Physical Database Tuning
- Teradata Application Utilities
- Teradata Parallel Transporter
- Teradata Warehouse Management
- Teradata Warehouse Administration

Teradata 14 Certified Solutions Developer

Exams Required:
- TE0-141 – Teradata 14 Basics
- TE0-142 – Teradata 14 SQL
- TE0-143 – Teradata 14 Physical Design and Implementation
- TE0-145 – Teradata 14 Solutions Development

4 Exams to be passed in sequential order

Recommended Teradata Experience:
2-3 years

Recommended Preparation Courses:
- Introduction to the Teradata Database
- Teradata SQL
- Advanced Teradata SQL
- Physical Database Design
- Physical Database Tuning
- Teradata Application Utilities
- Teradata Parallel Transporter
- Teradata Application Design and Development

Teradata 14 Certified Enterprise Architect

Exams Required:

- TE0-141 – Teradata 14 Basics
- TE0-142 – Teradata 14 SQL
- TE0-143 – Teradata 14 Physical Design and Implementation
- TE0-145 – Teradata 14 Solutions Development
- TE0-146 – Teradata 14 Enterprise Architecture

5 Exams to be passed in sequential order

Recommended Teradata Experience:
2-3 years

Recommended Preparation Courses:

- Introduction to the Teradata Database
- Teradata SQL
- Advanced Teradata SQL
- Physical Database Design
- Physical Database Tuning
- Teradata Application Utilities
- Teradata Parallel Transporter
- Teradata Warehouse Management
- Teradata Warehouse Administration
- Teradata Application Design and Development

Teradata 14 Certified Master*

Exams Required:

- TE0-141 - TE0-146: Successful completion of all exams **PLUS:**
- TE0-147 – Teradata 14 Comprehensive Mastery Exam

7 Exams to be passed in sequential order

*Path for Teradata 12 Certified Masters

- TE0-147 – Teradata 14 Comprehensive Mastery Exam

Recommended Teradata Experience:
A minimum 5 years practical hands-on experience is highly recommended

Recommended Preparation Courses:

- Introduction to the Teradata Database
- Teradata SQL
- Advanced Teradata SQL
- Physical Database Design
- Physical Database Tuning
- Teradata Application Utilities
- Teradata Parallel Transporter
- Teradata Warehouse Management
- Teradata Warehouse Administration
- Teradata Application Design and Development

Note: Formal education recommendations may vary based on previous training and relevant job experience.

Certification… Knowledge Building to Mastery

Competition is fierce. Differentiate yourself while building critical IT technology knowledge and skills. Trust Teradata Certification to help you build the expertise employers are looking for in a demanding, data-driven global business environment. Teradata developed a new generation of certification exams that bring premium value to Teradata 14 Certification credentials.

Top 10 "What's new about the Teradata 14 Certification Track?"

1. Seven exams with all new content based upon the following database releases: Teradata Database 13.0, Teradata Database 13.1, Teradata Database 14.0 (including SLES 11)
2. The "*Teradata 14 Bridge from Teradata 12*" Exam allows Teradata 12 certified candidates to move, or "bridge", from the Teradata 12 Certification track to the Teradata 14 Certification track without starting the track from the beginning.
3. Eligibility-based exams to ensure compliance with Teradata Certification requirements (Bridge and Masters exams only)
4. Teradata 12 Certified Masters will take just one exam to update to Teradata 14 Certified Master status.
5. A Qualification exam is not required for those that have achieved a Teradata 12 Master Certification.
6. A new Candidate Agreement and revised security measures are in place to protect the value of your investment and integrity of all exams and certifications.
7. Newly designed electronic certificates, wallet cards, and logos.
8. An easy Certification verification process for individuals and employers.
9. More rigorous certification criteria including a combination of training, study, and practical, hands-on experience.

10. A team of dedicated, experienced, and knowledgeable individuals with a passion to help you achieve your Teradata Certification goals!

Path to Teradata 14 Mastery

A Teradata Certified Master enjoys a distinct advantage in the global marketplace. Employers seek Teradata Certified staff with verifiable knowledge and skills that support their business-critical Teradata systems. The TCPP process helps those individuals who want to deepen their knowledge and build their skills to the highest level.

The path to achieve Teradata 14 Certified Master status is summarized in the matrix below.

If You Are...	Exams Required for Teradata 14 Master Certification
Starting on the Teradata 14 Certification Track	• TE0-141 – TE0-147 All 7 Exams required
Teradata 12 Certified Master	TE0-147: Teradata 14 Comprehensive Mastery Exam

Exam Registration

All Teradata Certification exams are administered and proctored by authorized Prometric Testing Centers. Schedule exams at any authorized Prometric Testing Center by phone or online. In the US and Canada, you may call 1-877-887-6868. A listing of Prometric telephone numbers, by country, is available at:

www.prometric.com/Teradata. Some countries do not offer online registration.

Where to Find More Information

Teradata Corporation's official certification exams and credentials are developed, copyrighted, and managed solely by the Teradata Certified Professional Program (TCPP) team. There are no other Teradata authorized exams, certifications, or legitimate credentials in the IT industry. To achieve your training and certification goals, pursue only authorized processes and approved courses of study as outlined on the official TCPP Website: www.Teradata.com/Certification. A mobile app with access to all study guides, practice questions, and many more Teradata Certification and related resources is also available for a variety of devices. Please refer to the web site for additional information.

Chapter 2: SELECT Command

Certification Objectives

- ✓ Identify the correct use of comparison operators in logical expressions.
- ✓ Evaluate expressions involving NULLs.
- ✓ Identify the correct use of multiple logical expressions in a conditional expression using AND, OR, NOT.
- ✓ Identify a correctly written SELECT statement.
- ✓ Describe the characteristics of the IN, NOT IN logical predicate.
- ✓ Describe usage of built-in Teradata key words (e.g., CURRENT_DATE).

Before You Begin

You should be familiar with the following terms and concepts.

Terms	Key Concepts
Where Clause	How to use with compound comparisons
Like	Character string evaluations
Derived Columns	Arithmetic operations and column alias
Order By	Sorting data ascending and descending

Structured Query Language

Teradata uses the Teradata Structured Query Language, which runs on the Teradata Database to manage objects, data, and permissions.

SELECT Statement

The most frequently used SQL command is the SELECT statement. Because the SQL language also has INSERT, UPDATE, and DELETE statements, many people think that SELECT means "Read". It is the WHERE clause that controls reading. In the SQL language, SELECT means "return for display or processing."

The following chart shows the basic components of a SELECT statement.

SELECT	*column names and/or expressions*
FROM	*table or view name*
WHERE	*search condition(s)*
ORDER BY	*column name(s)*

Here is an example of a simple SELECT statement.

```
SELECT   *
FROM     student_table
WHERE    class_cd = 'FR'
ORDER BY last_name;
```

Figure 2.1

Note: It is recommended that every SQL statement ends with a semicolon.

Derived Columns

Frequently, the data residing in a table needs to be changed for display or reporting purposes. A derived column is created when a column in a SELECT performs a calculation.

The following example demonstrates displaying the annual salary amount of employees as a monthly salary amount.

```
SELECT  salary
        ,salary/12
FROM    employee_table;

Result: 9 rows returned

    Salary   (Salary/12)
----------   -----------
  32800.50       2733.38
  48800.00       4066.67
  64300.00       5358.33
  54590.00       4549.17
  48850.00       4070.83
  54590.00       4549.17
  35000.00       2916.67
  42788.88       3565.74
  40200.00       3350.00
```

Figure 2.2

Note: The derived column name defaults to the expression. Also, notice the column heading in the result. Each output column heading has initial capitalizations, but the column names in the SELECT are all lower case. This is because the CREATE TABLE for each of the columns headings has initial capitalizations.

Alias Column Names

In the previous example (Figure 2.2), the derived column name defaulted to the expression (salary/12). Though this might be acceptable in some cases, it isn't user-friendly.

To give an output column a different name, use AS <name> following the expression. This allows you to give user-friendly names to derived columns.

If <name> contains a blank or is a reserved word, put it inside double quotes (").

As shown below, the calculation of the annual salary amount as a weekly salary amount has a different column name.

```
SELECT  salary
        ,salary/52 AS "Weekly Salary"
FROM    employee_table;

Result: 9 rows returned

    Salary  Weekly Salary
----------  -------------
  32800.50         630.78
  48800.00         938.46
  64300.00        1236.54
  54590.00        1049.81
  48850.00         939.42
  54590.00        1049.81
  35000.00         673.08
  42788.88         822.86
  40200.00         773.08
```

Figure 2.3

ORDER BY

Relational theory states that the order of columns and the order of rows in a table are arbitrary. When you perform a query, the system will return the rows in a random manner. To request that rows be returned in some sequence, include an ORDER BY clause.

The ORDER BY clause specifies the column(s) to be used in a sort operation, which is performed on the final result set.

The following example sorts all students by their class code.

```
SELECT      last_name
            ,class_code
FROM        student_table
ORDER BY class_code;

Result: 10 rows returned

Last_name              Class_code
--------------------   ----------
Johnson                ?
Garrett                FR
Kojack                 FR
Lamp                   FR
Rieter                 JR
Bond                   JR
McCann                 SO
McCormick              SO
Phillips               SR
Craig                  SR
```

Figure 2.4

Note: ASC (ascending) is the default sort order. Nulls, represented by a "?", sort low.

The order of the output rows can be changed from ascending to descending by specifying DESC to get a descending sort, as illustrated below.

```
SELECT     last_name
           ,class_code
FROM       student_table
ORDER BY class_code DESC;

Result: 10 rows returned

Last_name                 Class_code
--------------------      ----------
Phillips                  SR
Craig                     SR
McCann                    SO
McCormick                 SO
Rieter                    JR
Bond                      JR
Garrett                   FR
Kojack                    FR
Lamp                      FR
Johnson                   ?
```

Figure 2.5

Note: Nulls sort low.

When writing queries, it can become tedious having to write the same column name repeatedly. As a convenience, the SQL language allows you to use numeric designators to specify the output columns to be used for sorting.

The following example illustrates this. It uses the class_code column position instead of the column name.

```
SELECT     last_name
           ,class_code
FROM       student_table
ORDER BY 2 DESC;

Result: 10 rows returned

Last_name              Class_code
--------------------   ----------
Phillips               SR
Craig                  SR
McCann                 SO
McCormick              SO
Rieter                 JR
Bond                   JR
Garrett                FR
Kojack                 FR
Lamp                   FR
Johnson                ?
```

Figure 2.6

Note: Using numeric column designators should be discouraged. If the order of columns following SELECT changes, the system will still sort on whatever output column is in that position. Using explicit column names will always yield the desired result regardless of their output position.

Multiple ORDER BY Columns

You are probably asking yourself these questions, "Can I mix ASCending and DESCending? Is the first column the major sort key?" The answer to both of these questions is "YES". The first column specified is the major sort column. The second and subsequent columns are minor sort columns. Separate the column names with commas.

The example below uses the column class_code as the major descending sort key, and the last_name column as an ascending sort key.

```
SELECT     last_name
           ,class_code
FROM       student_table
ORDER BY class_code DESC, last_name;

Result: 10 rows returned

Last_name              Class_code
--------------------   ----------
Craig                  SR
Phillips               SR
McCann                 SO
McCormick              SO
Bond                   JR
Rieter                 JR
Garrett                FR
Kojack                 FR
Lamp                   FR
Johnson                ?
```

Figure 2.7

DISTINCT Option

Suppose you are interested in determining the unique values that exist in a column. You could list all of the rows and do a visual scan. If the table contains thousands of rows, having the system do the scan and report just the unique values is a better solution.

The DISTINCT option specifies only one row is to be returned from any set of duplicate values that might result from the query.

DISTINCT will return only one row for each specified value. The following example returns each distinct class code.

```
SELECT     DISTINCT class_code
FROM       student_table
ORDER BY class_code;

Result: 5 rows returned

Class_code
----------
?
FR
JR
SO
SR
```

Figure 2.8

When additional columns are added to the SELECT, a row will be returned for every unique value combination of the listed columns. As illustrated below, if multiple rows have the same class_code + grade_pt values, only one of the rows will be returned.

```
SELECT    DISTINCT class_code, grade_pt
FROM      student_table
ORDER BY class_code, grade_pt;

Result: 10 rows returned

Class_code  Grade_Pt
----------  --------
?                  ?
FR               .00
FR              2.88
FR              4.00
JR              1.90
JR              3.95
SO              2.00
SO              3.80
SR              3.00
SR              3.35
```

Figure 2.9

WHERE

Other than the DISTINCT option, all of the queries we've seen returned an output row for every table row. For small tables this is probably fine. However, for large tables you will probably want to limit the output to only those rows meeting certain criteria.

The WHERE clause enables you to retrieve only the rows you need, by specifying a search condition. The following illustrates the general layout of a query with a WHERE clause.

```
SELECT  <column-names>
FROM    <table-name>
WHERE  <column-name>  <comparison>  <data-value> ;
```

Figure 2.10

The chart below lists the comparison operations that are available.

Comparison Operators:

OPERATOR	MEANING
=	Equal
< >	Not Equal
>	Greater Than
<	Less Than
>=	Greater Than or Equal To
<=	Less Than or Equal To
BETWEEN . . . AND	Inclusive range
[NOT] IN	Test against predefined set
IS [NOT] NULL	Test for nulls
EXISTS	Test for existence
LIKE	Test for partial string

Figure 2.11

The following example limits the output to only those students who have a grade_pt *Greater Than or Equal to* 3.0.

```
SELECT   student_id
        ,last_name
        ,grade_pt
FROM     student_table
WHERE    grade_pt >= 3.0 ;

Result: 5 rows returned

Student_ID  Last_name             Grade_Pt
----------  --------------------  --------
    324652  Craig                     3.35
    231222  McCormick                 3.80
    234121  Garrett                   4.00
    322133  Bond                      3.95
    123250  Phillips                  3.00
```

Figure 2.12

Compound Comparisons

Suppose you want to retrieve only those rows meeting multiple conditions. You just can't put them into a comma-separated list like you can the column names in an Order By clause.

Complex comparisons are created by combining different comparisons using Logical operators to form compound comparisons.

Figure 2.13 lists the Logical Operators.

LOGICAL OPERATOR	MEANING
AND	All specified conditions must be met.
OR	Rows meeting either condition are selected.
NOT	Negates the specified condition or specified operator.

Figure 2.13

The following example shows the generic syntax of a query with a compound condition in the WHERE clause.

```
SELECT  <column-name>
FROM    <table-name>
WHERE <column-name> <comparison> <data-value> { AND | OR }
        <column-name> <comparison> <data-value>;
```

Figure 2.14

Look at the following query, and see if you can determine how many rows will be returned.

```
SELECT    last_name
         , first_name
         , grade_pt
FROM     student_table
WHERE   grade_pt  =  3.0 AND grade_pt  =  4.0;
```

Figure 2.15

Remember, the AND operator says **both** conditions must be met. The OR condition says **either** condition must be met. Since a column in a row can only contain one value, the correct answer to the question is 'None'.

The following query changes the AND to OR and produces the output as shown.

```
SELECT    last_name
         , first_name
         , grade_pt
FROM     student_table
WHERE    grade_pt = 3.0 OR grade_pt = 4.0;

Result: 2 rows returned

Last_name              First_name    Grade_Pt
--------------------   ------------  --------
Garrett                Wendy             4.00
Phillips               Beth              3.00
```

Figure 2.16

Using AND and OR

As the WHERE clause becomes more complex, the use of parentheses in coding compound conditional statements is vital to getting the correct results. Examine the following query and its output.

```
SELECT  last_name
        ,class_code
        ,grade_pt
FROM    student_table
WHERE   grade_pt = 3.0
     OR grade_pt = 4.0
    AND class_code = 'FR' ;

Result: 2 rows returned

Last_name             Class_code  Grade_Pt
--------------------  ----------  --------
Garrett               FR              4.00
Phillips              SR              3.00
```

Figure 2.17

Can you determine why Phillips was selected? He's not a FR(eshman).

The answer lies in knowing where the SQL Parser logically puts parentheses if you don't, as illustrated in Figure 2.18.

```
SELECT  last_name
        ,class_code
        ,grade_pt
FROM    student_table
WHERE   (grade_pt = 3.0)
       OR
        (grade_pt = 4.0 AND class_code = 'FR') ;
```

Figure 2.18

As you can see, ORed conditions are treated separately from ANDed conditions. ANDed conditions are grouped together. So, to combine multiple OR conditions against a column and then have them ANDed to another test, use parentheses.

The example below illustrates this.

```
SELECT   last_name
        ,class_code
        ,grade_pt
FROM     student_table
WHERE    ( grade_pt = 3.0  OR  grade_pt = 4.0 )
         AND  class_code = 'FR' ;

Result: 1 row returned

Last_name             Class_code  Grade_Pt
--------------------  ----------  --------
Garrett               FR              4.00
```

Figure 2.19

Using the NOT Operator

Sometimes it's difficult to figure out the inverse of a complex compound conditional phrase. The solution to this is to have the system figure it out for you. Simply put the entire conditional phrase inside a set of parentheses, and preface it with the NOT logical operator.

The following example utilizes both the NOT and the AND comparison in order to identify all seniors, along with lower classmates with grade points less than 3.0.

```
SELECT     last_name
          ,first_name
          ,class_code
          ,grade_pt
FROM       student_table
WHERE NOT  ( grade_pt >= 3.0
              AND class_code  <>  'SR' ) ;

Result: 6 rows returned

Last_name              First_name    Class_code  Grade_Pt
---------------------  ------------  ----------  --------
Lamp                   Mike          FR               .00
McCann                 Andy          SO              2.00
Rieter                 Richard       JR              1.90
Kojack                 Henry         FR              2.88
Craig                  Danny         SR              3.35
Phillips               Beth          SR              3.00
```

Figure 2.20

The NOT operator reverses condition testing, including changing the AND to OR.

The WHERE clause, above,

WHERE NOT (grade_pt >= 3.0 AND class_code <> 'SR')

is equivalent to

WHERE (grade_pt < 3.0 OR class_code = 'SR')

Comparisons Against Nulls

NULL represents the absence of a data value.
NULL indicates a column has no data.
NULL represents an unknown or non-existent value.
NULL is an SQL keyword.
NULL is neither a data type nor a characteristic of data.
NULL columns may be COMPRESSed to occupy zero space in a row.

The following chart shows the result of actions on nulls.

Col1	Operator	Col2	Result
10	+	NULL	NULL
10	-	NULL	NULL
10	*	NULL	NULL
10	/	NULL	NULL
10	>	NULL	Unknown/False
10	<	NULL	Unknown/False
10	>=	NULL	Unknown/False
10	<=	NULL	Unknown/False
10	=	NULL	Unknown/False
10	<>	NULL	Unknown/False
NULL	>	NULL	Unknown/False
NULL	<	NULL	Unknown/False
NULL	>=	NULL	Unknown/False
NULL	<=	NULL	Unknown/False
NULL	=	NULL	Unknown/False
NULL	<>	NULL	Unknown/False

Figure 2.21

Based upon the chart above, the next query will return zero rows.

```
SELECT   student_id
         , last_name
         , grade_pt
         , class_code
FROM  student_table
WHERE   grade_pt = NULL   AND  class_code = NULL ;
```

Figure 2.22

Simply change the equal sign to the reserved word IS.

```
SELECT   student_id
         , last_name
         , grade_pt
         , class_code
FROM  student_table
WHERE   grade_pt IS NULL   AND  class_code IS NULL ;

Result: 1 row returned

Student_ID  Last_name                  Grade_Pt  Class_code
----------- -------------------- --------  ----------
     260000  Johnson                          ?  ?
```

Figure 2.23

Note: Numeric data is right-aligned and character data is left-aligned. This includes the default symbol (?) for a null.

Using IN and NOT IN

Suppose you want to test a column for multiple values. You could write multiple ORed comparisons, such as

WHERE <col> <condition> <val1> OR <col> <condition> <val2> OR . . .

The IN comparison operator is an easier alternative to using OR comparisons (requires less typing than the OR) and allows values to be listed within parenthesis. This is illustrated in the following query.

```
SELECT    last_name
         , class_code
         , grade_pt
FROM     student_table
WHERE    grade_pt IN ( 2.0, 3.0, 4.0 ) ;

Result: 3 rows returned

Last_name              Class_code  Grade_Pt
---------------------  ----------  --------
Garrett                FR              4.00
McCann                 SO              2.00
Phillips               SR              3.00
```

Figure 2.24

To reverse the logic, simply use NOT IN as shown below.

```
SELECT      last_name
          , class_code
          , grade_pt
FROM      student_table
WHERE     grade_pt NOT IN ( 2.0, 3.0, 4.0 ) ;

Result: 6 rows returned

Last_name              Class_code  Grade_Pt
--------------------   ----------  --------
Lamp                   FR               .00
McCormick              SO              3.80
Rieter                 JR              1.90
Bond                   JR              3.95
Kojack                 FR              2.88
Craig                  SR              3.35
```

Figure 2.25

Using BETWEEN

There is another conditional operator, called BETWEEN, that can be used to test a column for values within a given range.

BETWEEN is simpler than either a compound OR comparison, or an IN comparison (a lengthy value list of sequential numbers would be required). A query using the BETWEEN comparison operator is shown below in Figure 2.26.

```
SELECT    Grade_Pt
FROM      Student_Table
WHERE     Grade_Pt BETWEEN 2.0 and 4.0 ;

Result: 7 rows returned

Grade_Pt
--------
    2.88
    3.80
    3.35
    3.95
    4.00
    2.00
    3.00
```

Figure 2.26

An important thing to remember is that BETWEEN is inclusive. Notice, in the above example, that 2.0 and 4.0 are included in the answer set.

Using the LIKE operator

Another frequently used comparison operator is the LIKE operator. The LIKE operator can only be used to search for a string of consecutive characters within character data. It cannot be used on numeric data.

The following shows the general syntax and meaning of the LIKE components.

Syntax: *expression* [NOT] LIKE [ALL | ANY | SOME] *pattern_expression* [ESCAPE *escape_character*]

Syntax Element . . .	**Specifies . . .**
expression	a character string or character string expression argument to be searched for the substring *pattern_expression.*
pattern_expression	a character expression for which *expression* is to be searched.
ANY SOME	Compares a value to each value in a list or returned by a query. SOME is a synonym for ANY.
ALL	Compares a single value against a set of data from a query.
ESCAPE *escape_character*	Defines a wildcard character to be treated as a normal, non-control character.

Figure 2.27

In creating a search pattern, you can use wildcard characters to represent one or more characters that can be ignored by the comparison logic.

The following chart describes the wildcard characters and their meaning.

Character	Description
% (Percent sign)	Represents any string of zero or more arbitrary characters. Any string of characters is acceptable as a replacement for the percent.
_ (Underscore)	Represents exactly one arbitrary character. Any single character is acceptable in the position in which the underscore character appears, but a character must exist in that position.

Figure 2.28

The following example returns all employee rows where the last name of the employee begins with 'St'.

```
SELECT last_name
FROM    employee_table
WHERE last_name  LIKE 'St%' ;

Result: 2 rows returned

Last_name
--------------------
Student
Strickland
```

Figure 2.29

In doing comparisons against character data, it is vital to know whether you are running in Teradata (BT/ET) transaction mode, or in ANSI transaction mode. The issue is case sensitivity. Teradata is NOT CASESPECIFIC, whereas ANSI is CASESPECIFIC.

The results from the following query illustrate this issue.

SELECT last_name
FROM employee_table
WHERE last_name LIKE 'st%' ;

In BTET transaction mode:

```
Result: 2 rows returned

Last_name
--------------------
Student
Strickland
```

In ANSI transaction mode:

```
*** Query completed. No rows found.
*** Total elapsed time was 1 second.
```

Figure 2.30

Built-In Functions

Teradata SQL contains built-in functions, which return information about the system. These built-in functions can be used anywhere that a literal can appear.

FUNCTION	INFORMATION RETURNED	ANSI
ACCOUNT	Returns the account string for the current user.	N
CURRENT_DATE	Returns the current date.	Y
CURRENT_ROLE	Returns the current role of the current authorized user.	N*
CURRENT_TIME	Returns the current time.	Y
CURRENT_TIMESTAMP	Returns the current timestamp.	Y
CURRENT_USER	Provides the user name of the current authorized user.	N*
DATABASE	Returns the name of the default database for the current user.	N
DATE	Returns the current date.	N
PROFILE	Returns the current profile for the session or NULL if none.	N
ROLE	Returns the session current role.	N
SESSION	Returns the number of the session for the current user.	N
TEMPORAL_DATE	Returns the current transaction date where the evaluation is based on the session time zone.	N
TEMPORAL_TIMESTAMP	Returns the current transaction timestamp where the evaluation is based on the session time zone.	N
TIME	Returns the current time.	N
USER	Provides the session user name.	Y

Figure 2.31

Note: *CURRENT_ROLE and *CURRENT_USER are consistent with ANSI SQL:2008 usage.

Chapter 2: Practice Questions

1. Using the numbers of 1-4, put the following values in proper descending order.
   a. __ 0.123
   b. __ Null
   c. __ 0.321
   d. __ 0.001

2. Given c1 values of 0,1,2,3,4,5,6,7,8,9, which query will return the most rows?
   a. SELECT * FROM t1 WHERE c1 IN (2,5);
   b. SELECT * FROM t1 WHERE c1 BETWEEN 2 AND 5 ;
   c. SELECT * FROM t1 WHERE c1 NOT IN (2,5);
   d. SELECT * FROM t1 WHERE c1 NOT BETWEEN 2 AND 5;

3. Given c1 values of 0,1,2,3,4,5,6,7,8,9, which query will return 6 rows?
   a. SELECT * FROM t1 WHERE c1 IN (2,5);
   b. SELECT * FROM t1 WHERE c1 BETWEEN 2 AND 5 ;
   c. SELECT * FROM t1 WHERE c1 NOT IN (2,5);
   d. SELECT * FROM t1 WHERE c1 NOT BETWEEN 2 AND 5;

4. Which built-in function is ANSI SQL:2008 compliant?
   a. DATE
   b. TIME
   c. ROLE
   d. USER
   e. ACCOUNT

5. Given the following WHERE clause, where will the Parser logically place parentheses?

   WHERE c1 NOT IN(1,2,3) AND c2 = 5 AND c3 = c4 OR c3 = c5 OR c5 < C6

   a. WHERE (c1 NOT IN(1,2,3) AND c2 = 5 AND c3 = c4) OR (c3 = c5 OR c5 < C6)
   b. WHERE c1 NOT IN(1,2,3) AND c2 = 5 AND c3 = c4 OR (c3 = c5 OR c5 < C6)
   c. WHERE (c1 NOT IN(1,2,3) AND c2 = 5 AND c3 = c4) OR (c3 = c5) OR (c5 < C6)
   d. WHERE c1 NOT IN(1,2,3) AND c2 = 5 AND (c3 = c4 OR c3 = c5) OR c5 < C6

6. Given the following Course_Table rows:

Course_ID	Course_name	Credits	Seats
100	Teradata Basics	3	50
200	Introduction to SQL	3	20
210	Advanced SQL	3	22
220	TD12 SQL Features	2	25
300	Physical Database Tuning	4	20
400	Database Administration	4	16

   How many rows will be returned by the following query?

   SEL * FROM course_table WHERE course_name LIKE '%t%u%' ORDER BY 1;

   a. 0
   b. 1
   c. 2
   d. 3
   e. 4

Chapter Notes

Utilize this space for notes, key points to remember, diagrams, areas of further study, etc.

Chapter 3: HELP, SHOW, EXPLAIN Commands

Certification Objectives

- ✓ Describe usage of HELP, SHOW, and EXPLAIN commands and their expected outputs.
- ✓ Identify characteristics of a query that indicates optimization opportunities.

Before You Begin

You should be familiar with the following terms and concepts.

Terms	Key Concepts
HELP	How to use the HELP commands
SHOW	Understand the types of SHOW commands
EXPLAIN	What are the key concepts of an Explain

HELP Commands

What columns does this table contain? What objects are stored in this database? Is my session in Teradata transaction mode or ANSI transaction mode? Whenever you need information like this, all you need to do is to ask for HELP.

The HELP commands display information about:

- Database objects
- Session Characteristics

- SQL syntax

The following chart in Figure 3.1, describe the various HELP commands.

COMMAND	**RETURNS**
HELP CAST	Returns the available cast operations for the specified UDT.
HELP COLUMN	Displays the attributes of a column, including whether it is a single-column primary or secondary index and, if so, whether it is unique.
HELP CONSTRAINT	Displays the attributes for a specific *named* constraint on a table.
HELP DATABASE	Displays the attributes, sorted by object name, for all tables, views, join indexes, hash indexes, SQL procedures, user-defined functions, and macros contained by the specified database.
HELP ERROR TABLE	Displays the attributes for the specified error table.
HELP FUNCTION	Reports the specific function name, list of parameters, the data types of the parameters, whether the function is used to compress or decompress character or graphic data, and any comments associated with the parameters for SQL, scalar, aggregate, and table functions.
HELP HASH INDEX	Displays the data types of the columns defined by a particular hash index.
HELP INDEX	Displays the attributes for the primary and secondary indexes defined for a base data table, hash index, or join index.
HELP MACRO	Displays the attributes for the specified macro.
HELP METHHOD	Displays the parameter list of the specified method.
HELP PROCEDURE	Displays the attribute and format parameters

	for each parameter of a procedure or just the creation time attributes for the specified procedure.
HELP SESSION	Displays attribute information for the user of the current session or just the row-level constraint attribute information for the user of the current session.
HELP STATISTICS	Reports the summary statistics that have been collected in *DBC.StatsTbl* for the specified table, join index, or hash index.
HELP TRANSFORM	Reports the *fromsql* and *tosql* transform routines for the specified UDT or predefined data type.
HELP TABLE	Displays the attributes for the specified base data table.
HELP TRIGGER	Displays the attributes for the specified trigger.
HELP TYPE	Displays the attributes for a UDT and, optionally, all the attributes of a structured UDT or all the methods associated with the UDT.
HELP USER	Displays the attributes, sorted by object name, for all tables, views, join indexes, hash indexes, SQL procedures, user-defined functions, and macros contained by the specified user.
HELP VIEW	Displays the attributes for the specified view or recursive view.
HELP VOLATILE TABLE	Displays the attributes for the requested volatile table.
HELP (Online Form)	Displays syntax help for any SQL statement or client utility command.

Figure 3.1

The following charts provide syntax examples to help you get started.

Databases and Users

HELP DATABASE	CSQL_CLASS;
HELP USER	CSQL01;

Figure 3.2

Tables, Views, and Macros

HELP TABLE	employee_table ;
HELP VIEW	employee_v ;
HELP MACRO	new_sales ;
HELP COLUMN	* FROM employee_table ; employee_table.* ; employee_table.last_name ; CSQL_VIEWS.employee_v.* ; CSQL_VIEWS.employee_v.last_name ;
HELP INDEX	employee_table ;
HELP STATISTICS	employee_table ;
HELP CONSTRAINT	employee_table.over_21 ;
HELP SESSION ;	

Figure 3.3

HELP DATABASE

The following figure shows a HELP DATABASE command and the information returned by the system.

HELP DATABASE CSQL_CLASS;

```
Table/View/Macro name          Kind Comment
------------------------------ ---- -----------------
b_words                        T     ?
Course_table                   T     ?
Customer_table                 T     ?
date_time                      T     ?
Department_table               T     ?
Employee_table                 T     ?
Emp_Job_table                  T     ?
Job_table                      T     ?
Names_table                    T     ?
Order_table                    T     ?
Sales_table                    T     ?
Stats_Table                    T     ?
Student_Course_table           T     ?
Student_table                  T     ?
```

Figure 3.4

HELP TABLE

The HELP command in Figure 3.5 returns information about the columns in the employee_table. The chart in Figure 3.6 describes the meaning of the Type code shown as the second column of output.

```
HELP TABLE employee_table ;

Column Name                    Type Comment
------------------------------ ---- ------------
Employee_No                    I    Primary Key
Dept_No                        I2   Foreign Key
Mgr_Employee_No                I    Foreign Key
Last_name                      CF
First_name                     CV
Salary                         D    ?
```

Figure 3.5

Data types on the HELP TABLE are:

DATA TYPE CODE	DESCRIPTION
A1	ARRAY (one dimensional)
AN	ARRAY (multidimensional)
AT	TIME
BF	BYTE
BO	BINARY LARGE OBJECT
BV	BYTE VARYING
CF	CHARACTER (fixed)
CO	CHARACTER LARGE OBJECT
CV	CHARACTER (varying)
D	DECIMAL
D	NUMERIC
DA	DATE

DH	INTERVAL DAY TO HOUR
DM	INTERVAL DAY TO MINUTE
DS	INTERVAL DAY TO SECOND
DY	INTERVAL DAY
F	DOUBLE PRECISION
F	FLOAT
F	REAL
HM	INTERVAL HOUR TO MINUTE
HR	INTERVAL HOUR
HS	INTERVAL HOUR TO SECOND
I	INTEGER
I1	BYTEINT
I2	SMALLINT
I8	BIGINT
MI	INTERVAL MINUTE
MO	INTERVAL MONTH
MS	INTERVAL MINUTE TO SECOND
N	NUMBER
PD	PERIOD(DATE)
PM	PERIOD(TIMESTAMP(n) WITH TIME ZONE)
PS	PERIOD(TIMESTAMP(n))
PT	PERIOD(TIME(n))
PZ	PERIOD(TIME(n) WITH TIME ZONE)
SC	INTERVAL SECOND
SZ	TIMESTAMP WITH TIME ZONE
TS	TIMESTAMP
TZ	TIME WITH TIME ZONE
UT	USER-DEFINED TYPE (all types)
YM	INTERVAL YEAR TO MONTH
YR	INTERVAL YEAR

Figure 3.6

HELP INDEX

The previous Help command showed the columns in the Employee_table, but not the indexes. To see the indexes, execute the following command.

```
HELP INDEX employee_table;

 *** Help information returned. 3 rows.
 *** Total elapsed time was 1 second.

                   Unique? Y
  Primary//or//Secondary? P
              Column Names Employee_No
                  Index Id 1
         Approximate Count 6
                Index Name ?
Ordered//or//Partitioned? H
                   Unique? N
  Primary//or//Secondary? S
              Column Names Last_name
                  Index Id 4
         Approximate Count 3
                Index Name ?
Ordered//or//Partitioned? H
                   Unique? N
  Primary//or//Secondary? S
              Column Names Dept_No
                  Index Id 8
         Approximate Count 3
                Index Name ?
Ordered//or//Partitioned? H
```

Figure 3.7

HELP 'SQL'

The system has a built-in syntax guide that is available through the following HELP command. Notice that SQL must be inside of single quotes. The output shown is just a partial listing.

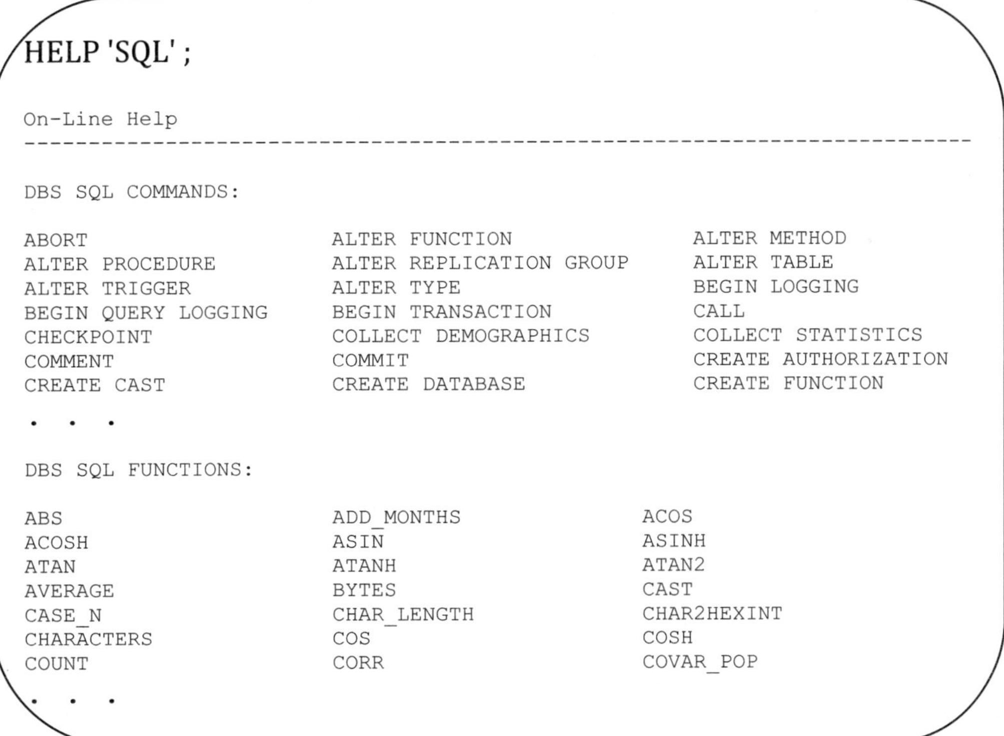

```
HELP 'SQL' ;

On-Line Help
---------------------------------------------------------------------------

DBS SQL COMMANDS:

ABORT                   ALTER FUNCTION              ALTER METHOD
ALTER PROCEDURE         ALTER REPLICATION GROUP     ALTER TABLE
ALTER TRIGGER           ALTER TYPE                  BEGIN LOGGING
BEGIN QUERY LOGGING     BEGIN TRANSACTION           CALL
CHECKPOINT              COLLECT DEMOGRAPHICS        COLLECT STATISTICS
COMMENT                 COMMIT                      CREATE AUTHORIZATION
CREATE CAST             CREATE DATABASE             CREATE FUNCTION
.  .  .

DBS SQL FUNCTIONS:

ABS                     ADD_MONTHS              ACOS
ACOSH                   ASIN                    ASINH
ATAN                    ATANH                   ATAN2
AVERAGE                 BYTES                   CAST
CASE_N                  CHAR_LENGTH             CHAR2HEXINT
CHARACTERS              COS                     COSH
COUNT                   CORR                    COVAR_POP
.  .  .
```

Figure 3.8

SHOW Commands

Though the HELP command returns useful information, it sometimes lacks the detail needed. To get the most information about an object, the SHOW command displays the actual CREATE syntax.

The following chart lists a few of the SHOW commands. To get a complete list, do HELP 'SQL SHOW';

Command	**Returns**
SHOW TABLE tablename ;	CREATE TABLE statement
SHOW VIEW viewname ;	CREATE VIEW statement
SHOW MACRO macroname ;	CREATE MACRO statement
SHOW STATISTICS ON objectname;	COLLECT STATISTICS statement
SHOW STATISTICS VALUES ON objectname;	Detailed statistics from the DBC.StatsTbl

Figure 3.9

SHOW TABLE

The SHOW TABLE commands return the fully expanded CREATE TABLE syntax. Compare the detail provided by the following SHOW command to the HELP command in Figure 3.5.

SHOW TABLE employee_table ;

```
CREATE SET TABLE CSQL_CLASS.employee_table ,NO FALLBACK ,
     NO BEFORE JOURNAL,
     NO AFTER JOURNAL,
     CHECKSUM = DEFAULT
     (
      Employee_No INTEGER,
      Dept_No SMALLINT,
      Mgr_Employee_No INTEGER,
      Last_name CHAR(20) CHARACTER SET LATIN
                NOT CASESPECIFIC,
      First_name VARCHAR(12) CHARACTER SET LATIN
                NOT CASESPECIFIC,
      Salary DECIMAL(8,2))
UNIQUE PRIMARY INDEX ( Employee_No )
INDEX ( Last_name )
INDEX ( Dept_No );
```

Figure 3.10

SHOW VIEW

Unlike the SHOW TABLE, the SHOW VIEW command returns just the syntax that was entered to create the view, exactly the way it was entered. This is illustrated by the following example.

SHOW VIEW CSQL_VIEWS.customer_v ;

```
CV  CSQL_VIEWS.Customer_v  (Cust_no, Cust_name, Phone)  AS
sel  customer_number, Customer_name, Phone_number
from CSQL_CLASS.customer_table;
```

Figure 3.11

SHOW MACRO

The following example shows the output from a SHOW MACRO command.

SHOW MACRO enrollments;

```
Create macro enrollments as
(select last_name
     ,first_name
     ,sc.course_id
     ,course_name
From      student_table as s
Inner join
      Student_course_table as sc
On    s.student_id = sc.student_id
Inner join
      Course_table c
On    sc.course_id = c.course_id
Order by sc.course_id, last_name;
);
```

Figure 3.12

SHOW STATISTICS

The following example shows the output from a SHOW STATISTICS command.

```
SHOW STATISTICS ON CSQL_CLASS.Employee_Table;

COLLECT STATISTICS
            COLUMN ( Last_name ) ,
            COLUMN ( Dept_No ) ,
            COLUMN ( Mgr_employee_no )
                ON CSQL_CLASS.Employee_table ;
```

Figure 3.13

EXPLAIN

When the word EXPLAIN appears in front of any SQL statement, the statement is fully parsed, but instead of the execution plan being sent to the AMPs, it is sent to the Explain facility which translates the processing steps into English and returns the translation to the user.

EXPLAIN is a powerful tool to help understand what the system will do if the SQL is actually executed.

The following is an example of an EXPLAIN of a simple SELECT.

EXPLAIN SELECT * FROM employee_table ;

```
*** Help information returned. 12 rows.
 *** Total elapsed time was 1 second.

Explanation
-------------------------------------------------------------------
  1) First, we lock a distinct CSQL_CLASS."pseudo table" for read
     on a RowHash to prevent global deadlock for
     CSQL_CLASS.employee_table.
  2) Next, we lock CSQL_CLASS.employee_table for read.
  3) We do an all-AMPs RETRIEVE step from
     CSQL_CLASS.employee_table by way of an all-rows scan with no
     residual conditions into Spool 1 (group_amps), which is built
     locally on the AMPs.  The size of Spool 1 is estimated with
     low confidence to be 12 rows (1,092 bytes).  The estimated
     time for this step is 0.03 seconds.
  4) Finally, we send out an END TRANSACTION step to all AMPs
     involved in processing the request.
  >  The contents of Spool 1 are sent back to the user as the
     result of statement 1.  The total estimated time is 0.03
     seconds.
```

Figure 3.14

EXPLAIN Terminology

Most EXPLAIN text is easy to understand. The following additional definitions may be helpful:

TERM	MEANING
... (Last Use) ...	A spool file is no longer needed and will be released when this step completes.
... with no residual conditions ...	All applicable conditions have been applied to the rows.
... END TRANSACTION ...	Transaction locks are released, and changes are committed.
... eliminating duplicate rows ...	(Duplicate rows only exist in spool files, not set tables.) Doing a DISTINCT operation.
... by way of the sort key in spool field1 ...	Field1 is created to allow a tag sort.
... we do an ABORT test ...	Caused by an ABORT or ROLLBACK statement.
... by way of a traversal of index #n extracting row ids only ...	A spool file is built containing the Row IDs found in a secondary index (index #n).
... we do a SMS (set manipulation step) ...	Combining rows using a UNION, EXCEPT, or INTERSECT operator.
... we do a BMSMS (bit map set manipulation step)	Doing a NUSI Bit Map operation.
... which is redistributed by hash code to all AMPs. *... which is duplicated on all AMPs.*	Relocating data in preparation for a join.
... (one_AMP) or (group_AMPs)	indicates one AMP or a subset of AMPs will be used instead of all AMPs.

... ("NOT (table_name.column_name IS NULL)")	feature in which the optimizer realizes that the column being joined to is NOT NULL or has referential integrity.
... Joined using a row id join ...	indicates a join back condition with a join index.

Figure 3.15

The various "confidence" phrases and their meaning are provided in the following chart.

PHRASE	**MEANING**
. . . with high confidence . . .	– Restricting conditions exist on index(es) or column(s) that have collected statistics.
. . . with low confidence . . .	– Restricting conditions exist on index(es) having no statistics, but estimates can be based upon a sampling of the index(es). – Restricting conditions exist on index(es) or column(s) that have collected statistics but are "ANDed" together with conditions on non-indexed columns. – Restricting conditions exist on index(es) or column(s) that have collected statistics but are "ORed" together with other conditions.
. . . with no confidence . . .	– Conditions outside the above.
. . . index join confidence . . .	- Only reported for join operations

Figure 3.16

Chapter 3: Practice Questions

1. Which of the following is invalid?
    a. EXPLAIN SELECT CURRENT_DATE;
    b. EXPLAIN HELP TABLE Employee_Table;
    c. EXPLAIN SHOW STATISTICS ON Employee_Table;
    d. EXPLAIN EXPLAIN;

2. Which of the following commands is invalid?
    a. HELP JOIN INDEX *joinindexname*;
    b. HELP HASH INDEX *hashindexname*;
    c. HELP ERROR TABLE *tablename*;
    d. HELP TRIGGER *triggername*;

3. The timings provided by EXPLAIN:
    a. Are measured clock time.
    b. Are anticipated execution times on a heavily-loaded system.
    c. Will change throughout the day.
    d. Are cost estimates for comparison purposes.

4. Which of the following phrases would not appear in an Explain of a UNION ALL operation?
    a. We do an SMS (Set Manipulation Step) . . .
    b. End Transaction
    c. last use
    d. eliminating duplicate rows . . .

5. Which of the following commands would be useful in interpreting the Explain phrase "by way of a traversal of index # 8"?
   a. SHOW INDEX
   b. HELP INDEX
   c. HELP TABLE
   d. SHOW JOIN INDEX

6. Which of the following will return online syntax about the MERGE INTO command?
   a. HELP 'SQL MERGE INTO';
   b. HELP MERGE INTO;
   c. HELP 'MERGE INTO';
   d. HELP 'SQL MERGE';

Chapter Notes

Utilize this space for notes, key points to remember, diagrams, areas of further study, etc.

Chapter 4: Data Conversions

Certification Objectives

- ✓ Given a scenario, identify the ramifications of explicit conversions from one data type to another.
- ✓ Given a scenario, identify the ramifications of implicit conversions from one data type to another.
- ✓ Given a scenario using CAST, identify the proper result.
- ✓ Identify formatting options for internationalization of various data types.
- ✓ Identify the characteristics of ANSI CAST and Teradata extensions for data conversion.

Before You Begin

You should be familiar with the following terms and concepts.

Terms	Key Concepts
Data Types	What are the data types supported and how to do conversions
Rounding	How is this handled with decimal data
Formatting	Options available including internationalizations

Data Types

All data in a database will have characteristics associated with it called attributes. Attributes would include a data type and length. A data type specifies the type and format of the data. The data value must conform to the rules and characteristics of the data type. A column in a relational database may only store one type of data and data types may not be mixed. Teradata supports most standard ANSI data types.

Teradata allows you to use either the specific data type name, or the data type alias when defining a column's data type, but will actually use the full data type name in the table definition. Teradata will convert data types when necessary.

The following charts, of Figure 4.1, show the characteristics of the supported data types.

Byte Data	**Description**
BLOB	Binary Large Object Max: 2,097,088,000 bytes which is the default
BYTE (size)	Fixed length Binary string. Default: (1) Max: 64,000 bytes
VARBYTE (size)	Variable length Binary string. Default: (1) Max: 64,000 bytes

Numeric Data	**Description**
BIGINT	Whole number Range: -9,223,372,036,854,775,808 to 9,223,372,036,854,775,807 8 bytes with the least significant byte first
BYTEINT	Whole number Range: -128 to 127 1 byte
SMALLINT	Whole number Range: -32,768 to 32,767 2 bytes
INTEGER	Whole number. Range: -2,147,483,648 to 2,147,483,647 4 bytes

<table>
<tr><td>DECIMAL [(n[,m])]</td><td>Decimal number of n digits, with m digits to the right of the decimal point.
Default: DECIMAL(5,0)
<table>
<tr><th>Number of digits (n)</th><th>Number of bytes</th></tr>
<tr><td>1 to 2</td><td>1</td></tr>
<tr><td>3 to 4</td><td>2</td></tr>
<tr><td>5 to 9</td><td>4</td></tr>
<tr><td>10 to 18</td><td>8</td></tr>
<tr><td>19 to 38</td><td>16</td></tr>
</table></td></tr>
<tr><td>NUMERIC [(n [, m])]</td><td>Synonym for DECIMAL</td></tr>
<tr><td>FLOAT (n)</td><td>Floating Point number.
IEEE format.
Range: $2.226*10^{-308}$ to $1.797*10^{308}$
8 bytes</td></tr>
<tr><td>DOUBLE PRECISION</td><td>Synonym for FLOAT</td></tr>
<tr><td>REAL</td><td>Synonym for FLOAT</td></tr>
<tr><td>NUMBER</td><td>Numeric value with optional precision and scale limitations.
Precision: 38 digits
0 to 18 bytes = Exponent (1)+ Mantissa(17)
May be used wherever DECIMAL or FLOAT are supported.</td></tr>
</table>

Date/Time	**Description**
DATE	Special type of integer. (((Calendar year) – 1900) * 10000) + MM * 100 + DD. Use ANSI Date form for compatibility. 4 bytes
TIME (n)	Stored as HHMMSS.nnnnnn 6 bytes
TIMESTAMP (n)	Stored as YYMMDDHHMMSS.nnnnnn 10 bytes
TIME (n) WITH TIME ZONE	Stored as HHMMSS.nnnnnn+HHMM 8 bytes
TIMESTAMP (n) WITH TIME ZONE	Stored as YYMMDDHHMMSS.nnnnnn+HHMM 12 bytes
PERIOD(DATE)	Stored as two DATE values 8 bytes
PERIOD(TIME)	Stored as two TIME values 16 bytes
PERIOD(TIME WITH TIME ZONE)	Stored as two TIME WITH TIME ZONE values 16 bytes
PERIOD(TIMESTAMP)	Stored as two TIMESTAMP values 16 or 24 bytes
PERIOD(TIMESTAMP WITH TIME ZONE)	Stored as two TIMESTAMP WITH TIME ZONE values 16 or 24 bytes

Interval data types	Description
INTERVAL YEAR [(n)]	Number of years (n) = 1 to 4 digits for years Default = 2 2 bytes
INTERVAL MONTH [(n)]	Number of months (n) = 1 to 4 digits for months Default = 2 2 bytes
INTERVAL DAY [(n)]	Number of days (n) = 1 to 4 digits for days Default = 2 2 bytes
INTERVAL YEAR [(n)] TO MONTH	Number of years and months (n) = 1 to 4 digits for years Default = 2 4 bytes
INTERVAL HOUR [(n)]	Number of hours (n) = 1 to 4 digits for years Default = 2 2 bytes
INTERVAL MINUTE [(n)]	Number of minutes (n) = 1 to 4 digits for days Default = 2 2 bytes
INTERVAL SECOND [(n)]	Number of seconds (n) = 1 to 4 digits for days Default = 2 (m) = 0 to 6 digits for fractional seconds Default = 6 6 bytes
INTERVAL DAY [(n)] TO HOUR	Number of days and hours (n) = 1 to 4 digits for days Default = 2 4 bytes

INTERVAL DAY [(n)] TO MINUTE	Number of days, hours and minutes (n) = 1 to 4 digits for days Default = 2 HOUR is always 2 digits and MINUTE is always 2 digits 8 bytes
INTERVAL DAY [(n)] TO SECOND [(m)]	Number of days, hours, minutes, and seconds (n) = 1 to 4 digits for days Default = 2 (m) = 0 to 6 digits for fractional seconds Default = 6 10 bytes
INTERVAL HOUR TO MINUTE	Number of hours and minutes (n) = 1 to 4 digits for hours Default = 2 4 bytes
INTERVAL HOUR [(n)] TO SECOND [(m)]	Number of hours, minutes and seconds (n) = 1 to 4 digits for hours Default = 2 (m) = 0 to 6 digits for fractional seconds Default = 6 8 bytes
INTERVAL MINUTE [(n)] TO SECOND [(m)]	Number of minutes and seconds (n) = 1 to 4 digits for minutes Default = 2 (m) = 0 to 6 digits for fractional seconds Default = 6 6 bytes

Character / Graphic Data Types	Description
CHAR (size)	Fixed length character data. Max: 64,000
CLOB	Character Large Object Max: 2,097,088,000 which is the default
VARCHAR (size) or CHARACTER VARYING (size)	Variable length character data Max: 64,000
LONG VARCHAR	Equivalent to VARCHAR(64000)
GRAPHIC (size)	Fixed length graphic data. 2 bytes per character Max: 32,000 double-byte characters
LONG VARGRAPHIC	Fixed length graphic data. 32,000 double-byte characters
VARGRAPHIC (size)	Variable length graphic data. 2 bytes per character Max: 32,000 double-byte characters

Figure 4.1

Note:

1. DATE is supported both in its Teradata form and in the preferred ANSI DateTime form. For new development, define DATE using ANSI DATE type.
2. The GRAPHIC types are equivalent to the type CHARACTER SET GRAPHIC, which is the form to use for all new development.
3. The CREATE TYPE statement determines the name of a UDT.

Data Conversions

Normally, operands must be of the same data type to do a comparison. One of the powerful abilities of Teradata SQL is the ability to compare operands of different data types. If two operands are not of the same data type, Teradata will automatically convert one, or both, to a common data type and then do the comparison.

As an example, comparisons between character and numeric data types require that the character field be convertible to a numeric value.

Implicit conversions (implied CAST) are a Teradata extension to the ANSI SQL-2003 standard.

If operand data types differ, then the Teradata Database performs an implied CAST according to the following table in Figure 4.2.

IF one expression operand is . . .	**AND the other expression operand is . . .**	**THEN Teradata compares the data as . . .**
Character	Character	Character
Character	Date	Date
Character	BYTEINT SMALLINT INTEGER FLOAT	FLOAT
Character	Period	Period
CHAR(k) VARCHAR(k) where k > 16	BIGINT DECIMAL (m,n) where m <= 16	FLOAT
CHAR(k) VARCHAR(k)`	NUMBER and k <=16	FLOAT
BYTEINT	SMALLINT	SMALLINT
BYTEINT	INTEGER	INTEGER

SMALLINT		
BYTEINT SMALLINT INTEGER BIGINT	BIGINT	BIGINT
BYTEINT	DECIMAL (m,n) where m <= 18 and m-n >= 3	DECIMAL (18,n)
SMALLINT	DECIMAL (m,n) where m <= 18 and m-n >= 5	DECIMAL (18,n)
INTEGER DATE	DECIMAL (m,n) where m <= 18 and m-n >= 10	DECIMAL (18,n)
BYTEINT	DECIMAL (m,n) where m > 18 or m-n < 3	DECIMAL(38, n)
SMALLINT	DECIMAL (m,n) where m > 18 or m-n < 5	DECIMAL(38, n)
INTEGER DATE	DECIMAL (m,n) where m > 18 or m-n < 10	DECIMAL(38, n)
BIGINT	DECIMAL(m,n)	DECIMAL(38, n)
DECIMAL (m,n)	DECIMAL(*k*,*j*) where max(*m*-*n*,*k*-*j*) + max(*j*,*n*) <= 18	DECIMAL(18,max(*j*,*n*))
DECIMAL (m,n)	DECIMAL(*k*,*j*) where max(*m*-*n*,*k*-*j*) + max(*j*,*n*) > 18	DECIMAL(38,max(*j*,*n*))
BYTEINT SMALLINT INTEGER BIGINT DECIMAL(m,n)	NUMBER(k,j) NUMBER(k) NUMBER(*,j) NUMBER	NUMBER

NUMBER(m,n) NUMBER(m) NUMBER(*,n) NUMBER		
DATE	BYTEINT SMALLINT INTEGER	INTEGER
DATE	BIGINT	BIGINT
DATE	FLOAT	FLOAT
FLOAT	BYTEINT SMALLINT INTEGER BIGINT DECIMAL(m,n) NUMBER(m,n) NUMBER(m) NUMBER(*,n) NUMBER	FLOAT
Period	Character	Period

Figure 4.2

CAST

When writing a query, it is sometimes necessary to redefine a data type. For example, a column with a character data type containing date information might need to be converted into a date data type in order to perform date calculations.

In the following example, notice that character data is left justified and numeric data is right justified.

```
SELECT CAST('ABCDE' AS CHAR(2) ) AS C1
       ,CAST(129 AS CHAR(6)) AS C2
       ,CAST(127 AS BYTEINT) AS B1
       ,CAST(128 AS SMALLINT) AS S1
       ,CAST(129 AS INTEGER ) AS I1;

Result: 1 row returned

C1  C2        B1      S1           I1
--  ------  ----  ------  -----------
AB  129      127     128          129
```

Figure 4.3

Notice that Teradata mode allowed the string value in the first line to be truncated. In ANSI mode, truncation of string data is forbidden, so the first line of the query would cause the entire query to fail with the following error message.

```
*** Failure 3996 Right truncation of string data.
```

By eliminating any truncation of string data, the query will work.

```
SELECT CAST('ABCDE' AS CHAR(6) )  AS C1
         ,CAST(129 AS CHAR(6))  AS C2
         ,CAST(127 AS BYTEINT) AS B1
         ,CAST(128 AS SMALLINT)  AS S1
         ,CAST(129 AS INTEGER )  AS I1;

Result: 1 row returned

C1       C2         B1       S1            I1
------   ------   ----   ------   -----------
ABCDE    129       127      128           129
```

Figure 4.4

Rounding

The rounding of fractional decimal values plays an important role in many financial and scientific calculations. Understanding the rules governing rounding becomes important to achieving the correct results.

The following chart describes how rounding is accomplished by Teradata.

IF the value of the digit to the right of the rounding digit is . . .	**THEN the value of the rounding digit . . .**
<5	does not change
>5	increases by one

<table>
<tr><th>IF the value of the digit to the right of the rounding digit is exactly 5 and . . .</th><th>THEN . . .</th></tr>
<tr><td>there are no trailing non-zero digits</td><td><table><tr><td>IF the value of the rounding digit is . . .</td><td>THEN the value of the rounding digit . . .</td></tr><tr><td>Odd</td><td>Increases by one</td></tr><tr><td>Even</td><td>Does not change</td></tr></table></td></tr>
<tr><td>there are trailing non-zero digits</td><td>rounding behaves as if the value of the digit to the right of the rounding digit is greater than five</td></tr>
</table>

Figure 4.5

The following query demonstrates these rules.

```
SELECT CAST(.014 AS DECIMAL(3,2))
       ,CAST(.015 AS DECIMAL(3,2))
       ,CAST(.025 AS DECIMAL(3,2))
       ,CAST(.0251 AS DECIMAL(3,2))
       ,CAST(.026 AS DECIMAL(3,2)) ;

Result: 1 row returned

.014   .015   .025   .0251   .026
-----  -----  -----  -----   -----
  .01    .02    .02    .03     .03
```

Figure 4.6

FORMAT

One of the relational database design guidelines is to store numbers in numeric data types. Following this guideline makes manipulating and searching the data easier. When it comes time to use these numeric columns in a report, being able to format the data makes it easier for end users to read the information. As an example, 832296468440.78 versus $832,296,468,440.78.

Teradata has an extension called FORMAT. It can be used with the Basic Teradata Query (BTEQ) tool to override the default format of data, both input and output. FORMAT cannot be used to specify any data conversions. SQL Assistant does not recognize the FORMAT clause.

The syntax is (FORMAT '*edit mask*')

The following chart shows some of the various symbols that may be used to create an edit mask.

Symbol	Meaning
$	Fixed or floating dollar sign
9	Decimal digit (no zero suppression)
Z	Zero-suppressed decimal digit
,	Comma – insert where specified
.	Decimal point position
-	Dash character – insert where specified
/	Slash character – insert where specified
%	Percent character – insert where specified
X	Character data – each X represents one character
G	Graphic data – each G represents on logical (double-byte) character
B	Blank data – insert a space and this point

Figure 4.7

In the following example, the multiple dollar signs ($) represent a floating dollar sign. The nines (9) represent an actual digit, even if it is a zero (0).

```
SELECT  salary(FORMAT '$$$,$$9.99')
FROM   employee_table
WHERE  employee_no = 1324657 ;


Result: 1 row returned

    Salary
----------
$42,788.88
```

Figure 4.8

Management has decided to give everyone in department number 400 a $1,000 raise, and wants to know what percentage pay increase that represents.

```
SELECT  last_name AS Employee
        , salary (FORMAT'$$$$$$$.99') AS "Current Salary"
        , (1000/salary) * 100
              (FORMAT 'ZZ9%')
              (TITLE 'Percent//Increase')
FROM    employee_table
WHERE  dept_no = 400
ORDER BY 2
;

Result: 3 rows returned
                                                   Percent
Employee                    Current Salary  Increase
--------------------  --------------  --------
Clooney                          $35000.00        3%
Strickland                       $54590.00        2%
Ford                             $54590.00        2%
```

Figure 4.9

In the above query, there are some things to notice:

- The Z characters represent zero suppression.
- There is a TITLE clause. The syntax is (TITLE '<value>')
- TITLEs cannot be referenced within a query.
- The double slant characters (//) can be used to stack the words in a TITLE up to three lines.

The following chart tests your understanding of proper FORMAT clause usage.

FORMAT	Data	Result?
FORMAT '999999'	08777	
FORMAT 'ZZZZZ9'	08777	
FORMAT '999-9999'	6494123	
FORMAT 'X(3)'	'Smith'	
FORMAT '$$9.99'	73.85	
FORMAT '999.99'	73.85	
FORMAT 'X(2)'	73.85	
FORMAT 'X(2)'	'73.85'	

Figure 4.10

Date Formats

There are two different ways to display dates. They are the ANSI recommended format of

FORMAT 'YYYY-MM-DD'

And the Teradata default format of

FORMAT 'YY/MM/DD'

Date formats that only display two digits of the year are not recommended. You should use the ANSI format for compatibility.

Some other ways of formatting dates:

Syntax	Result
FORMAT 'YYYY/MM/DD'	2010/07/26
FORMAT 'DDbMMMbYYYY'	26 Jul 2010
FORMAT 'mmmBdd,Byyyy'	Jul 26, 2010
FORMAT 'dd.mm.yyyy'	26.07.2010

Figure 4.11

As stated earlier, SQL Assistant does not recognize the FORMAT clause. Instead, the SQL Assistant provides the user with a choice of date display formats. Go to **Tools -> Options -> General**. There you can specify one of the following formats:

Display dates in this format	**Setting**
Local	Uses Windows format 07/25/2010
YYYY-MM-DD	This matches the ANSI format 2010-07-25
DD/MMM/YYYY	25/Jul/2010
DD/MM/YYYY	25/07/2010
MM/DD/YYYY	07/25/2010
YYYY/MM/DD	2010/07/25

Figure 4.12

Extracting Portions of Dates

The FORMAT clause can be used to extract portions of dates. However, since dates are stored as an Integer, you can also use normal integer arithmetic to do the same thing. In addition, there is also an EXTRACT function (shown below) that will be discussed in a later chapter.

The example below illustrates some of the EXTRACT methods.

```
SELECT order_date AS TDAT_Default
       , order_date (FORMAT 'yyyy-mm-dd')
                    AS ANSI_Format
       , order_date (FORMAT 'MMM-DD')
                    AS Format_Extract
       , order_date/100 MOD 100 AS Calc_Month
       , EXTRACT (MONTH FROM order_date) AS EXTRACT_Month
FROM order_table
ORDER BY 1;

Result: 6 rows returned

TDAT_Default  ANSI_Format  Format_Extract  Calc_Month  EXTRACT_Month
------------  -----------  --------------  ----------  -------------
           ?            ?               ?           ?              ?
    07/01/01   2007-01-01          Jan-01           1              1
    07/05/04   2007-05-04          May-04           5              5
    07/09/09   2007-09-09          Sep-09           9              9
    07/10/01   2007-10-01          Oct-01          10             10
    07/10/10   2007-10-10          Oct-10          10             10
```

Figure 4.13

Notice how confusing a date can appear with only two digits of the year displayed.

User Defined Functions (UDFs)

A User Defined Function (UDF) is a compiled function, which can perform calculations and complete SQL commands. UDFs are invoked as expressions from within SQL statements. UDFs are stored on their parent database/user's permanent space.

Teradata UDFs can be scalar functions that return single values, aggregate functions that return summary tables and table functions that return tables. UDFs are written in either the C or C++ programming language and must be compiled.

UDFs are very useful for performing calculations and summarizations of data. The ability to program in C or C++ allows for extended programming capability, beyond that of SQL. Examples of UDFs might include a function that checks if a value is numeric or a function that converts Fahrenheit into Celsius.

User Defined Types (UDTs)

A User Defined Type (UDT) is a custom data type that is defined by a user, often based on application or business rules. UDTs are usually a combination of one or more data types to form a new data type. UDTs reside in the Teradata SYSUDTLIB database, which is stored in permanent space. Teradata allows for two types of UDTs -- distinct and structured.

A distinct UDT is essentially a synonym for a regular Teradata type, such as a VARCHAR or INTEGER. A distinct UDT is useful when defining the data type for a column that may appear throughout a database. For instance, assume that customer id (cust_id) is used throughout several tables in our database, and it should always be assigned as an INTEGER. Unfortunately, it is very possible that two different table designing users might set the data types differently. By creating a distinct UDT for customer id, the table designing users would choose that UDT as the data type, as opposed to determining their own data type. Using the UDT ensures consistency across the data model for our customer id column.

A structured UDT is a made up of more than one different data types or UDTs. Structured UDTs are useful for creating custom data types that are specific to your application. For example, a structured UDT might be a unique identifier made up of a date, an integer value, and a character value (2008-12-3105STE).

Formatting for UDT

If you specify a FORMAT phrase to define the format for UDT columns, the format must be valid for the external type of the UDT, as specified by the transform that defines how to pass the UDT between the application and the server.

Formatting for Internationalizations

There is a *Specification for Data Formatting* (SDF) file available to the System Administrator. In addition to defining the default display formats for numeric, date, time, and timestamp data types, the SDF file defines strings that the Teradata Database displays in place of certain formatting characters that appear in a FORMAT phrase. The SDF file controls how the following kinds of information are formatted in the output.

- Day names
- Month names
- AM and PM names
- Numeric and currency separators
- Numeric and currency digit grouping rules
- Currency symbols
- Default display formats for data types

The SDF file also controls the default display formats for the following data types:

- BYTEINT
- SMALLINT
- BIGINT
- INTEGER
- NUMERIC and DECIMAL

- REAL, DOUBLE PRECISION, and FLOAT
- DATE
- TIME and TIME WITH TIME ZONE
- TIMESTAMP and TIMESTAMP WITH TIME ZONE
- NUMBER

Note: You cannot use the SDF file to control output formatting for the INTERVAL data type.

Chapter 4: Practice Questions

1. Which CAST will produce 0.27 as the result?
   a. CAST(0.2651 AS DEC(3,2))
   b. CAST(0.2646 AS DEC(3,2))
   c. CAST(0.265 AS DEC(3,2))
   d. CAST(0.2646 AS DEC(3,2))

2. Which of the following implicit comparison conversions will produce an error?
   a. BYTEINT to DATE
   b. BYTEINT to FLOAT
   c. BYTEINT to BYTE
   d. BYTEINT to VARCHAR

3. With 00000.67 as input, which FORMAT mask will cause an error?
   a. $$$,$$$.99'
   b. '$$$,$$9.99'
   c. 'ZZZZZ9.99'
   d. 'ZZZZ$9.99'

4. Given the following table definition:

```
CREATE TABLE CSQL_CLASS.department_table
     (Dept_No SMALLINT NOT NULL,
      Department_name CHAR(20,
      Mgr_No INTEGER,
      Budget DECIMAL(10,2))
UNIQUE PRIMARY INDEX ( Dept_No )
INDEX ( Department_name )
INDEX ( Mgr_No );
```

And the following data rows:

```
Dept_No  Department_name        Mgr_No        Budget
-------  --------------------  -------  ------------
    100  Marketing             1256349     500000.00
    200  Research and Develop  1000234     550000.00
    300  Sales                 1333454     650000.00
    400  Customer Support      1256349     500000.00
    500  Human Resources       1121334     450000.00
```

What will the result be if the following three queries are executed in ANSI mode?

```
SEL 'Query1', CAST(dept_no AS CHAR(3)) FROM
department_table;
SEL 'Query2', CAST(department_name AS CHAR(3)) FROM
department_table;
SEL 'Query3', CAST(mgr_no AS CHAR(3)) FROM
department_table;
```

a. Query1 will fail, Query2 will fail, Query 3 will succeed
b. Query1 will fail, Query2 will fail, Query3 will fail
c. Query1 will fail, Query2 will succeed, Query3 will fail
d. Query1 will fail, Query2 Will succeed, Query3 will succeed
e. Query1 will succeed, Query2 will fail, Query3 will fail

5. Which query will return the value of .89?
   a. SEL CAST(0.884622 AS DEC(3,2));
   b. SEL CAST(0.884645 AS DEC(3,2));
   c. SEL CAST(0.885501 AS DEC(3,2));
   d. SEL CAST(0.885000 AS DEC(3,2));

6. Which numeric data type has the largest maximum size?
   a. BIGINT
   b. DECIMAL
   c. FLOAT
   d. NUMBER
   e. NUMERIC

Chapter Notes

Utilize this space for notes, key points to remember, diagrams, areas of further study, etc.

Chapter 5: Aggregation

Certification Objectives

- ✓ Describe the characteristics of properly using GROUP BY, WHERE and HAVING.
- ✓ Given a scenario, identify which extended GROUP BY operator (e.g., ROLLUP) to use.
- ✓ Identify the impact of NULLs on the aggregate functions.
- ✓ Identify the use of GROUP BY, HAVING, DISTINCT, and WHERE.

Before You Begin

You should be familiar with the following terms and concepts.

Terms	Key Concepts
Aggregations	Identify all the math aggregates and how do they work
Group by	Group By Sets, Rollup, and Cube options
Having	How is this option applied and what does it do

Aggregations

Aggregation functions are used to perform basic arithmetic operations on data values. Aggregate functions can be used together within the same SELECT on either the same or different columns. The following list describes the most common Aggregate functions:
COUNT(*) – Counts all of the rows.

COUNT(*column-name*) – Counts every non-null value, within the specified column, and returns the resulting total as a single value.

SUM(*column-name*) – Sums up all of the non-null values within the specified column and returns the resulting total as a single value.

AVG(*column-name*) – Sums up all of the non-null values within the specified column and then divides by the count of all rows (provided that the value is not NULL), and returns the average number of all values as a single value.

MIN(*column-name*) – Compares all values within the specified column and returns the smallest of all the values.

MAX(*column-name*) – Compares all values within the specified column and returns the largest of all the values.

It is important to note that Aggregate functions can only return a single row as the next query demonstrates.

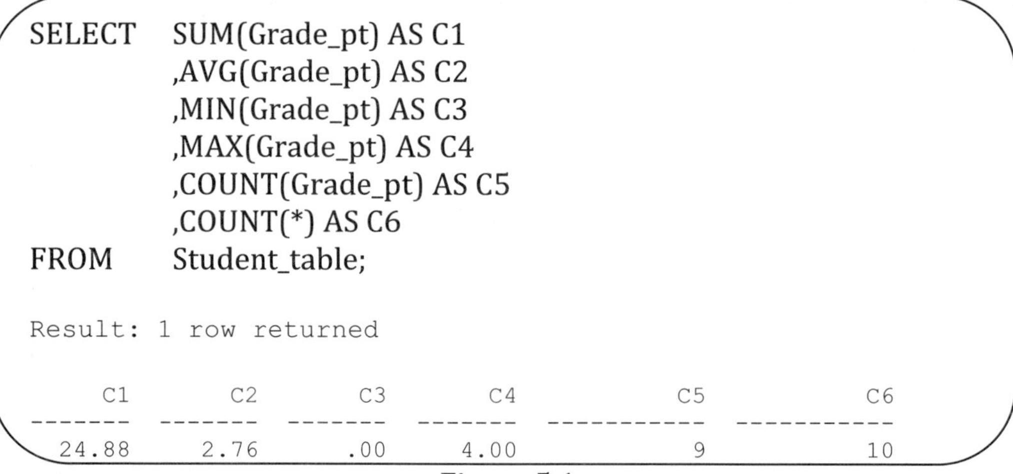

```
SELECT   SUM(Grade_pt) AS C1
         ,AVG(Grade_pt) AS C2
         ,MIN(Grade_pt) AS C3
         ,MAX(Grade_pt) AS C4
         ,COUNT(Grade_pt) AS C5
         ,COUNT(*) AS C6
FROM     Student_table;

Result: 1 row returned

     C1       C2       C3       C4          C5          C6
-------  -------  -------  -------  ----------  ----------
  24.88     2.76      .00     4.00           9          10
```

Figure 5.1

DISTINCT

The DISTINCT operator can be used to remove duplicate rows from an answer set. Two rows are considered duplicates only if each value in one is equal to the corresponding value in the other.

In Figure 5.2, the first query shows all the department number values present in the Employee table. The second query shows the use of the DISTINCT operator on that column.

```
SELECT dept_no FROM employee_table;

Dept_No
-------
      ?
    200
    100
    200
     10
    400
    400
    400
    300

SELECT DISTINCT dept_no FROM employee_table;

Dept_No
-------
    400
      ?
    200
    300
    100
     10
```

Figure 5.2

In query in Figure 5.3 shows the use of DISTINCT along with COUNT.

```
SELECT COUNT(*)
        , COUNT(dept_no)
        , COUNT(DISTINCT dept_no)
        FROM employee_table;

   Count(*)   Count(Dept_No)   Count(Distinct(Dept_No))
-----------   --------------   ------------------------
          9                8                          5
```

Figure 5.3

Aggregates Example with Derived Data

The following SELECT sums all employee salaries, provides the average salary, and demonstrates the effect of giving all employees a raise of either 5% or 10%.

```
SELECT    SUM(salary)
          ,SUM(salary*1.05) AS "5% Raise"
          ,SUM(salary*1.10) AS "10% Raise"
          ,AVG(salary)   AS "Avg Salary"
          ,SUM(salary) / COUNT(salary) AS "Computed Avg"
FROM employee_table;

Result: 1 row returned

Sum(Salary)   5% Raise      10% Raise      Avg Salary   Computed Avg
-----------   -----------   -----------    ----------   -----------
421919.38     443015.35     464111.32      46879.93     46879.93
```

Figure 5.4

Using a GROUP BY with Aggregation

Aggregates can only return a single row. In the following query, the first column requests a row for every department number, while the remaining columns can only return a single row.

The following example utilizes the GROUP BY in order to return the aggregated values for each department number within the column.

Think of GROUP BY as *FOR EACH.*

```
SELECT    dept_no   -- For each dept_no, return . . .
          ,SUM(salary) AS SumSal
          ,MAX(salary) AS MaxSal
          ,MIN(salary) AS MinSal
          ,AVG(salary) AS AvgSal
FROM employee_table
GROUP BY dept_no;

Result: 6 rows returned

Dept_No      SumSal      MaxSal      MinSal      AvgSal
-------  ----------  ----------  ----------  ----------
    200    91588.88    48800.00    42788.88    45794.44
      ?    32800.50    32800.50    32800.50    32800.50
    400   144180.00    54590.00    35000.00    48060.00
    100    48850.00    48850.00    48850.00    48850.00
    300    40200.00    40200.00    40200.00    40200.00
     10    64300.00    64300.00    64300.00    64300.00
```

Figure 5.5

If NULL values are allowed, there is potential for the NULL to impact the final outcome of compound tests. Using the IS NOT NULL option is a good technique when NULLs are allowed in a column. However, this does require another comparison and could be written as:

```
SELECT    dept_no  -- For each dept_no, return . . .
          ,SUM(salary) AS SumSal
          ,MAX(salary) AS MaxSal
          ,MIN(salary) AS MinSal
          ,AVG(salary) AS AvgSal
FROM employee_table
WHERE dept_no IS NOT NULL
GROUP BY dept_no;
```

Figure 5.6

HAVING

HAVING is the "WHERE clause of the GROUP BY" – it is used to limit output values of the GROUP BY. The system first does the GROUP BY and then casts off any groups not matching the HAVING condition.

The following example aggregates all rows, by class code. The result set is restricted to return only those students with a Grade Point Average higher than 3.00.

```
SELECT   Class_code
         ,SUM(Grade_Pt)   AS "Total"
         ,AVG(Grade_Pt)   AS "Average"
         ,COUNT(Grade_Pt) AS "Count"
FROM     student_table
GROUP BY 1
HAVING "Average" > 3.00
ORDER BY 1;

Result: 1 row returned

Class_code     Total  Average         Count
----------  -------  -------  -----------
SR             6.35     3.18              2
```

Figure 5.7

To use a reserved word as a column heading, put it inside double quotes. Also, use quotes when referenced elsewhere in a query such as a HAVING clause as shown above.

GROUP BY ROLLUP

Starting in Teradata 12, the ANSI standard extended grouping functions are supported. These functions allow for aggregations that would normally take multiple queries or unions to produce. Given *n* column references, ROLLUP groups data at *n* levels of detail in one dimension. Doing a ROLLUP on a single column is the same as doing a normal GROUP BY.

The following query produces the normal detail lines, but then adds summary lines for each PID and a grand total.

ROLLUP summarizes on a single dimension only, PID in this example.

```
SELECT Product_id AS PID
        , sale_date
        , SUM(daily_sales) AS Sales
FROM  sales_table
GROUP BY ROLLUP (pid, sale_date)
ORDER BY pid, sale_date
;

Result: 22 rows returned

        PID  Sale_Date        Sales
-----------  ---------  -----------
          ?          ?    869577.35
       1000          ?    346526.72
       1000   07/09/28     45850.40
       1000   07/09/29     64500.22
       1000   07/09/30     36000.07
       1000   07/10/01     45700.43
       1000   07/10/02     33700.50
       1000   07/10/03     66200.00
       1000   07/10/04     54575.10
       2000          ?    302956.81
       2000   07/09/28     42787.88
       2000   07/09/29     46090.00
       2000   07/09/30     44850.03
       2000   07/10/01     58850.29
       2000   07/10/02     35599.93
       2000   07/10/03     41900.18
       2000   07/10/04     32878.50
       3000          ?    220093.82
       3000   07/09/28     60903.77
       3000   07/09/29     34654.13
       3000   07/09/30     42338.86
       3000   07/10/01     27000.00
       3000   07/10/02     18767.94
       3000   07/10/03     21553.79
       3000   07/10/04     14875.33
```

Figure 5.8

GROUP BY GROUPING SETS

Now notice the change when we make the GROUP BY columns GROUPING SETS:

```
SELECT Product_id AS PID
       , sale_date
       , SUM(daily_sales) AS Sales
FROM  sales_table
GROUP BY GROUPING SETS (pid, sale_date)
ORDER BY pid, sale_date
;

Result: 10 rows returned

        PID  Sale_Date        Sales
-----------  ---------  -----------
          ?   07/09/28    149542.05
          ?   07/09/29    145244.35
          ?   07/09/30    123188.96
          ?   07/10/01    131550.72
          ?   07/10/02     88068.37
          ?   07/10/03    129653.97
          ?   07/10/04    102328.93
       1000          ?    346526.72
       2000          ?    302956.81
       3000          ?    220093.82
```

Figure 5.9

Notice that we get summary lines for each PID and date.

To get a sales total across all dates and product IDs, add a null column to the GROUPING SETS definition:

```
SELECT Product_id AS PID
        , sale_date
        , SUM(daily_sales) AS Sales
FROM  sales_table
GROUP BY GROUPING SETS (pid, sale_date, ( ) )
ORDER BY pid, sale_date
;

Result: 11 rows returned

        PID  Sale_Date        Sales
-----------  ---------  -----------
          ?          ?    869577.35
          ?   07/09/28    149542.05
          ?   07/09/29    145244.35
          ?   07/09/30    123188.96
          ?   07/10/01    131550.72
          ?   07/10/02     88068.37
          ?   07/10/03    129653.97
          ?   07/10/04    102328.93
       1000          ?    346526.72
       2000          ?    302956.81
       3000          ?    220093.82
```

Figure 5.10

In the previous examples, nulls are used to represent an empty set, not missing information. In this case, the nulls mean that information is not reported at the grouping level represented, not that the information is missing from the *sales_table*. The next chart provides a better understanding on how the nulls are utilized.

IF	AND	THEN
PID is null	Sale_date is null	Sales is the sum of all products across all dates
PID is null	Sale_date is not null	Sales is the sum of all products for that date
PID is not null	Sale_date is null	Sales is the sum of that product across all dates.

Figure 5.11

GROUP BY CUBE

CUBE analyzes data by grouping it into multiple dimensions. For *n* dimensions, it creates 2^n groups as illustrated in the next figure. Therefore, each group reports as a single row.

GROUP NUMBER	Dimension 1	Dimension 2
1	X	X
2	X	
3		X
4		

Figure 5.12

The following query has 2 dimensions in the GROUP BY CUBE, which will produce 4 groups in the report.

```
SELECT Product_id AS PID
       , sale_date
       , SUM(daily_sales) AS Sales
FROM  sales_table
GROUP BY CUBE (pid, sale_date)
ORDER BY pid, sale_date ;
```

```
Result: 32 rows returned

   PID        Sale_Date        Sales
-----------  ---------  -----------
         ?           ?    869577.35
         ?    07/09/28    149542.05
         ?    07/09/29    145244.35
         ?    07/09/30    123188.96
         ?    07/10/01    131550.72
         ?    07/10/02     88068.37
         ?    07/10/03    129653.97
         ?    07/10/04    102328.93
      1000           ?    346526.72
      1000    07/09/28     45850.40
      1000    07/09/29     64500.22
      1000    07/09/30     36000.07
      1000    07/10/01     45700.43
      1000    07/10/02     33700.50
      1000    07/10/03     66200.00
      1000    07/10/04     54575.10
      2000           ?    302956.81
      2000    07/09/28     42787.88
      2000    07/09/29     46090.00
      2000    07/09/30     44850.03
      2000    07/10/01     58850.29
      2000    07/10/02     35599.93
      2000    07/10/03     41900.18
      2000    07/10/04     32878.50
      3000           ?    220093.82
      3000    07/09/28     60903.77
      3000    07/09/28     60903.77
      3000    07/09/29     34654.13
      3000    07/09/30     42338.86
      3000    07/10/01     27000.00
      3000    07/10/02     18767.94
      3000    07/10/03     21553.79
      3000    07/10/04     14875.33
```

Figure 5.13

Chapter 5: Practice Questions

1. Given the following values for column c2

   (1, 4, ?, 3, ?, 2, 0, 5, 7, ?, 0, 6, 9, 8, 0)

   which of the following queries will return an answer of 3.75?

   a. SELECT AVG(c2) FROM T1;
   b. SELECT AVG(DISTINCT c2) FROM T1;
   c. SELECT SUM(c2) / COUNT(*) FROM T1;
   d. SELECT SUM(DISTINCT c2) / COUNT(c2) FROM T1;

2. Which of the following queries is correct?
   a. SELECT c3, SUM(c2), c4 FROM t1;
   b. SELECT c3, SUM(c2), c4 FROM t1 ORDER BY c3, c4;
   c. SELECT c3, SUM(c2), c4 FROM t1 GROUP BY c2;
   d. SELECT c3, SUM(c2), c4 FROM t1 GROUP BY 1,3;

3. Which of the following queries is correct?
   a. SELECT c1 AS View, c2 AS Column, c3 AS Tables FROM T1;
   b. SELECT c1 AS "View", c2 AS Column, c3 AS Table FROM T1;
   c. SELECT c1 AS 'View', c2 AS 'Column', c3 AS 'Table' FROM T1;
   d. SELECT c1 AS Views, c2 AS Columns, c3 AS "Table" FROM T1;

4. If c2 has the values (7, 0, 5, 0, 3, ?, 1, ?, 8, 9, 6, 0, 4, ?, 2), which aggregate function will return the value of 10?
    a. MAX(c2)
    b. COUNT(DISTINCT(c2))
    c. COUNT(c2)
    d. COUNT(*)

5. Which query will produce the following report?

```
        PID  Sale_Date        Sales
-----------  ---------  -----------
          ?          ?    869577.35
          ?   07/09/28    149542.05
          ?   07/09/29    145244.35
          ?   07/09/30    123188.96
          ?   07/10/01    131550.72
          ?   07/10/02     88068.37
          ?   07/10/03    129653.97
          ?   07/10/04    102328.93
       1000          ?    346526.72
       2000          ?    302956.81
       3000          ?    220093.82
```

a.
```
SELECT Product_id AS PID
        , sale_date
        , SUM(daily_sales) AS Sales
FROM  sales_table
GROUP BY GROUPING SETS (pid, sale_date, ( ) )
ORDER BY pid, sale_date;
```

b.
```
SELECT Product_id AS PID
        , sale_date
        , SUM(daily_sales) AS Sales
FROM  sales_table
GROUP BY GROUPING SETS (pid, sale_date)
ORDER BY pid, sale_date;
```

c. SELECT Product_id AS PID
        , sale_date
        , SUM(daily_sales) AS Sales
   FROM sales_table
   GROUP BY ROLLUP (pid, sale_date)
   ORDER BY pid, sale_date;

d. SELECT Product_id AS PID
        , sale_date
        , SUM(daily_sales) AS Sales
   FROM sales_table
   GROUP BY CUBE (pid, sale_date)
   ORDER BY pid, sale_date ;

6. Which query will produce the following report?

```
        PID  Sale_Date        Sales
-----------  ---------  -----------
          ?   07/09/28    149542.05
          ?   07/09/29    145244.35
          ?   07/09/30    123188.96
          ?   07/10/01    131550.72
          ?   07/10/02     88068.37
          ?   07/10/03    129653.97
          ?   07/10/04    102328.93
       1000          ?    346526.72
       2000          ?    302956.81
       3000          ?    220093.82
```

a. SELECT Product_id AS PID
        , sale_date
        , SUM(daily_sales) AS Sales
   FROM sales_table
   GROUP BY GROUPING SETS (pid, sale_date, ( ))
   ORDER BY pid, sale_date;

b.
```
SELECT Product_id AS PID
          , sale_date
          , SUM(daily_sales) AS Sales
FROM  sales_table
GROUP BY GROUPING SETS (pid, sale_date)
ORDER BY pid, sale_date;
```
c.
```
SELECT Product_id AS PID
          , sale_date
          , SUM(daily_sales) AS Sales
FROM  sales_table
GROUP BY ROLLUP (pid, sale_date)
ORDER BY pid, sale_date;
```
d.
```
SELECT Product_id AS PID
          , sale_date
          , SUM(daily_sales) AS Sales
FROM  sales_table
GROUP BY CUBE (pid, sale_date)
ORDER BY pid, sale_date ;
```

7. Which of the following queries is wrong?
   a. SEL c1, SUM(c2) GROUP BY c1 FROM t1 HAVING c1 > 8 WHERE c2 IS NOT NULL;
   b. SEL c1, SUM(c2) HAVING c1 > 8 FROM t1 WHERE c2 IS NOT NULL GROUP BY c1;
   c. SEL c1, SUM(c2) WHERE c2 IS NOT NULL HAVING c1 > 8 GROUP BY c1 FROM t1;
   d. SEL c1, SUM(c2) HAVING c1 > 8 FROM t1 WHERE c2 IS NOT NULL ORDER BY c1;

Chapter Notes

Utilize this space for notes, key points to remember, diagrams, areas of further study, etc.

Chapter 6: Subquery Processing

Certification Objectives

- ✓ Given a scenario, identify the SQL statement for a correlated scalar subquery to qualify a subset of data.
- ✓ Given a scenario, identify the SQL statement for a noncorrelated scalar subquery to qualify a subset of data.
- ✓ Identify the characteristics of a scalar subquery.
- ✓ Given a scenario, identify the SQL statement for a correlated subquery to qualify a subset of data.
- ✓ Given a scenario, identify the SQL statement for a noncorrelated subquery to qualify a subset of data.

Before You Begin

You should be familiar with the following terms and concepts.

Terms	Key Concepts
Subquery	How does a subquery work
Table Alias	Understand the reasons for utilizing an Alias for a table
Correlated Subquery	What are the key differences vs. a non-correlated subquery

Non-Scalar Subquery

A Subquery is used to select rows from one table, based on the values from another table. It is a SELECT statement within another SELECT statement that generates a set of values based on an IN or NOT IN list. Therefore, in subquery processing, the lowest level is processed first and those results are input to the next level. This continues until the top level is reached. Lastly, a subquery will always produce a distinct set of values.

The next example utilizes a subquery in order to retrieve all customers with an order exceeding $10,000.

```
SELECT   Customer_name
         ,phone_number
FROM     customer_table
WHERE    customer_number IN
  ( SELECT customer_number
    FROM   order_table
    WHERE order_total > 10000 ) ;

Result: 3 rows returned

Customer_name          Phone_number
--------------------   ------------
Best Electronics       559-9987
XYZ Landscapers        447-7954
Database Pros          622-1012
```

Figure 6.1

Note: By comparison, non-scalar correlated subqueries execute once for each row of the outer query. For more details, refer to the non-scalar correlated subqueries section later on in this chapter.

SUBQUERY using a NOT IN

NOT IN is used when you want to retrieve the rows that do NOT match the specified criteria. This query lists all customers who do not have an order.

```
SELECT  customer_name
        ,phone_number
FROM    customer_table
WHERE  customer_number  NOT IN
      ( SELECT customer_number  FROM order_table) ;

Result: 1 row returned

Customer_name          Phone_number
--------------------   ------------
Acme Designs           555-5564
```

Figure 6.2

SUBQUERY using a NOT IN with NULLs

With NOT IN, there is a potential for including a NULL in the value list, since a NULL will compare either a False or UNKNOWN.

```
SELECT   customer_name
        ,phone_number
FROM     customer_table
WHERE    customer_number  NOT IN
         ( SELECT customer_number
           FROM    order_table
           WHERE customer_number IS NOT NULL) ;

Result: 1 row returned

Customer_name          Phone_number
--------------------   ------------
Acme Designs           555-5564
```

Figure 6.3

Note: The NOT IN has the potential for a NULL to be returned in the result set. It is recommended to code an IS NOT NULL compound comparison to remove the NULLs.

Non-Scalar Correlated Subquery Processing

The second type of subquery is a non-scalar correlated subquery. Non-scaler correlated subqueries differ for non-scalar subqueries because each row from the outer query is retrieved and compared to the criteria in the subquery result generated based on column values from the outer row that are referenced in the subquery. These types of queries are often used when the basis of comparison is an aggregate value from the same table.

The following query returns the highest paid employee, by department. Notice the word "AS", which is used to alias the table name. Table aliasing is described in more detail in Chapter 7.

```
SELECT   last_name
        , first_name
        , dept_no
        , salary
FROM    employee_table  AS emp
WHERE  salary  =
      ( SELECT MAX(salary)
        FROM employee_table  AS  emt
        WHERE  emp.dept_no = emt.dept_no )
ORDER BY 3,1 ;

Result: 6 rows returned

Last_name             First_name    Dept_No      Salary
--------------------  ------------  -------  ----------
Gere                  Richard            10    64300.00
Student               Mandee            100    48850.00
Roberts               Julia             200    48800.00
Mcfly                 Loraine           300    40200.00
Ford                  Harrison          400    54590.00
Strickland            Stan              400    54590.00
```

Figure 6.4

Note: The column emp.dept_no from the outer query is referenced in the subquery. This is what makes the subquery a correlated subquery.

Scalar Subquery

A scalar function can only return one value. A scalar subquery can be either a noncorrelated subquery (does not reference columns of the outer query) or correlated subquery (does reference columns of the outer query). An example of scalar functions are the CASE and COALESCE functions (covered in a later chapter).

A scalar subquery is a subquery expression that can return a maximum of one value.

Scalar Correlated Subquery

In the following subquery, the WHERE clause evaluates to TRUE for those rows in Emp_Job_Table that do not match any rows in the Employee_Table.

```
SELECT employee_no, last_name, first_name
FROM    employee_table AS e
WHERE (SELECT 1
          FROM    emp_job_table AS j
          WHERE e.employee_no = j.emp_no) IS NULL;

 *** Query completed. One row found. 3 columns returned.
 *** Total elapsed time was 1 second.

Employee_No  Last_name             First_name
-----------  --------------------  ------------
    2312225  Mcfly                 Loraine
```

Figure 6.5

Subquery Processing with Derived tables

The third subquery processing type is the derived table. A derived table is a temporary table that is named, getting its results from a subquery. These tables are created in the user's spool space, can be used in other parts of the query and are deleted when the query finishes.

This derived table example shows the employees whose salary is greater than their department average.

```
SELECT  last_name AS LAST
        ,salary       (FORMAT '$,$$$,$99.99') AS sal
        ,dept_no      AS dep
        ,avgsal       (FORMAT '$,$$$,$99.99')
FROM   (SELECT AVG (salary)
              ,dept_no
        FROM  employee_table
        GROUP BY dept_no)
        my_temp (avgsal, deptno)
       , employee_table
WHERE deptno = dept_no AND sal > avgsal
ORDER BY 2 DESC;

Result: 3 rows returned

LAST                          sal     dep          avgsal
--------------------  ------------  ------  ------------
Ford                   $54,590.00     400    $48,060.00
Strickland             $54,590.00     400    $48,060.00
Roberts                $48,800.00     200    $45,794.44
```

Figure 6.6

Chapter 6: Practice Questions

1. The where does the space for derived tables comes from?
    a. PERM
    b. SPOOL
    c. TEMP
    d. AMP Memory

2. When are Derived tables dropped?
    a. At the end of a multi-statement request.
    b. When the user finally logs off.
    c. At the end of the query.
    d. At the next DBC restart.

3. Which query will identify those employees in each department who are making more than the lowest paid employee in each department?
    a. SELECT last_name , first_name, dept_no, salary FROM employee_table AS emp WHERE salary > (SELECT MIN(salary) FROM employee_table AS emt WHERE emp.dept_no = emt.dept_no) ORDER BY 3,1 ;
    b. SELECT last_name , first_name, dept_no, salary FROM employee_table AS emp WHERE salary >= (SELECT MIN(salary) FROM employee_table AS emt WHERE emp.dept_no = emt.dept_no) ORDER BY 3,1 ;
    c. SELECT last_name , first_name, dept_no, salary FROM employee_table WHERE salary < (SELECT MIN(salary) FROM employee_table) ORDER BY 3,1;
    d. SELECT last_name , first_name, dept_no, salary FROM employee_table WHERE salary <> (SELECT MIN(salary) FROM employee_table) ORDER BY 3,1 ;

4. Which query will produce the following report showing the employees whose salary is greater than their department average?

```
dep   emp      sal          minsal       avgsal
----- -------- ----------   ----------   ----------
200  1333454  $48,800.00  $42,788.88  $45,794.44
400  1256349  $54,590.00  $35,000.00  $48,060.00
400  1121334  $54,590.00  $35,000.00  $48,060.00
```

a.
```
SELECT dept_no AS dep, employee_no AS emp, salary
(FORMAT '$,$$$,$99.99') AS sal, minsal (FORMAT
'$,$$$,$99.99'), avgsal (FORMAT '$,$$$,$99.99')
FROM (SELECT AVG (salary),MIN(salary), dept_no
      FROM employee_table
      GROUP BY dept_no)
      my_temp (avgsal, minsal, deptno)
,employee_table
WHERE deptno = dept_no AND sal < avgsal
ORDER BY 1;
```

b.
```
SELECT dept_no AS dep, employee_no AS emp, salary
(FORMAT '$,$$$,$99.99') AS sal, maxsal (FORMAT
'$,$$$,$99.99'), avgsal (FORMAT '$,$$$,$99.99')
FROM (SELECT AVG (salary),MAX(salary), dept_no
      FROM employee_table
      GROUP BY dept_no)
      my_temp (avgsal, maxsal, deptno)
, employee_table
WHERE deptno = dept_no AND sal > avgsal
ORDER BY 1;
```

c. SELECT dept_no AS dep, employee_no AS emp, salary (FORMAT '$,$$$,$99.99') AS sal, minsal (FORMAT '$,$$$,$99.99'), avgsal (FORMAT '$,$$$,$99.99')
```
FROM (SELECT AVG (salary),MIN(salary), dept_no
     FROM employee_table
     GROUP BY dept_no)
     my_temp (avgsal, minsal, deptno)
,employee_table
WHERE deptno = dept_no AND sal > avgsal
ORDER BY 1;
```
d. SELECT dept_no AS dep, employee_no, salary (FORMAT '$,$$$,$99.99') AS sal, minsal (FORMAT '$,$$$,$99.99'), avgsal (FORMAT '$,$$$,$99.99')
```
FROM (SELECT AVG (salary),MIN(salary), dept_no
     FROM employee_table
     GROUP BY dept_no)
     my_temp (avgsal, minsal, deptno)
,employee_table
WHERE deptno = dept_no AND sal > avgsal
ORDER BY 1;
```

Chapter Notes

Utilize this space for notes, key points to remember, diagrams, areas of further study, etc.

Chapter 7: Join Processing

Certification Objectives

- ✓ Given a scenario, determine the type of join to code to get the desired result set.
- ✓ Given a scenario, identify the evaluation order of various join types.
- ✓ Identify proper and improper use of aliasing in table joins.
- ✓ Identify the characteristics of outer joins.

Before You Begin

You should be familiar with the following terms and concepts.

Terms	Key Concepts
Inner Join	Syntax of an INNER JOIN
Outer Join	OUTER JOIN and how they process
Product Joins	What to look for with a PRODUCT JOIN
Residuals	PPI, and WHERE clause considerations with JOINs

Table Aliasing

An alias is a user-specified, temporary name given to a table, within the SQL. Aliases are useful for shortening long table names, especially when a table is referenced multiple times in the SQL.

Syntax:

```
SELECT * FROM <table name>   AS <table alias name>;
```

The alias is simply a reference to an existing table name - the real table name is not changed. Use double quotes " " around an alias name when using spaces or SQL keywords in the alias. The keyword "AS" is optional.

Join Processing

A JOIN occurs when two or more tables are linked together within the same SELECT statement. Tables are joined together using one or more columns that create a common domain between the tables. Joins can be performed on either equality or inequality comparison but are usually used for equal comparisons. As with a single table SELECT, each table is listed following the FROM clause.

The objective of an INNER JOIN is to return the matching rows between two or more tables.

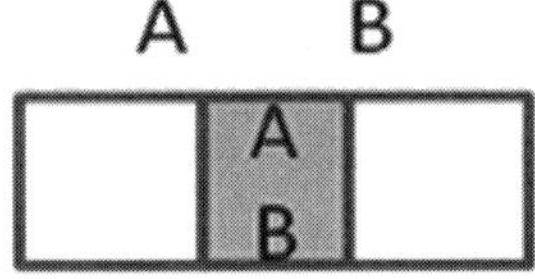

INNER JOIN

The next example uses an INNER JOIN to find all customers with valid orders based on the common column (or domain) they share -- customer number.

```
SELECT  cust.customer_number AS Cust_no
        ,cust.customer_name
        ,ord.order_number
        ,ord.order_total
FROM    customer_table AS cust
INNER JOIN
        order_table AS ord
ON      cust.customer_number = ord.customer_number
ORDER BY 2 ;

Result: 6 rows returned

    Cust_no  Customer_name      Order_Number  Order_Total
-----------  ----------------  ------------  ------------
   31323134  ABC Consulting          123552       5311.47
   31323134  ABC Consulting          999999             ?
   11111111  Best Electronics        123512       7995.91
   11111111  Best Electronics        123456      12447.53
   87323456  Database Pros           123585      16231.62
   57896883  XYZ Landscapers         123777      25454.84
```

Figure 7.1

INNER JOIN - Three Table Example using AND Clause

The following query is a three-table INNER JOIN that finds all students that are enrolled in a 'SQL" course. The common columns (or domain) between the tables being joined in the ON clauses are the student_id and course_id.

```
SELECT   s.last_name AS "Last Name"
         ,CAST(s.student_id AS CHAR(6))
         ,CAST(c.course_name AS CHAR(20)) AS Course
FROM     Student_table  AS s
INNER JOIN
         student_course_table  AS  sc
ON       s.student_id = sc.student_id
INNER JOIN
         course_table  AS c
ON       c.course_id = sc.course_id
AND      course_name LIKE '%SQL%'
ORDER BY course, last_name;

Result: 7 rows returned

Last Name             Student_ID  Course
--------------------  ----------  --------------------
McCormick             231222      Advanced SQL
Rieter                280023      Advanced SQL
Craig                 324652      Introduction to SQL
Kojack                125634      Introduction to SQL
Bond                  322133      TD12 SQL Features
Kojack                125634      TD12 SQL Features
McCormick             231222      TD12 SQL Features
```

Figure 7.2

OUTER JOIN

An OUTER JOIN returns all rows from the Outer Table and the rows from the INNER table based on the join condition. OUTER JOINs are useful because they show the rows that match as well as the rows that don't. There are three types of OUTER JOINs:

left_table **LEFT OUTER JOIN** *right_table* – left table is the outer table. All rows from the left table will be in the result set.

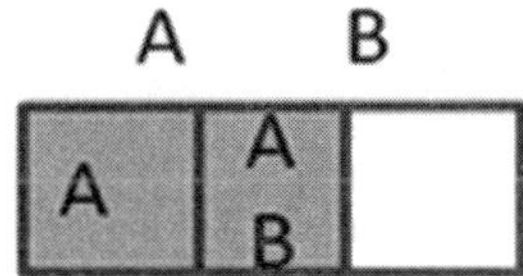

left_table **RIGHT OUTER JOIN** *right_table* – right table is the outer table. All rows from the right table will be in the result set.

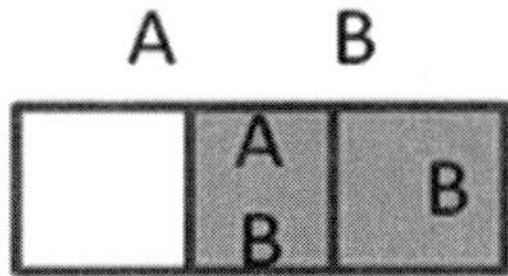

left_table **FULL OUTER JOIN** *right_table* – both are outer tables. All rows from both the left and right tables will be in the result set.

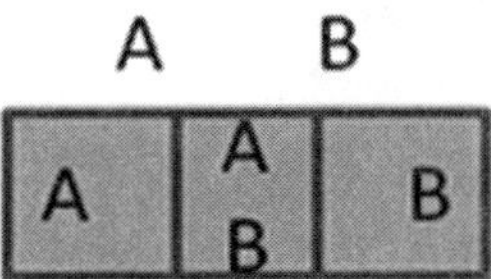

The next series of pages illustrate specific examples that emphasize the points above.

LEFT OUTER JOIN

The following example returns customers with orders along with those who have NOT placed an order. This helps to identify the non-buying customers. It also shows how to use aliases.

```
SELECT  cust.customer_name
        ,ord.order_number
        ,ord.order_total
FROM    customer_table  cust
LEFT OUTER JOIN
        order_table  ord
ON      cust.customer_number = ord.customer_number
ORDER BY 1;

Result: 7 rows returned

Customer_name         Order_Number   Order_Total
--------------------  ------------  ------------
ABC Consulting              123552       5311.47
Acme Designs                     ?             ?
Best Electronics            123456      12447.53
Best Electronics            123512       7995.91
Database Pros               123585      16231.62
XYZ Landscapers             123777      25454.84
```

Figure 7.3

RIGHT OUTER JOIN

All rows from the right table – order table - will be in the result set. The query below returns orders with matching customers along with those orders that do NOT have customers. This helps to identify incorrect orders.

```
 SELECT  cust.customer_name
         ,ord.order_number
         ,ord.order_total
FROM     customer_table  cust
RIGHT OUTER JOIN
         order_table  ord
ON       cust.customer_number = ord.customer_number
ORDER BY 1 ;

Result: 6 rows returned

Customer_name          Order_Number   Order_Total
--------------------   ------------  ------------
?                            999999             ?
ABC Consulting               123552       5311.47
Best Electronics             123512       7995.91
Best Electronics             123456      12447.53
Database Pros                123585      16231.62
XYZ Landscapers              123777      25454.84
```

Figure 7.4

FULL OUTER JOIN

All rows from both the left and right tables will be in the result set. The following example uses a FULL OUTER JOIN to return all customers with orders, orders without customers, and customers without orders.

```
SELECT  cust.customer_name
        ,ord.order_number
        ,ord.order_total
FROM    customer_table cust
FULL OUTER JOIN
        order_table ord
ON      cust.customer_number = ord.customer_number
ORDER BY 1 ;

Result: 7 rows returned

Customer_name         Order_Number   Order_Total
--------------------  ------------  ------------
?                           999999             ?
ABC Consulting              123552       5311.47
Acme Designs                     ?             ?
Best Electronics            123456      12447.53
Best Electronics            123512       7995.91
Database Pros               123585      16231.62
XYZ Landscapers             123777      25454.84
```

Figure 7.5

Residual Conditions

Including a WHERE clause adds residual conditions to be applied to the joined rows. The following eliminates the two rows that have a null for the course name:

```
SELECT  s.student_id
        ,sc.course_id
        ,c.course_name
FROM   student_table  AS  s
FULL OUTER JOIN
        student_course_table  AS  sc
ON      s.student_id = sc.student_id
FULL OUTER JOIN
        course_table  AS c
ON      c.course_id = sc.course_id
WHERE c.course_name IS NOT NULL
ORDER BY 2;
```

```
Result: 14 rows returned

 Student_ID  Course_ID  Course_name
-----------  ---------  ------------------------------
     234121        100  Teradata Basics
     123250        100  Teradata Basics
     125634        100  Teradata Basics
     324652        200  Introduction to SQL
     125634        200  Introduction to SQL
     231222        210  Advanced SQL
     280023        210  Advanced SQL
     231222        220  TD12 SQL Features
     125634        220  TD12 SQL Features
     322133        220  TD12 SQL Features
     322133        300  Physical Database Tuning
     333450        400  Database Administration
     260000        400  Database Administration
```

Figure 7.6

The following rules and recommendations apply to coding ON and WHERE clauses for outer joins:

1. One or more join conditions, or connecting terms, are required in the ON clause for each table in an outer join. These join conditions define the rows in the outer table that take part in the match to the inner table.

2. The best practice is to use *only* join conditions in ON clauses. However, when a search condition is applied to the *inner* table it should be applied in the ON clause and not in the WHERE clause. A search condition in the ON clause of the inner table does *not* limit the number of rows in the answer set. Instead, it defines the rows that are eligible to take part in the match to the outer table.

3. An outer join can also include a WHERE clause; however, the results you get with a WHERE clause may be surprising and not obvious or even intuitive. To limit the number of qualifying rows in the outer table (and therefore the answer set), the search condition for the outer table must be in the WHERE clause. Note that the Optimizer *logically* applies the WHERE clause condition only after a join has been produced. The *actual* application of conditions always depends on how the Optimizer chooses to implement the query.

4. If a search condition on the inner table is placed in the WHERE clause, the join is logically equivalent to an inner join, even if you explicitly specify the keywords LEFT/RIGHT/FULL OUTER JOIN in the query. The Optimizer always treats such a join as an inner join to simplify the query, rewriting it to roll the entire complex process into a single step.

Evaluation Order

The result of an inner join of two tables does not change if rows from one table are joined to rows from another. This is because inner joins are both commutative and associative. Therefore, the Optimizer can select the best join order and the end result is always the same.

Outer joins however, are rarely commutative or associative. In this case, the Optimizer cannot select the best join order for outer joins because it does not have any way of knowing the specific result that was intended with the query.

Given the above, if you have a three table outer join, then you must specify their join order explicitly by placing the ON clause in an appropriate position within the FROM clause to ensure that the join is evaluated correctly. The Optimizer adheres to the following rules when generating join orders for outer joins:

- The first ON clause in the query - reading from left to right - is evaluated first.
- Any ON clause applies to its immediately preceding join operation.
- Parentheses can be used to override the left to right order

Self-Join

The following example joins the Employee table to itself in order to find all of the managers (not all employees are managers). In addition, the Department table is joined in order to return each manager's department information.

```
SELECT   mgr.employee_no  AS "Manager Number"
         , mgr.last_name      AS "Manager Name"
         , dept.dept_no
FROM     employee_table AS Emp
INNER JOIN
         employee_table  AS Mgr
ON       mgr.employee_no  =  emp.mgr_employee_no
INNER JOIN
         department_table  AS Dept
ON       mgr.dept_no = dept.dept_no
ORDER BY 2 ;

Result: 7 rows returned

Manager Number  Manager Name          Dept_No
--------------  --------------------  -------
       1256349  Ford                      400
       1256349  Ford                      400
       1333454  Roberts                   200
       1333454  Roberts                   200
       1121334  Strickland                400
       1121334  Strickland                400
       1121334  Strickland                400
```

Figure 7.7

Note: The employee_table is referenced twice but with different aliases. Each alias acts like a separate instance of the table.

Cross Join

A CROSS JOIN takes <u>every</u> row from the left table and joins it to <u>every</u> row in the right table. The following example demonstrates a CROSS JOIN that introduces a WHERE clause to retrieve a specific course_id and then joins it to every row in the student_table.

```
SELECT  course_name
        ,student_id
FROM    student_table
CROSS JOIN
        course_table
WHERE Course_ID  = 100 ;

Result: 10 rows returned

Course_name                       Student_ID
------------------------------  -----------
Teradata Basics                       423400
Teradata Basics                       231222
Teradata Basics                       280023
Teradata Basics                       322133
Teradata Basics                       125634
Teradata Basics                       333450
Teradata Basics                       324652
Teradata Basics                       260000
Teradata Basics                       234121
Teradata Basics                       123250
```

Figure 7.8

Note: Not all students listed are enrolled in this class.

Cross Join - Continued

The following example uses a WHERE clause to limit the rows for the customer "Best Electronics" and associate the result with every row in the Order Table. This type of join can have a major impact on system performance and is normally avoided.

```
SELECT  customer_name
        ,order_number
        ,order_total
FROM    customer_table  AS cust
        ,order_table    AS ord
WHERE   customer_name = 'Best Electronics';

Result: 6 rows returned

Customer_name          Order_Number   Order_Total
--------------------   ------------  ------------
Best Electronics             999999             ?
Best Electronics             123777      25454.84
Best Electronics             123585      16231.62
Best Electronics             123456      12447.53
Best Electronics             123512       7995.91
Best Electronics             123552       5311.47
```

Figure 7.9

Note: Product Joins can be prohibited on a user / group basis.

Join Consideration and PPI

Teradata has made the optimizer aware of join operations that would occur between PI and PPI tables. This merge join might be slightly slower than a traditional PI merge join. However, if you have a solid partition elimination strategy on the PPI table, then performance should be equal to that of a traditional merge join.

The Optimizer has (3) methods when joining PPI to non-PPI (NPPI) tables, and when joining two PPI tables that have different partitioning columns defined. These are as follows:

1. When joining two PPI tables that have different partition columns, the Optimizer could choose to spool one or both of the PPI tables in order to convert it to a NPPI table(s) in spool and then complete the merge join.

2. When joining an NPPI with a PPI table, the optimizer may opt to spool the non-PPI table and convert it into a PPI table in spool. This approach would create the new PPI table in spool with the same partition strategy as the base PPI table which will enable the join to complete on a row-key based merge join.

3. When joining NPPI and PPI tables that have the same Primary Index (PI), the optimizer can match the rows based on the PI. From there, the optimizer can determine how many partitions are required from the PPI table to complete the join. In this case, spool will not be utilized to complete the join operation.

Finally, it is important to make sure statistics are collected on the primary indexes, the partitioning columns in the PPI table and on the columns in the NPPI table that are the same as the partition column in the PPI table.

Chapter 7: Practice Questions

1. Which of the following statements is true about Product joins?.
    a. They can only join numeric columns because they produce the product of col_1 * col_2.
    b. They can be prohibited on a user/group basis.
    c. They are the most efficient of the join plans.
    d. They always require a join condition.

2. Which of the following is true about the ON and WHERE clauses of an outer join?
    a. Put the inner table join conditions in the ON clause and the outer table join conditions in the WHERE clause.
    b. Put the inner table search conditions in the WHERE clause and the outer table search conditions in the ON clause.
    c. Put the inner table search conditions in the ON clause and the outer table search conditions in the WHERE clause.
    d. Put all join and search conditions in the ON clause.

3. Given two tables T1 and T2, which diagram represent a Product Join?

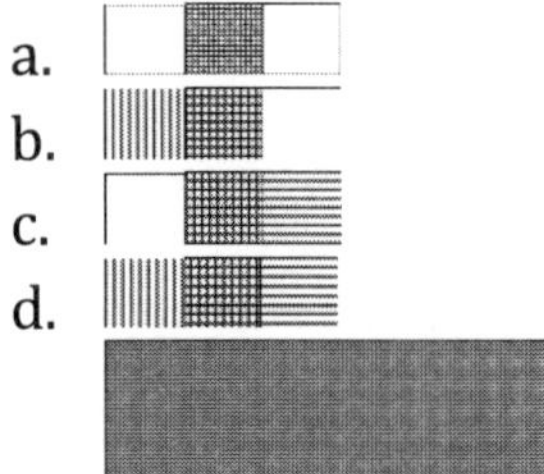

4. Given two tables T1 and T2, which diagram represent an Inner Join?

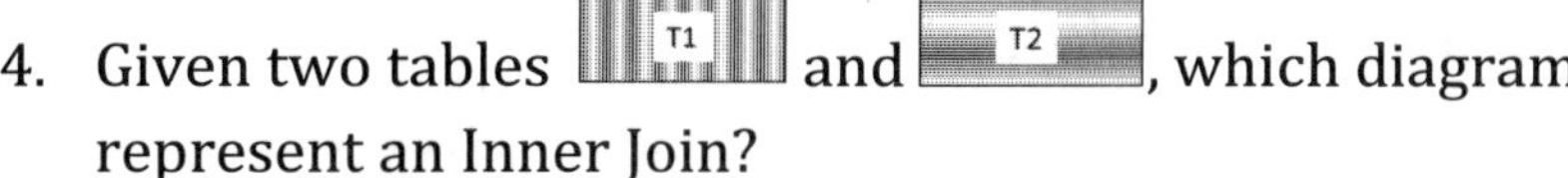

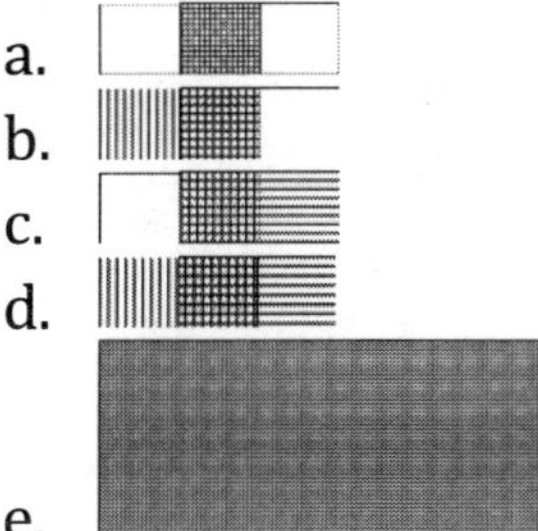

a.
b.
c.
d.
e.

5. Which of the following statements are TRUE when joining PPI and NPPI tables?
   a. Collect statistics on the primary indexes of both tables.
   b. Collect statistics on the partition columns of the PPI table.
   c. Collect statistics on the NPPI columns that match the PPI partition columns.
   d. All of the above.

Chapter Notes

Utilize this space for notes, key points to remember, diagrams, areas of further study, etc.

Chapter 8: Date and Time Processing

Certification Objectives

- ✓ Given a date, identify valid date calculations in a Teradata database.
- ✓ Identify the correct use of Intervals in expressions involving computations, conversions, literals, date intervals, and extractions.
- ✓ Identify the correct use of Time/Date in expressions involving computations, conversions, literals, and extractions.
- ✓ Identify the correct use of Timestamp in expressions involving computations, conversions, literals, and extractions.

Before You Begin

You should be familiar with the following terms and concepts.

Terms	Key Concepts
Date Forms	Differences with ANSI vs. Teradata dates
Date Processing	Methods for processing dates
Time	Timestamp data type options and SQL operations with time
Intervals	Arithmetic and casting options

Temporal Data Types

In this chapter, we will review the temporal data types, which allow you to store date, time, and time-interval information. These data types allow you to deal with past/present/future events.

The figure below reviews the temporal data types that are supported.

Date/Time	Description
DATE	Special type of integer. ((YEAR - 1900) * 10000) + (MONTH * 100) + DAY Use ANSI Date form for compatibility. 4 bytes
TIME (n)	Stored as HHMMSS.nnnnnn 6 bytes
TIMESTAMP (n)	Stored as YYMMDDHHMMSS.nnnnnn 10 bytes
TIME (n) WITH ZONE	Stored as HHMMSS.nnnnnn+HHMM 8 bytes
TIMESTAMP (n) WITH ZONE	Stored as YYMMDDHHMMSS.nnnnnn+HHMM 12 bytes

Figure 8.1

Temporal Functions

Though portions of dates can be accessed using standard integer arithmetic, Teradata provides the following functions to make handling temporal values easier.

Function	Description
ADD_MONTHS (d, n)	The function returns the date *d* plus the *n* months. You can use any integer for *n* months. If *d* is the last day of the month, or if the resulting month has fewer days than the day component, then the result is the last day of the resulting month. Otherwise, the result has the same day component as *d*.

EXTRACT (*period* FROM *value*)	PERIOD	SPECIFIES . . .
	YEAR	that the integer value for YEAR is to be extracted from the date represented by *value*.
	MONTH	that the integer value for MONTH is to be extracted from the date represented by *value*.
	DAY	that the integer value for DAY is to be extracted from the date represented by *value*.
	HOUR	that the integer value for HOUR is to be extracted from the time represented by *value*.
	MINUTE	that the integer value for MINUTE is to be extracted from the time represented by *value*.
	SECOND	that the integer value for SECOND is to be extracted from the time represented by *value*.
	TIMEZONE_HOUR	that the integer value for TIMEZONE_HOUR is to be extracted from the time represented by *value*.
	TIMEZONE_MINUTE	that the integer value for TIMEZONE_MINUTE is to be extracted from the time represented by *value*.

(d1) OVERLAPS (d2)	The function determines if two time intervals overlap. Teradata SQL supports the standard SQL overlaps predicate. Each time period to the left and right of the OVERLAPS keyword is one of the following expression types: • DateTime, DateTime • DateTime, Interval • Row subquery

Figure 8.2

DATEFORM

The display of DATE values is supported both in its Teradata form and the ANSI DateTime form. Though date values are stored as an integer, the default display of date values is controlled by the system parameter *Current DateForm.* This parameter is set by the system administrator.

DATE data can be set to be treated either using the ANSI date format (DATEFORM=ANSIDATE) or using the Teradata date format (DATEFORM=INTEGERDATE).

The following table explains the differences.

Option	**Description**
INTEGERDATE	Sets the DATEFORM option to import and export DATE values as encoded integers. INTEGERDATE results in a default DATE format in field mode of 'YY/MM/DD' for date columns created and for date constants in character form. INTEGERDATE is the default.

ANSIDATE	Sets the DATEFORM option to import and export DATE values as CHARACTER(10). Results in a 'YYYY-MM-DD' date format for date columns created and for date constants in character form.

Figure 8.3

You can see the setting of this parameter through the HELP SESSION; command.

Date Arithmetic

As mentioned earlier, dates are stored internally in an INTEGER as ((YEAR - 1900) * 10000) + (MONTH * 100) + DAY

Here is an example:

```
SELECT CURRENT_DATE, CAST(CURRENT_DATE AS INTEGER);

Result: 1 row returned

    Date             Date
--------    -----------
10/08/26        1100826
```

Figure 8.4

Note: Please see Figure 8.3 for more information regarding the above examples.

Because Teradata stores dates as an integer data type, arithmetic operations can be used to extract portions of dates as shown in this figure:

```
SELECT CAST(CURRENT_DATE AS INTEGER) AS INT_Date
        , CURRENT_DATE / 10000 + 1900 AS "Year"
        , CURRENT_DATE / 100 MOD 100 AS "Month"
        , CURRENT_DATE MOD 100 AS "Day"
;

Result: 1 row returned

   INT_Date         Year         Month           Day
-----------  -----------  -----------  -----------
    1100826         2010            8           26
```

Figure 8.5

When doing addition and subtraction on dates, the system converts the dates to a linear number of days, does the math, and then converts the result back to a calendar date.

EXTRACT

The EXTRACT function retrieves portions of date and time, such as year or hour, from DATE, TIME, or TIMESTAMP values. The following example illustrates this.

```
SELECT CURRENT_TIMESTAMP
, EXTRACT(YEAR FROM CURRENT_DATE)  AS Yr_Part
, EXTRACT(MONTH FROM CURRENT_DATE)  AS Mth_Part
, EXTRACT(DAY FROM CURRENT_TIMESTAMP)   AS Day_Part
, EXTRACT(HOUR FROM CURRENT_TIMESTAMP)   AS Hr_Part
, EXTRACT(MINUTE FROM CURRENT_TIME) AS Min_Part
, EXTRACT(SECOND FROM CURRENT_TIME) AS Sec_Part
,EXTRACT(TIMEZONE_HOUR FROM CURRENT_TIMESTAMP)AS TZ_Hr
,EXTRACT(TIMEZONE_MINUTE FROM CURRENT_TIMESTAMP) AS
TZ_Min ;

Result: 1 row returned

Current TimeStamp(6)  2010-07-26 08:33:14.140000+00:00
            Yr_Part          2010
           Mth_Part             7
           Day_Part            26
            Hr_Part             8
           Min_Part            33
           Sec_Part            14
              TZ_Hr             0
             TZ_Min             0
```

Figure 8.6

EXTRACT with Aggregates

The following example will display the selling month along with how many of each product was sold and the average sales revenue by product for the month.

```
SELECT  product_id
        , EXTRACT(MONTH FROM sale_date) AS Sale_month
        ,AVG(daily_sales) AS Avg_sale
        , COUNT(*) AS Sales_count
FROM   sales_table
GROUP BY 1,2
ORDER BY 2,3 ;
```

The same query using integer arithmetic on a date:

```
SELECT  product_id
        , sale_date /100 MOD 100 AS Sale_month
        ,AVG(daily_sales) AS Avg_sale
        , COUNT(*) AS Sales_count
FROM   sales_table
GROUP BY 1,2
ORDER BY 2,3 ;
```

```
Result: 6 rows returned
```

Product_ID	Sale_month	Avg_sale	Sales_count
2000	9	44575.97	3
3000	9	45965.59	3
1000	9	48783.56	3
3000	10	20549.26	4
2000	10	42307.22	4
1000	10	50044.01	4

Figure 8.7

Though both queries produced the desired report, the first one, using the EXTRACT, is easier to understand.

Date and Time Literals

Teradata SQL is written to handle date literals in either the Teradata format ('yy/mm/dd') or the ANSI format ('yyyy-mm-dd').

The ANSI date literal form is DATE 'yyyy-mm-dd', which does not depend on format settings/defaults.

Regardless of the Transaction mode (BTET, ANSI), the following query will execute because the literal is in ANSI format.

```
SELECT CAST('2002-11-21' AS DATE);

Result: 1 row returned

'2002-11-21'
------------
    02/11/21
```

Figure 8.8

Note: Figure 8-8 takes a character string and casts it as a date – it is the cast as date (which is ANSI) that allows the character string to have the format 'yyyy-mm-dd' and other formats. There is no other date literal form than DATE 'yyyy-mm-dd' in Teradata. There are character strings that can be implicitly or explicitly cast/converted to a date (based on an implicit/default or explicitly specified format) and there are numeric literals that can be implicitly/explicitly cast/converted to a date.

This query will also execute, regardless of the Transaction mode (BTET, ANSI), because the literal matches the Teradata default for dates.

```
SELECT CAST('2002/11/21' AS DATE);

Result: 1 row returned

'02/11/21'
----------
  2002/11/21
```

Figure 8.9

Without a FORMAT clause, the following query will fail since the literal does not match either the ANSI or Teradata format.

```
SELECT CAST('Nov 21, 2002' AS DATE);

*** Failure 2665 Invalid date.
                Statement# 1, Info =0
```

Figure 8.10

You can use a FORMAT clause to tell the system how to interpret a non-standard date value as shown below.

```
SELECT CAST('Nov 21, 2002' AS DATE FORMAT 'MMMbDD,bYYYY');

Result: 1 row returned

'Nov 21, 2002'
--------------
  Nov 21, 2002
```

Figure 8.11

The following example will change the order_date for one row in the order_table using a non-standard date format.

```
UPDATE order_table
SET order_date =
CAST('21/2002/11' AS DATE FORMAT 'dd/y4/mm')
WHERE order_number = 123777;

*** Update completed. One row changed.

SELECT *
FROM order_table
WHERE order_number = 123777;

Result: 1 row returned

Order_Number  Customer_number  Order_Date   Order_Total
------------  ---------------  ----------  ------------
      123777         57896883    02/11/21      25454.84
```

Figure 8.12

The following SQL will change the order_date back to its original value. Notice how much cleaner the SQL is when a standard format is used for the date value.

```
UPDATE order_table
SET order_date = '2007-09-09'
WHERE order_number = 123777;

*** Update completed. One row changed.

SELECT *
FROM order_table
WHERE order_number = 123777;

Result: 1 row returned

Order_Number  Customer_number  Order_Date   Order_Total
------------  ---------------  ----------  ------------
      123777         57896883    07/09/09      25454.84
```

Figure 8.13

INTERVAL Processing

In creating an Interval clause, it is important to remember that the literal string can only be interpreted in the context of the interval type where it is explicitly declared. In other words INTERVAL '30' is ambiguous because it could imply 30 years, 30 months, or 30 days.

In the following example, notice how the system adjusts for the length of the months involved.

```
SELECT   product_id
         , sale_date
         , sale_date + INTERVAL '30' DAY AS Due_Date
         , sale_date + INTERVAL '20' DAY AS Discount_Date
FROM     sales_table
WHERE product_id = 1000;

Result: 7 rows returned

 Product_ID  Sale_Date  Due_Date  Discount_Date
-----------  ---------  --------  -------------
       1000   07/09/28  07/10/28       07/10/18
       1000   07/09/29  07/10/29       07/10/19
       1000   07/09/30  07/10/30       07/10/20
       1000   07/10/01  07/10/31       07/10/21
       1000   07/10/02  07/11/01       07/10/22
       1000   07/10/03  07/11/02       07/10/23
       1000   07/10/04  07/11/03       07/10/24
```

Figure 8.14

As seen above in Figure 8.14, the literal value for an interval goes inside of quote marks. Any arithmetic operator is placed outside the leading quote mark. As an example: INTERVAL –'30' DAY

In the INTERVAL YEAR TO MONTH example below, the system interprets the literal '3-07' as a number of years (3) and a number of months (07).

SELECT (INTERVAL '3-07' YEAR TO MONTH) * 4;

```
Result: 1 row returned

( 3-07*4)
---------
    14-04
```

This is the equivalent of:
SELECT (((3*12) + 7)*4)/12 , (((3*12) + 7)*4) MOD 12

Figure 8.15

Note: 3 years 7 months = 43 months
43 * 4 = 172 months
172 months /12 = 14 years 4 months

Suppose you want to know how much time elapsed between a start time and an ending time. This is shown in the example below.

SELECT call_et, call_st, (call_et - call_st) SECOND(4)
FROM phcall
WHERE area_code = 650 AND phone_no = 5601140;

```
Result: 1 row returned

call_et       call_st       (call_et - call_st) SECOND
2006-01-23 09:00:06   2006-01-23 08:49:41  625.000000
```

Figure 8.16

You can use CAST to convert one interval type to another interval type. The only requirement is that both types must belong to the same Interval group, either the Year-Month or the Day-Time group.

The following example converts a DAY TO SECOND interval to a given number of hours.

```
SELECT CAST(INTERVAL '135 12:37:25.26' DAY TO SECOND AS
INTERVAL HOUR(4));

Result: 1 row returned

 135 12:37:25.26
----------------
            3252
```

Figure 8.17

OVERLAPS

The OVERLAP operater is used to test whether two time periods overlap one another. It returns either TRUE or FALSE.

Each side of the OVERLAPS must specify a starting and ending point in time.

The following query will not return a row since the two time spans DO NOT overlap. They meet at CURRENT_TIME(0).

```
SELECT 'OVERLAPS'
WHERE (CURRENT_TIME(0), INTERVAL '1' HOUR)
OVERLAPS (CURRENT_TIME(0), INTERVAL -'1' HOUR);
```

Figure 8.18

This query will return a row since the time periods overlap by one second.

```
SELECT 'OVERLAPS'
WHERE (CURRENT_TIME(0), INTERVAL '1' HOUR) OVERLAPS
 (CURRENT_TIME(0) + INTERVAL '1' SECOND, INTERVAL -'1' HOUR);

Result: 1 row returned

'OVERLAPS'
----------
OVERLAPS
```

Figure 8.19

This query will also return a row.

```
SELECT 'OVERLAPS'
WHERE (DATE '2000-01-15', DATE '2002-12-15')
OVERLAPS (DATE '2001-06-15', DATE '2005-06-15');

Result: 1 row returned

'OVERLAPS'
----------
OVERLAPS
```

Figure 8.20

Chapter 8: Practice Questions

1. What will the following date calculation return?

```
SELECT CAST( CURRENT_DATE/10000*10000 +
(EXTRACT(MONTH FROM CURRENT_DATE)-1)/3*300+101 AS
DATE);
```

   a. The first day of the current month
   b. The first day of the previous month
   c. The first day of the next quarter
   d. The first day of the current quarter

2. What will the following date calculation return?

```
SELECT ADD_MONTHS(CURRENT_DATE, 1)
- EXTRACT(DAY FROM ADD_MONTHS(CURRENT_DATE,1));
```

   a. The first day of the next month
   b. The first day of the previous month
   c. The last day of the current month
   d. The last day of the previous month

3. What will the following query return as the answer?

```
SELECT MIN(calendar_date), MAX(calendar_date)
FROM sys_calendar.calendar
WHERE calendar_date BETWEEN
ADD_MONTHS(CURRENT_DATE, -3) - EXTRACT(DAY FROM
ADD_MONTHS(CURRENT_DATE ,-3) -1)
AND
ADD_MONTHS(CURRENT_DATE, 0) - EXTRACT(DAY FROM
ADD_MONTHS(CURRENT_DATE, 0)) ;
```

   a. The first and last dates of the current quarter
   b. The first and last dates of the previous three months
   c. The first and last dates of the current month and previous two months
   d. The first and last dates of the previous quarter

4. What will the following query return as the answer?

```
SELECT CURRENT_DATE (FORMAT 'EEEE') (CHAR(9));
```

   a. The name of the current day of the week in long form
   b. The name of the current day of the week in short form
   c. The name of the current month in long form
   d. The name of the current month in short form
   e. An error

Chapter Notes

Utilize this space for notes, key points to remember, diagrams, areas of further study, etc.

Chapter 9: Character String Processing

Certification Objectives

- ✓ Identify the correct use of new embedded services functions (e.g., TO_CHAR, TO_NUMBER, NVL, etc.).
- ✓ Identify the attribute functions and identify how they work within SQL.
- ✓ Identify the correct use of string manipulation functions and attributes.

Before You Begin

You should be familiar with the following terms and concepts.

Terms	Key Concepts
Character Data	Functions used to transform character data
Trim	How to apply along with understand the options
Substring	When to use properly
Concatenation	Utilizing SQL to combine column fields
Imbedded Services Functions	How to use them

Teradata SQL provides many ways to manipulate character data. Most of the ways are ANSI standard, while a few are Teradata extensions.

The following chart summarizes your choices:

IF you want to . . .	THEN use . . .
Concatenate strings	Concatenation character ||
Get the starting position of a substring within another string	POSITION or INDEX INDEX is a Teradata extension
Convert a character string to lowercase	LOWER
Convert a character string to uppercase	UPPER Note: This is a Teradata extension
Extract a substring from another string	SUBSTRING or SUBSTR SUBSTR is a Teradata extension
Trim specified pad characters or bytes from a character or byte string	TRIM
Count the number of characters in a string	CHARACTER_LENGTH is a synonym for the Teradata CHARACTERS function
Count the number of bytes in a byte string	BYTES Note: This is a Teradata extension
See the default value assigned to a column in the CREATE TABLE	SELECT DEFAULT(*columnname*) This is a Teradata extension
See the display format assigned to a column in the CREATE TABLE	SELECT FORMAT(*columnname*) This is a Teradata extension

Figure 9.1

TRIM

VARCHAR does not automatically trim trailing spaces as stated. Therefore, it is recommended to use TRIM for both CHAR and VARCHAR. VARBYTE will automatically trim trailing bytes of binary 00 but not leading bytes of binary 00.

Most frequently, TRIM is used on fixed-length data along with concatenation.

The following example shows the variations of a TRIM.

```
SELECT '**1234**'
        , TRIM(LEADING '*' FROM '**1234**')
        , TRIM(TRAILING '*' FROM '**1234**')
        , TRIM(BOTH '*' FROM '**1234**');

Result: 1 row returned

                          '**1234**'   **1234**
 Trim(LEADING '*' FROM '**1234**')   1234**
Trim(TRAILING '*' FROM '**1234**')   **1234
    Trim(BOTH '*' FROM '**1234**')   1234
```

Figure 9.2

Implicit Data Conversion

The TRIM function is designed to operate on character data. If numeric data is supplied, it will be converted to character data first.

The following is an example where the literal supplied is numeric.

```
SELECT employee_no
    ,TRIM(LEADING 0 FROM employee_no)
FROM  employee_table;

*** Failure 5388 The Pad Expression for TRIM has an
incorrect data type or length.
```

Figure 9.3

In this next example, the literal was changed to alphanumeric to match the implicit numeric to character conversion of the input.

```
SELECT employee_no
   ,TRIM(LEADING '0' FROM employee_no)
FROM  employee_table;

Result: 9 rows returned

Employee_No  Trim(LEADING '0' FROM Employee_No)
-----------  ----------------------------------
    2000000      2000000
    1333454      1333454
    1000234      1000234
    1256349      1256349
    1232578      1232578
    1121334      1121334
    2341218      2341218
    1324657      1324657
    2312225      2312225
```

Figure 9.4

TRIM and Concatenation

As mention above, TRIM is frequently combined with concatenation. The following example shows two ways of displaying names.

```
SELECT TRIM(last_name) || ', ' || first_name AS Example1
        ,first_name || ' ' || TRIM(last_name) AS Example2
FROM   employee_table
ORDER BY 1;
```

```
Result: 9 rows returned

Example1                            Example2
----------------------------------  ----------------------------------
Clooney, George                     George
Clooney
Ford, Harrison                      Harrison Ford
Gere, Richard                       Richard Gere
Mcfly, Loraine                      Loraine Mcfly
Roberts, Julia                      Julia Roberts
Strickland, Stan                    Stan Strickland
Student, Mandee                     Mandee Student
Travolta, John                      John Travolta
Willis, Bruce                       Bruce Willis
```

Figure 9.5

The *first_name* column is VARCHAR and does not need to be trimmed.

CHARACTER_LENGTH and CHARACTERS Functions

The CHARACTER_LENGTH (ANSI) and the CHARACTERS (Teradata) functions are only meaningful with VARCHAR and VARBYTE data. They return the length of a string as a count of logical characters or bytes.

You can use the TRIM function to transform a fixed length string into a variable length string, as shown below.

```
SELECT last_name
       , CHARACTERS(last_name)
       , CHARACTER_LENGTH( TRIM(last_name))
FROM employee_table
ORDER BY last_name;
```

Result: 9 rows returned

Last name	Characters(Last name)	Characters(Trim(BOTH FROM Last name))
Clooney	20	7
Ford	20	4
Gere	20	4
Mcfly	20	5
Roberts	20	7
Strickland	20	10
Student	20	7
Travolta	20	8
Willis	20	6

Figure 9.6

Note: Notice the heading for column 3.

OCTET Function

This function returns the length of *string_expression* in octets when it is converted to the named character set (taking the export width value into consideration). Since our character set is ASCII, the results will match the CHARACTERS count.

```
SELECT job_desc
       , CHARACTERS (job_desc)
       , OCTET_LENGTH (job_desc)
FROM job_table
ORDER BY 2;

Result: 5 rows returned

job_desc              Characters(job_desc)  Octet_Length(job_desc)
--------------------  --------------------  ----------------------
Manager                                  7                       7
Developer                                9                       9
Programmer                              10                      10
Security Guard                          14                      14
Project Manager                         15                      15
```

Figure 9.7

POSITION

Another useful function is POSITION. It returns the starting position of *string-1* within *string-2.* It is frequently combined with the SUBSTRING or SUBSTR function. In addition, if *string-1 and string-2* are numeric, they will be converted to CHARACTER.

The following is a simple example of the POSITION function.

```
SELECT  job_desc
        , POSITION ('Ma' IN job_desc)
FROM    job_table
ORDER BY 1;

Result: 5 rows returned

job_desc              Position('Ma' in job_desc)
--------------------  ---------------------------
Developer                                       0
Manager                                         1
Programmer                                      0
Project Manager                                 9
Security Guard                                  0
```

Figure 9.8

INDEX

As shown in the Figure 9.9, the INDEX function is a Teradata extension. It functions just like POSITION, and returns the starting position of string-2 within string-1. Use POSITION for ANSI compatibility.

The following query is the same as the previous query (Figure 9.8) but uses the INDEX function.

```
SELECT job_desc
        , INDEX(job_desc, 'ma')
FROM   job_table
ORDER BY 1;

Result: 5 rows returned

job_desc                  Index(job_desc,'ma')
--------------------      --------------------
Developer                                    0
Manager                                      1
Programmer                                   0
Project Manager                              9
Security Guard                               0
```

Figure 9.9

SUBSTRING and SUBSTR

The SUBSTRING and SUBSTR functions operate identically to extract a substring from a string starting at a specified character position for a given number of characters. SUBSTRING is the ANSI version of the Teradata SUBSTR. If the string is numeric, it is converted to CHARACTER.

ANSI syntax: SUBSTRING (string-1 FROM p-1 [FOR c-1])

Teradata syntax: SUBSTR (string-1, p-1 [,c-1])

Where p-1 is the starting position and c-1 is the length of the substring to be extracted. If c-1 is omitted, the default is end-of-string.

The following example uses both functions to extract the first 5 characters from each course name.

```
SELECT course_name
       , SUBSTRING (course_name FROM 1 FOR 5) AS "Substring"
       , SUBSTR (course_name, 1, 5) AS "Substr"
FROM   course_table
ORDER BY 1;

Result: 6 rows returned

Course_name                      Substring  Substr
------------------------------   ---------  ------
Advanced SQL                     Advan      Advan
Database Administration          Datab      Datab
Introduction to SQL              Intro      Intro
Physical Database Tuning         Physi      Physi
TD12 SQL Features                TD12       TD12
Teradata Basics                  Terad      Terad
```

Figure 9.10

SUBSTRING and POSITION

If the starting position for an extract varies from row to row, based upon some defined value, use POSITION to locate the value and extract from that point.

The next example extracts all words of the course name after the first word.

```
SELECT course_name
       , SUBSTRING(course_name FROM
         POSITION(' ' IN course_name)) AS "SUBSTRING"
FROM course_table
ORDER BY 1 ;

Result: 6 rows returned

Course_name                     SUBSTRING
------------------------------  ------------------
Advanced SQL                     SQL
Database Administration          Administration
Introduction to SQL              to SQL
Physical Database Tuning         Database Tuning
TD12 SQL Features                SQL Features
Teradata Basics                  Basics
```

Figure 9.11

Because POSITION returns the value of the first space character in this example, the space is included in the result. To eliminate this space, do the following.

```
SELECT course_name
       , SUBSTRING(course_name FROM
         POSITION(' ' IN course_name) + 1) AS "SUBSTRING"
FROM course_table
ORDER BY 1 ;

Result: 6 rows returned

Course_name                      SUBSTRING
------------------------------   -----------------
Advanced SQL                     SQL
Database Administration          Administration
Introduction to SQL              to SQL
Physical Database Tuning         Database Tuning
TD12 SQL Features                SQL Features
Teradata Basics                  Basics
```

Figure 9.12

Imbedded Services Functions

The following functions, in Figure 9.13, all exist in the TD_SYSFNLIB database, and can be used to convert data from one data type to another.

You can invoke an embedded services function using the function name alone. You can also qualify the function name by adding the TD_SYSFNLIB database name.

If you try to invoke an embedded services function using the function name alone, but you also have a customer-developed UDF with the same name in the current database or in the SYSLIB database,

Teradata Database will execute the customer-developed UDF instead of the embedded services function.

FUNCTION	**PURPOSE**	**EXAMPLE**
TO_BYTES	Decodes a sequence of characters in a given encoding into a sequence of bits.	The following query: SELECT TO_BYTES ('5A', 'base16'); returns '01011010'.
FROM_BYTES	Encodes a sequence of bits into a sequence of characters representing its encoding.	The following query: SELECT from_bytes('5A1B'XB, 'base10'); returns '23067'.
TO_NUMBER	Converts *string_expr* to a NUMBER data type.	The following query: SELECT TO_NUMBER ('1789.96', '9999.99'); returns the result 1789.96.
TO_CHAR (Numeric)	Converts *numeric_expr* to a character string.	The following query: SELECT TO_CHAR(50000, '$99,999.99'); returns '$50,000.00'.
TO_CHAR (DateTime)	Converts a *date_timestamp_value* to a character string.	The following query: SELECT TO_CHAR(DATE '2003-12-23', 'DD-MON-YYYY'); returns a result of '23-DEC-2003'.
TO_DATE	Converts *string_expr* to a DATE data type.	The following query: SELECT TO_DATE ('January 15, 1989, 11:00 A.M.', 'Month dd, YYYY, HH: MI A.M.'); returns the result 15-JAN-89.
TO_TIMESTAMP	Converts *string_expr* to a TIMESTAMP data type.	The following query: SELECT TO_TIMESTAMP ('January 15, 1989, 11:00 A.M.', 'Month dd, YYYY,

		HH:MI A.M.'); returns the result 1989-01-15 11:00:00.000000.
TO_TIMESTAMP_TZ	Converts *string_expr* to a TIMESTAMP WITH TIME ZONE data type.	The following query: SELECT TO_TIMESTAMP_TZ ('January 15, 1989, 11:00 A.M.', 'Month dd, YYYY, HH: MI A.M.'); returns the result 1989-01-15 11:00:00.000000+00:00.
TO_YMINTERVAL	Converts *string_value* specified into an INTERVAL YEAR(4) TO MONTH value.	The following query SELECT TO_YMINTERVAL('04-10'); returns the result '04-10'.
TO_DSINTERVAL	Converts *string_value* specified into an INTERVAL DAY(4) TO SECOND(6) value.	The following query SELECT TO_DSINTERVAL('100 04:23:59'); returns the result '100 04:23:59.000000'.
NUMTODSINTERVAL	Converts *numeric_value* into an INTERVAL DAY(4) TO SECOND(6) value.	The following query: SELECT NUMTODSINTERVAL(100, 'HOURS'); returns the result '4 04:00:00.000000', which is 4 days, 4 hours.
NUMTOYMINTERVAL	Converts *numeric_value* into an INTERVAL YEAR(4) TO MONTH value.	The following query: SELECT NUMTOYMINTERVAL(100, 'MONTHS'); returns the result '08-04', which is 8 years, 4 months.

Figure 9.13

Here's an example using the TO_DATE function.

```
SELECT c1 AS c1_int
        , c2 AS  c2_char12
        , TD_SYSFNLIB.TO_DATE(c2, 'Mon dd, yyyy')  AS c2_to_date
        FROM test;


 *** Query completed. 3 rows found. 3 columns returned.
 *** Total elapsed time was 1 second.

     c1_int  c2_char12     c2_to_date
-----------  ------------  ----------
          3  Apr 01, 1900    00/04/01
          1  Feb 28, 2011    11/02/28
          2  Dec 25, 2000    00/12/25
```

Figure 9.14

Chapter 9: Practice Questions

1. Choose the correct result for the following query.

   SELECT trim(leading from '   St') || trim(' ud ') || trim('y h') || substring('pwardyvo' from -3 for 7);

   a. Study hard
   b. Study hpwa
   c. Study hwar
   d. Study hrdy

2. What will the following query return?

   SELECT 'Good   ' || substring('guest' from -3 for 4) || substring('nopqrs' from 7 for -1);

   a. Error
   b. Good guess
   c. Good gs
   d. Good gus

3. What will the following query return?

   SELECT POSITION('e' IN (SUBSTRING('a b c d e f g' FROM (POSITION(' ' IN 'a b c d e f g')))));

   a. 6
   b. 7
   c. 8
   d. 9
   e. Error

4. In which database are the embedded functions stored?
    a. SYSLIB
    b. SYSUDTLIB
    c. TD_SYSFNLIB
    d. TDPUSER

Chapter Notes

Utilize this space for notes, key points to remember, diagrams, areas of further study, etc.

Chapter 10: OLAP Functions

Certification Objectives

- ✓ Describe the functionality of RESET WHEN in the Window Aggregate function.
- ✓ Describe the functionality of Ordered Analytic Functions.
- ✓ Describe the functionality of QUALIFY in the Window Aggregate function.
- ✓ Describe the functionality of RANK in the Window Aggregate function.
- ✓ Given a scenario, identify the result set returned by SAMPLE (e.g., replacement vs. no replacement).
- ✓ Identify the processing differences between TOP N and SAMPLE.

Before You Begin

You should be familiar with the following terms and concepts.

Terms	Key Concepts
Sum / Over	Understand the SQL syntax for cumulative summation of data
Rank	How to apply and reset capabilities
Row_Number	Utilization of this function to number resulting rows
Sample / Top	How do these functions work and the differences

Teradata On-Line Analytical Processing Functions

The OLAP and aggregate functions are close cousins, but are very different in their use. Like traditional aggregates, OLAP functions operate on groups of rows and permit qualification and filtering of the group result. Unlike aggregates that return a single aggregated value, OLAP functions also return the individual row detail.

The following chart contains the Teradata OLAP aggregates and their functions. These are supported only for backward compatibility.

Teradata Extensions

DEPRECATED TERADATA EXTENSIONS	DESCRIPTION	EQUIVALENT ANSI SQL-2003 WINDOW FUNCTIONS
CSUM	Cumulative sum of a referenced value, for a range or dimension.	SUM
MAVG	Computation of a moving average of a referenced value based on a specified window.	AVG
MDIFF	Computation of a moving difference between two referenced data values based on a specified window.	Composable from SUM
MLINREG	Computation of a moving linear regression between two referenced data values based on a specified window.	Composable from SUM and COUNT

MSUM	Computation of a moving sum of a referenced value based on a specified window.	SUM
RANK	Ranking based on high order or low order of a referenced data value based on a specified value.	RANK

Figure 10.1

Though there are more OLAP functions, the following chart shows some of the more frequently used ANSI OLAP commands and their functions:

ANSI OLAP Functions

Command	Functionality
SUM/OVER	Cumulative sum of a referenced value, for a range or dimension.
SUM / OVER (Moving Sum)	Computation of a moving sum of a referenced value, based on a specified window.
RANK / OVER	Ranking based on high order or low order of a referenced data value, based on a specified value.
RANK / OVER (QUANTILE)	Categorize a referenced data value, based on a number of partitions.
ROW_NUMBER / OVER	Assigns a unique number to each row to which it is applied, either each row in the partition or each row returned by the query. In the ordered sequence of rows specified in the order by clause, the rows begin with the number one.

Figure 10.2

In the following chart, the OVER Windows definitions are presented.

OVER (. . .) WINDOW DEFINITIONS

<table>
<tr><td>PARTITION BY col1 [, ... , coln]</td><td colspan="2">Defines the "GROUP" or "Window" of rows over which the aggregate function operates. If there is no PARTITION BY clause, then the entire result set, delivered by the FROM clause, constitutes a single group or partition.</td></tr>
<tr><td>ORDER BY value_expression [ASC | DESC]</td><td colspan="2">The ordering of rows within the Group, not the final result.</td></tr>
<tr><td>RESET WHEN</td><td colspan="2">This determines the group or partition, over which the ordered analytical function operates.</td></tr>
<tr><td rowspan="4">ROWS</td><td colspan="2">The starting point for the aggregation group within the partition. The aggregation group end is the current row. The aggregation group of a row R is a set of rows, defined relative to R in the ordering of the rows within the partition.

If there is no ROWS or ROWS BETWEEN clause, the default aggregation group is ROWS BETWEEN UNBOUNDED PRECEDING AND UNBOUNDED FOLLOWING.</td></tr>
<tr><td>UNBOUNDED PRECEDING</td><td>Include all group rows preceding the current row.</td></tr>
<tr><td>Value PRECEDING</td><td>Include the specified number of rows before the current row.</td></tr>
<tr><td>CURRENT ROW</td><td>Report only on the current row.</td></tr>
</table>

<table>
<tr><td rowspan="5">ROWS BETWEEN</td><td colspan="2">The aggregation group start and end, which defines a set of rows relative to the current row in the ordering of the rows within the partition. The row specified by the group start must precede the row specified by the group end.

If there is no ROWS or ROWS BETWEEN clause, the default aggregation group is ROWS BETWEEN UNBOUNDED PRECEDING AND UNBOUNDED FOLLOWING.</td></tr>
<tr><td>UNBOUNDED PRECEDING AND</td><td>UNBOUNDED FOLLOWING
value PRECEDING
CURRENT ROW
value FOLLOWING</td></tr>
<tr><td>value PRECEDING AND</td><td>UNBOUNDED FOLLOWING
value PRECEDING
CURRENT ROW
value FOLLOWING</td></tr>
<tr><td>CURRENT ROW AND</td><td>UNBOUNDED FOLLOWING
CURRENT ROW
value FOLLOWING</td></tr>
<tr><td>value FOLLOWING AND</td><td>UNBOUNDED FOLLOWING
value FOLLOWING</td></tr>
</table>

Figure 10.3

General Syntax:

aggregate_function OVER([PARTITION BY] [RESET WHEN] [ORDER BY] [ROWS | ROWS BETWEEN])

The best way to understand the OLAP functions is by studying the following examples.

Cumulative SUM - SUM / OVER

The next example demonstrates the ANSI SUM / OVER. It produces the same result as the Teradata CSUM function.

```
SELECT Product_ID
       ,Sale_Date
       ,Daily_Sales
       ,SUM(Daily_Sales)
         OVER ( ORDER BY Sale_Date
         ROWS UNBOUNDED PRECEDING) AS Like_CSum
FROM Sales_table
WHERE Product_ID BETWEEN 1000 and 2000 ;
```

```
Result: 14 rows returned

Product_ID  Sale_Date  Daily_Sales    Like_CSum
----------- ---------  -----------  -----------
       1000  07/09/28     45850.40     45850.40
       2000  07/09/28     42787.88     88638.28
       1000  07/09/29     64500.22    153138.50
       2000  07/09/29     46090.00    199228.50
       2000  07/09/30     44850.03    244078.53
       1000  07/09/30     36000.07    280078.60
       2000  07/10/01     58850.29    338928.89
       1000  07/10/01     45700.43    384629.32
       2000  07/10/02     35599.93    420229.25
       1000  07/10/02     33700.50    453929.75
       2000  07/10/03     41900.18    495829.93
       1000  07/10/03     66200.00    562029.93
       2000  07/10/04     32878.50    594908.43
       1000  07/10/04     54575.10    649483.53
```

Figure 10.4

Note: In this example, all rows participate as a single group.

SUM Using SUM / OVER and PARTITION BY

The ANSI method does not use GROUP BY. Instead, it uses the OVER to designate that a partition or group can be established using the PARTITION BY indicator.

```
SELECT Product_ID
         ,Sale_Date
         ,Daily_Sales
         ,SUM(Daily_Sales)
           OVER ( PARTITION BY Sale_Date
            ORDER BY Sale_Date  ROWS UNBOUNDED PRECEDING)
          (format '$$$$,$$$.99')  AS  Like_CSum
FROM  Sales_table
WHERE Sale_Date between 1071001 and 1071003 ;

Result: 9 rows returned

Product_ID  Sale_Date  Daily_Sales    Like_CSum
----------- ---------  -----------  -----------
       2000  07/10/01     58850.29   $58,850.29
       3000  07/10/01     27000.00   $85,850.29
       1000  07/10/01     45700.43  $131,550.72
       1000  07/10/02     33700.50   $33,700.50
       2000  07/10/02     35599.93   $69,300.43
       3000  07/10/02     18767.94   $88,068.37
       1000  07/10/03     66200.00   $66,200.00
       2000  07/10/03     41900.18  $108,100.18
       3000  07/10/03     21553.79  $129,653.97
```

Figure 10.5

Ranking Data using the ANSI RANK / OVER

The output of the RANK / OVER function is the highest or the lowest data values in the column, depending on the sort requested. A query can return a specified number of the "best" rows (highest values) or the "worst" rows (lowest values). These capabilities and output options will be demonstrated below.

Here is the syntax for RANK / OVER:

RANK() OVER ([PARTITION BY <column-name> [...,<column-number>]] ORDER BY <column-list> [DESC | ASC])

The next SELECT operates over all of the rows in the Sales table, ranking daily sales in best-to-worst (DESC) order.

```
SELECT        Product_ID
              ,Sale_Date
              ,Daily_Sales
              ,RANK() OVER (ORDER BY daily_sales DESC)  AS
"RANK"
FROM   Sales_table ;

Result: 21 rows returned

Product_ID  Sale_Date  Daily_Sales          RANK
----------- --------- -----------  -----------
       1000  07/10/03     66200.00            1
       1000  07/09/29     64500.22            2
       3000  07/09/28     60903.77            3
       2000  07/10/01     58850.29            4
       1000  07/10/04     54575.10            5
       2000  07/09/29     46090.00            6
       1000  07/09/28     45850.40            7
       1000  07/10/01     45700.43            8
       2000  07/09/30     44850.03            9
       2000  07/09/28     42787.88           10
       3000  07/09/30     42338.86           11
       2000  07/10/03     41900.18           12
       1000  07/09/30     36000.07           13
       2000  07/10/02     35599.93           14
       3000  07/09/29     34654.13           15
       1000  07/10/02     33700.50           16
       2000  07/10/04     32878.50           17
       3000  07/10/01     27000.00           18
       3000  07/10/03     21553.79           19
       3000  07/10/02     18767.94           20
       3000  07/10/04     14875.33           21
```

Figure 10.6

To make the report show daily sales in worst-to-best ranking order, change the ORDER BY to ASC (default).

QUALIFY to Find Top Best or Bottom Worse

The above report could have been created without the window functions by simply listing all rows in decreasing sales amount. With a small number of rows, the best and the worst is readily available. However, when there are hundreds or millions of rows, returning all the rows takes far too much time.

The QUALIFY function operates on window group output the same way the HAVING clause does for GROUP BY groups. It's either GROUP BY ... HAVING, or OVER(...) QUALIFY.

The following SELECT is the same as the above, but uses the QUALIFY to limit the output to the best 3 (highest values) rows:

```
SELECT      Product_ID
            ,Sale_Date
            ,Daily_Sales
            ,RANK() OVER (ORDER BY Daily_Sales DESC) AS
"RANK"
FROM   Sales_table
QUALIFY "RANK" < 4 ;

Result: 3 rows returned

Product_ID  Sale_Date  Daily_Sales          RANK
----------- ---------  -----------   -----------
       1000  07/10/03     66200.00             1
       1000  07/09/29     64500.22             2
       3000  07/09/28     60903.77             3
```

Figure 10.7

The next SELECT is the same as the above, with one exception. It uses the ASC to reverse the default sequence of DESC. Now, the worst (lowest) 3 values are returned:

```
SELECT      Product_ID
            ,Sale_Date
            ,Daily_Sales
            ,RANK() OVER (ORDER BY Daily_Sales ASC) AS "RANK"
FROM   Sales_table
QUALIFY "RANK" < 4 ;

Result: 3 rows returned

Product_ID  Sale_Date  Daily_Sales         RANK
----------- ---------  -----------  -----------
       3000  07/10/04     14875.33            1
       3000  07/10/02     18767.94            2
       3000  07/10/03     21553.79            3
```

Figure 10.8

RANK with Reset Capabilities

There is a method available to reset a RANK / OVER function to provide the best or worst rank of a group of rows that contain a common value in another column. Use the PARTITION BY designation to specify a data value that, when it changes, causes the accumulation value to be reset back to zero. Figure 10.9 demonstrates the reset option.

Using RANK/OVER with PARTITION BY

The following SELECT ranks the daily sales for each product using the PARTITION BY and creates an alias for the RANK column to use in the QUALIFY to find the best 2 days:

```
SELECT      Product_ID
            ,Sale_Date
            ,Daily_Sales
            ,RANK()  OVER (PARTITION BY Product_ID
                           ORDER BY Daily_Sales DESC )  AS Ranked
FROM   Sales_table
QUALIFY Ranked <= 2 ;

Result: 6 rows returned

Product_ID  Sale_Date  Daily_Sales       Ranked
----------- ---------  -----------  -----------
       1000  07/10/03     66200.00            1
       1000  07/09/29     64500.22            2
       2000  07/10/01     58850.29            1
       2000  07/09/29     46090.00            2
       3000  07/09/28     60903.77            1
       3000  07/09/30     42338.86            2
```

Figure 10.9

Numbering of the Rows Using ROW_NUMBER / OVER

The following ANSI syntax is used with ROW_NUMBER to provide OLAP functionality. At the same time, it can be used to generate a sequential number.

```
ROW_NUMBER() OVER ( [ PARTITION BY <value-column-data> ]
                    ORDER BY <column-list>)
```

The next SELECT uses ROW_NUMBER to produce a report for the dates in September:

```
SELECT      Product_ID
            ,Sale_Date
            ,Daily_Sales    (Format '$$$,$$$.99')
            ,ROW_NUMBER() OVER ( ORDER BY product_id,
                       daily_sales desc) AS "Row Number"
FROM   Sales_table
WHERE EXTRACT(MONTH FROM Sale_Date) = 9 ;

Result: 9 rows returned

Product_ID  Sale_Date  Daily_Sales   Row Number
----------- ---------  -----------   -----------
       1000  07/09/29   $64,500.22             1
       1000  07/09/28   $45,850.40             2
       1000  07/09/30   $36,000.07             3
       2000  07/09/29   $46,090.00             4
       2000  07/09/30   $44,850.03             5
       2000  07/09/28   $42,787.88             6
       3000  07/09/28   $60,903.77             7
       3000  07/09/30   $42,338.86             8
       3000  07/09/29   $34,654.13             9
```

Figure 10.10

The next SELECT uses ROW_NUMBER / OVER to produce a similar report as the previous functions, sorting and breaking on the Product ID:

```
SELECT      Product_ID
            ,Sale_Date
            ,Daily_Sales          (Format '$$$,$$$.99')
            ,ROW_NUMBER() OVER
                 (PARTITION BY product_id
                  ORDER BY product_id, daily_sales desc
                 ) AS "Row Number"
FROM   Sales_table
WHERE EXTRACT(MONTH FROM Sale_Date) = 9;
```

```
Result: 9 rows returned

 Product_ID  Sale_Date  Daily_Sales   Row Number
-----------  ---------  -----------  -----------
       1000   07/09/29   $64,500.22            1
       1000   07/09/28   $45,850.40            2
       1000   07/09/30   $36,000.07            3
       2000   07/09/29   $46,090.00            1
       2000   07/09/30   $44,850.03            2
       2000   07/09/28   $42,787.88            3
       3000   07/09/28   $60,903.77            1
       3000   07/09/30   $42,338.86            2
       3000   07/09/29   $34,654.13            3
```

Figure 10.11

RESET WHEN

Depending on the evaluation of the specified condition, RESET WHEN determines the group or partition, over which the ordered analytical function operates. If the condition evaluates to TRUE, a new dynamic partition is created inside the specified window partition.

If there is no RESET WHEN phrase or PARTITION BY phrase, then the entire result set, delivered by the FROM clause, constitutes a single partition, over which the ordered analytical function executes.

A window specification that specifies a RESET WHEN clause must also specify an ORDER BY clause.

The condition in the RESET WHEN clause is equivalent in scope to the condition in a QUALIFY clause with the additional constraint that nested ordered analytical functions cannot specify conditional partitioning.

The condition is applied to the rows in all designated window partitions to create subpartitions within the particular window partitions.

A RESET WHEN condition can contain the following:

- Ordered analytical functions that do not include the RESET WHEN clause
- Scalar subqueries
- Aggregate operators
- DEFAULT functions

The following query finds sequences of increasing sales by month.

```
SELECT product_id
       , sale_date / 100 MOD 100 AS sale_month, daily_sales
       , ROW_NUMBER( ) OVER
              (PARTITION BY product_id
               ORDER BY sale_date
               RESET WHEN daily_sales <=
               SUM(daily_sales) OVER
                     (PARTITION BY product_id
                      ORDER BY sale_date
                      ROWS BETWEEN 1 PRECEDING
                      AND 1 PRECEDING
                     )
              ) -1 AS sales_increase
FROM csql_class.sales_table;
```

Product_ID	sale_month	Daily_Sales	sales_increase
1000	9	45850.40	0
1000	9	64500.22	1
1000	9	36000.07	0
1000	10	45700.43	1
1000	10	33700.50	0
1000	10	66200.00	1
1000	10	54575.10	0
2000	9	42787.88	0
2000	9	46090.00	1
2000	9	44850.03	0
2000	10	58850.29	1
2000	10	35599.93	0
2000	10	41900.18	1
2000	10	32878.50	0
3000	9	60903.77	0
3000	9	34654.13	0
3000	9	42338.86	1
3000	10	27000.00	0
3000	10	18767.94	0
3000	10	21553.79	1
3000	10	14875.33	0

Figure 10.12

SAMPLE and SAMPLEID

The SAMPLE function reduces the number of rows to be considered for further processing by returning one or more samples of rows specified either as a list of fractions of the total number of rows or as a list of numbers of rows from the SELECT query. This is a Teradata extension.

Syntax:

SAMPLE [WITH REPLACEMENT] [RANDOMIZED ALLOCATION]
{ [{*fraction_description* | *count_description* } |
WHEN *condition* THEN {*fraction_description* | *count_description* }
[ELSE {*fraction_description* | *count_description*] } END
}

Syntax element . . .	Specifies . . .
WITH REPLACEMENT	whether sampling is done by returning each sampled row to the table for possible redundant sampling or by withholding sampled rows from resampling. If you specify WITH REPLACEMENT, then it is possible to request more samples than there are rows in the table. Sampling without replacement is the default. You select it implicitly by not specifying WITH REPLACEMENT.

RANDOMIZED ALLOCATION	whether rows are sampled randomly across AMPS (RANDOMIZED ALLOCATION) or proportionate to the number of qualified rows per AMP (proportional allocation). The proportional allocation option does not provide a simple random sample of the entire population. It provides a random sample stratified by AMPs, but it is much faster, especially for very large samples. Proportional is the default. You select it implicitly by not specifying RANDOMIZED ALLOCATION.
fraction_description	any set of unsigned floating point constant numbers in the closed interval (0,1) that specifies the percentage of rows to be sampled for a true search condition. This is a comma-separated list of fractions, the sum of which must not exceed 1. The value set specifies the percentage of the homogeneous subgroup defined by *search_condition* to be sampled for the report. No more than 16 samples can be requested per fraction description.

count_description	a set of positive integer constants that specifies the number of rows to be sampled for a true search condition. A warning is returned if there are not enough rows in the result to satisfy the sampling request completely. No more than 16 samples can be requested per count description.
WHEN	to test a set of conditions for truth.
condition	an evaluation predicate that defines each homogeneous subgroup in the sample set.
THEN	to apply the specified sampling fraction description or count description to the sample.
ELSE	to apply the specified sampling fraction description or count description to the sample if none of the WHEN *condition* predicates evaluates to true.
END	the termination of the WHEN ... THEN ... ELSE clause.

Figure 10.13

In the following query, all of the rows will be included in the sample since the fraction description sums to 100%.

```
SELECT product_id
       , sale_date
       , daily_sales
FROM sales_table
SAMPLE .1, .2, .3, .4
ORDER BY sale_date, product_id;

Result: 20 rows returned

Product_ID  Sale_Date  Daily_Sales
----------  ---------  -----------
      1000   07/09/28     45850.40
      2000   07/09/28     42787.88
      3000   07/09/28     60903.77
      1000   07/09/29     64500.22
      2000   07/09/29     46090.00
      3000   07/09/29     34654.13
      1000   07/09/30     36000.07
      2000   07/09/30     44850.03
      1000   07/10/01     45700.43
      2000   07/10/01     58850.29
      3000   07/10/01     27000.00
      1000   07/10/02     33700.50
      2000   07/10/02     35599.93
      3000   07/10/02     18767.94
      1000   07/10/03     66200.00
      2000   07/10/03     41900.18
      3000   07/10/03     21553.79
      1000   07/10/04     54575.10
      2000   07/10/04     32878.50
      3000   07/10/04     14875.33
```

Figure 10.14

SAMPLEID, which is a Teradata extension, identifies the sample to which a row belongs in the left-to-right order of the SAMPLE clause specification; from 1 through *n* (where *n* is the number of samples requested in the SAMPLE clause).

Since the sales_table contains 21 rows, the first sample of .1 (or 10%) will contain 2 rows, the second sample .2 (or 20%), etc..

The following query shows the SampleId generated values.

```
SELECT product_id
       , sale_date
       , daily_sales
       , SAMPLEID
FROM sales_table
SAMPLE .1, .2, .3, .4
ORDER BY  sale_date, product_id;

Result:  20 rows returned

Product_ID  Sale_Date  Daily_Sales     SampleId
----------- ---------  -----------  -----------
       1000  07/09/28     45850.40            3
       2000  07/09/28     42787.88            3
       3000  07/09/28     60903.77            3
       1000  07/09/29     64500.22            3
       2000  07/09/29     46090.00            2
       3000  07/09/29     34654.13            4
       1000  07/09/30     36000.07            1
       2000  07/09/30     44850.03            4
       3000  07/09/30     42338.86            2
       1000  07/10/01     45700.43            2
       2000  07/10/01     58850.29            3
       3000  07/10/01     27000.00            3
       1000  07/10/02     33700.50            4
       3000  07/10/02     18767.94            4
       1000  07/10/03     66200.00            4
       2000  07/10/03     41900.18            4
       3000  07/10/03     21553.79            1
       1000  07/10/04     54575.10            4
       2000  07/10/04     32878.50            2
       3000  07/10/04     14875.33            4
```

Figure 10.15

TOP [n] [WITH TIES]

The TOP n allows the user to specify how many rows are to be returned from the query result set. The value of n may be specified as either a positive integer or a positive decimal number. If PERCENT is not specified, the decimal number may not contain a decimal point. If *n* is greater than the actual number of rows, all rows are returned without error.

```
SELECT TOP 3
        student_id
       , last_name
       , class_code
FROM student_table;

Result: 3 rows returned

Student_ID  Last_name             Class_code
----------- --------------------  ----------
     280023  Rieter                JR
     423400  Lamp                  FR
     322133  Bond                  JR
```

Figure 10.16

The WITH TIES option only applies to a SELECT statement that also specifies an ORDER BY clause. In addition to returning the specified number or percentage of rows in the ordered set produced by the ORDER BY clause, the query should return any rows where the sort value is the same as the sort value in the last row that satisfies the specified number or percentage of rows. The next query demonstrates this.

```
SELECT TOP 3 WITH TIES
         student_id
        , last_name
        , class_code
FROM student_table
ORDER BY class_code ;

Student_ID  Last_name             Class_code
----------- --------------------  ----------
     260000 Johnson                ?
     423400 Lamp                   FR
     234121 Garrett                FR
     125634 Kojack                 FR
```

Figure 10.17

Note: Though we requested only three rows, four were returned. In best-case scenarios, the TOP option provides better performance over SAMPLE. In worst-case scenarios, the TOP option provides equivalent performance.

Chapter 10: Practice Questions

1. Which of the following is not a deprecated Teradata function?
   a. CSUM
   b. RANK ( )
   c. MDIFF
   d. RANK
   e. MSUM

2. Which of the following statements about ROW_NUMBER is true?
   a. Ignores window partition boundaries.
   b. Resets back to 1 for each window partition.
   c. Generates random values.
   d. Must be associated with a PARTITION BY.

3. If there is no ROWS or ROWS BETWEEN clause as part of an OVER(. . .) window definition, the default aggregation group is ____________________________.
   a. CURRENT ROW AND UNBOUNDED FOLLOWING
   b. ROWS BETWEEN UNBOUNDEC PRECEDING AND UNBOUNDED FOLLOWING
   c. UJNBOUNDED PRECEDING AND CURRENT ROW
   d. value PRECEDING AND value FOLLOWING

4. Which of the following are not Teradata extensions to ANSI SQL?
    a. TOP n
    b. WITH TIES
    c. SAMPLE
    d. SAMPLEID
    e. QUALIFY

Chapter Notes

Utilize this space for notes, key points to remember, diagrams, areas of further study, etc.

Chapter 11: Set Operators

Certification Objectives

- ✓ Given a request and a set operator, identify the outcome.
- ✓ Given a Venn diagram, identify the set operator.

Before You Begin

You should be familiar with the following terms and concepts.

Terms	Key Concepts
Set Operators	Considerations and restrictions
UNION / INTERSECT	Knowledge on how to apply
EXCEPT / MINUS	How do these functions eliminate rows
Multiple Operators	Understand the order of precedence

The set operator(s) let you combine the results from two or more SELECT statements to construct more complex queries. Teradata supports three classes of set operations:

UNION [DISTINCT] and UNION ALL
INTERSECT [DISTINCT] and INTERSECT ALL
EXCEPT [DISTINCT] or MINUS [DISTINCT] and EXCEPT ALL, MINUS ALL

The ALL option (which allows duplicate rows to be returned), and the MINUS operator, are Teradata extensions.

Set Operations - Restrictions

SQL statements that contain set operators are called compound queries. In order for a compound query to work successfully, the following conditions must exist:

- The result sets of both queries must have the same number of columns.
- The corresponding columns in the queries must have the same data type or must be implicitly convertible to the same data type.
- If the names of the columns match, SQL uses that column name in the answer set.
- If the column names are different, SQL uses the names from the first query in the set operation. Use an AS clause in the first query if you want to rename a column.
- You can specify an optional ORDER BY clause only in the final query in the set statement. SQL applies the sort to the final combined result.
- You can specify GROUP BY and HAVING only in individual queries. You cannot use them to affect the result.
- WITH and WITH ... BY cannot be used.

UNION

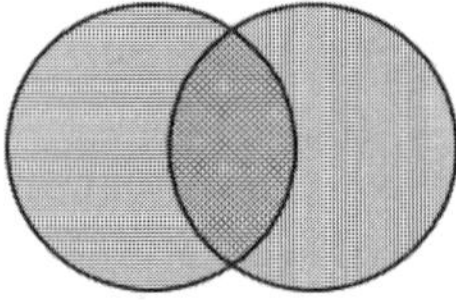

The UNION operation combines the results of two subqueries into a single result that consists of all of the rows from both queries. A UNION removes duplicate rows from the result set.

The following query shows the UNION operator.

```
SELECT dept_no FROM department_table
UNION
SELECT dept_no FROM employee_table
ORDER BY 1 ;

Result: 7 rows returned

Dept_No
-------
      ?
     10
    100
    200
    300
    400
    500
```

Figure 11.1

Note: Set operator results evaluate to the data type of the columns defined in the first SELECT statement in the operation. When a column in the first SELECT is defined as an explicit NULL, the data type of the result is not intuitive.

UNION ALL

A UNION ALL expression allows for all the duplicates to be displayed. Remember that the ALL option is a Teradata extension. The next example demonstrates this.

```
SELECT dept_no FROM department_table
UNION ALL
SELECT dept_no FROM employee_table
ORDER BY 1 ;

Result: 14 rows returned

Dept_No
-------
      ?
     10
    100
    100
    200
    200
    200
    300
    300
    400
    400
    400
    400
    500
```

Figure 11.2

The following query answers the questions, "Who is manager 1121334, and who works for him?".

```
SELECT  first_name
        , last_name
        , 'employee' AS Employee_Type
FROM    employee_table
WHERE mgr_employee_no = 1121334
UNION
SELECT first_name
        , last_name
        , 'manager'
FROM    employee_table
WHERE employee_no = 1121334
ORDER BY 3 DESC , 2 ;

Result: 4 rows returned

first_name    last_name              Employee_Type
------------  ---------------------  -------------
Stan          Strickland             manager
Richard       Gere                   employee
Julia         Roberts                employee
John          Travolta               employee
```

Figure 11.3

Remember that the first query determines the column names for the output.

INTERSECT

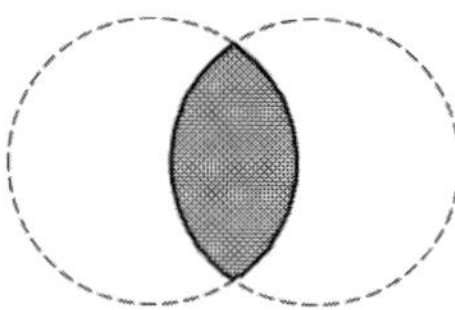

The INTERSECT operator combines the results of two queries into a single result set that consists of only the common rows they share.

List all managers having subordinate employees.

```
SELECT mgr_employee_no FROM employee_table
INTERSECT
SELECT mgr_no FROM department_table
ORDER BY 1 ;

Result: 4 rows returned

Mgr_Employee_No
---------------
        1000234
        1121334
        1256349
        1333454
```

Figure 11.4

EXCEPT/MINUS

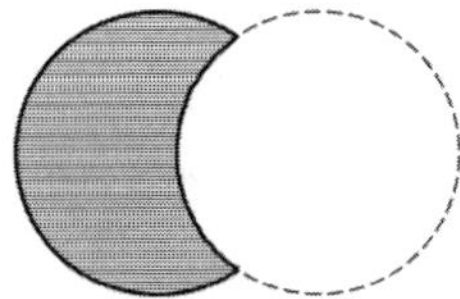

The EXCEPT/MINUS operation returns only the rows that are unique to the first query, removing any rows that it has in common with the second query. The MINUS operator is a Teradata extension.

The next query answers the request, "Find the departments that do not have any employees".

```
SELECT   Dept_no  AS Department_Number
FROM     Department_Table
EXCEPT
SELECT Dept_no
FROM    Employee_Table ;

or

SELECT   Dept_no  AS Department_Number
FROM     Department_Table
MINUS
SELECT Dept_no
FROM    Employee_Table ;

Result: 1 row returned

Department_Number
-----------------
              500
```

Figure 11.5

Multiple Set Operators and Precedence Order

If multiple operators appear in the same query, SQL executes them from left to right. The INTERSECT function takes higher precedence and will be done first before all other Operators, unless parentheses specify a different order. For example, consider the following example:

```
SELECT statement_1
UNION
SELECT statement_2
EXCEPT
SELECT statement_3
INTERSECT
SELECT statement_4;
```

The operations are performed in the following order:

1. Intersect the results of statement_3 and statement_4.
2. Union the results of statement_1 and statement_2.
3. Subtract the intersected rows from the union.

In any set operator, the first select (logically) determines:

1. The resulting data type
2. The TITLE (if specified using TITLE)
3. The resulting column name
4. The resulting format

For any column in any of the subsequent selects, the column aliases, titles and formats are allowed but ignored.

As stated earlier in this chapter, the corresponding columns in the queries must have the same data type or must be implicitly convertible to the same data type. The following query satisfies this requirement, but produces results that are meaningless. It combines employee numbers and job numbers in the same column.

```
SELECT emp_no FROM emp_job_table
WHERE job_no=20010
INTERSECT
SELECT employee_no FROM employee_table
UNION
SELECT job_no FROM job_table
WHERE job_desc LIKE 'Prog%' ;

Result: 4 rows returned

     emp_no
-----------
      20010
    1121334
    1324657
    2341218
```

Figure 11.6

Though the corresponding columns in the queries have the same data type, the data values come from different domains.

Chapter 11: Practice Questions

1. Which Venn diagram represents the EXCEPT operator?
    a. 
    b. 
    c. 
    d.

2. Which of the following queries will not cause an error?
    a. SELECT dept_no FROM employee_table EXCEPT SELECT dept_no AS department_number FROM department_table ORDER BY 1;
    b. SELECT dept_no FROM employee_table AS 'Dept Num' EXCEPT SELECT dept_no FROM department_table ORDER BY 1;
    c. SELECT dept_no FROM employee_table ORDER BY 1 EXCEPT SELECT dept_no AS department_number FROM department_table1;
    d. SELECT dept_no FROM employee_table EXCEPT SELECT department_name FROM department_table ORDER BY 1;

3. Given the following SQL statement, in which order will the Set operators be executed?

    sel . . . UNION sel . . . EXCEPT sel . . . INTERSECT sel . . . UNION sel . . . ;

    a. INTERSECT, UNION, UNION, EXCEPT
    b. UNION, EXCEPT, INTERSECT, UNION
    c. UNION, UNION, EXCEPT, INTERSECT
    d. INTERSECT, UNION, EXCEPT, UNION
    e. EXCEPT, UNION, INTERSECT, UNION

4. Which of the following are Teradata extensions?
    a. ALL
    b. EXCEPT
    c. INTERSECT
    d. UNION

Chapter Notes

Utilize this space for notes, key points to remember, diagrams, areas of further study, etc.

Chapter 12: Data Manipulation

Certification Objectives

- ✓ Identify a correctly written INSERT statement.
- ✓ Identify a correctly written DELETE statement.
- ✓ Identify a correctly written MERGE INTO statement.
- ✓ Identify the factors that influence the decision to use ANSI MERGE INTO and UPDATE (upsert processing).
- ✓ Identify a correctly written UPDATE statement.

Before You Begin

You should be familiar with the following terms and concepts.

Terms	Key Concepts
Data Maintenance	Consideration and safeguards
DML	INSERT, UPDATE, UPSERT, and DELETE commands
Merge-Into	Understanding how this function works, and the benefits

The following Data Manipulation Language (DML) commands enable you to remove, add, and modify data:

- DELETE - Removes rows from a table
- INSERT- Adds a new row to a table
- INSERT/SELECT adds rows to a table from another table
- UPDATE- Replaces values of columns in a table
- UPSERT – Updates a row or inserts a new one

DELETE

The DELETE command is used to remove rows from a table that satisfy a condition based on a WHERE clause. This example illustrates a DELETE statement that has a join to another table. This is a Teradata extension to an ANSI standard delete.

```
DELETE FROM order_table_new
WHERE        customer_table.customer_number =
order_table_new.customer_number
AND    order_table_new.order_date='07-01-2009';
```

Figure 12.1

To remove all rows from a table, do the following:

```
DELETE FROM order_table_new;
or
DELETE FROM order_table_new ALL;
```

Figure 12.2

A DELETE FROM <tablename> ALL is very efficient. Since table and index rows of every table are contained within their own data blocks, Teradata simply moves those blocks to the Free Space list. The ALL is the default and is used when a WHERE condition is not specified. Lastly, the ALL option is a non-ANSI Teradata extension.

Tip: Do not use DROP TABLE just to empty a table. In addition to deleting all data and index rows, DROP TABLE also removes the table's definition which can cause a high degree of dictionary overhead.

INSERT

Next statement is the INSERT which is used to add rows into a table. This example inserts a single row to the employee table with the fields in the CREATE TABLE column order:

```
INSERT INTO employee_table
VALUES (3121445,  , null, 'Redding', 'Lisa', 53560.00);
```

Figure 12.3

Notice the two ways of specifying missing data values: skipping the column by just entering a comma, and using the keyword NULL.

To specify a different order of data input, list the columns in the order of the data values:

```
INSERT INTO employee_table (first_name, last_name,
                                  employee_no, salary)
VALUES ('Lisa', 'Redding', 3121445, 53560.00);
```

Figure 12.4

Note: Since the column names for dept_no and mgr_employee_no do not appear in the column list, the system will insert nulls. If a column has been declared NOT NULL, then a value for that column must be supplied. You can also specify a logging option with an INSERT which will do error handling.

INSERT/SELECT

This command is used to copy rows, or a subset of rows, from one table to another. The following is a simple INSERT/SELECT example:

```
INSERT INTO emp_new
SELECT * FROM employee_table;
```

Figure 12.5

Assumptions:

- A complete replica of employee_table is required
- The emp_new and employee_table need to have the same number of columns defined. They do not have to have the same datatypes defined for each column (exact replica is not required).
- The target table must have datatypes that can be implicitly converted from non-matching datatypes in the source.
- Default values can be different as well as other characteristics such as null ability or compression values.

Two different optimizations can occur:

1. If the PI of the source AND destination tables are identical, an AMP local operation is used.
2. If the target table is empty,
    a.) Transient Journaling is reduced
    b.) 64K block transfers are used

If both conditions are satisfied, both optimizations are used. Below is a more complex example:

```
CREATE TABLE sales_analysis
(sales_count SMALLINT, yr_mo INTEGER, sales_total DECIMAL (9,2))
PRIMARY INDEX (sales_count);

INSERT INTO sales_analysis
SELECT COUNT(*), sale_date/100, SUM(daily_sales)
FROM sales_table
GROUP BY 2 ;

SELECT * FROM sales_analysis;

Result: 2 rows returned

sales_count        yr_mo  sales_total
-----------  -----------  -----------
          9        10709    417975.36
         12        10710    451601.99
```

Figure 12.6

UPSERT

Teradata has another extension to the Update command called an UPSERT. The query checks to see if the row exists in the table and updates it if found. If nothing is found, a new row is inserted.

There are several restrictions that need to be considered when deciding to use an UPSERT, which are outlined below:

1. The update and the insert portions must reference the same row of the same table using the rows PI value to do the operation. The PI cannot be an Identity column. If these rules are not followed, an error is returned.

2. For tables with PPI, there are additional restrictions. Both statements have to specify the same partition. The update can't modify partitioning columns and all the partitioning columns must be in the WHERE clause.

The example below shows a simple UPSERT statement.

```
UPDATE job_table
SET job_desc = 'Gopher'
WHERE job_no = 12345  /* Non-existent job number */
ELSE
INSERT INTO job_table
VALUES (12345, 'Gopher');
```

Figure 12.7

MERGE

The MERGE-INTO command merges a source row set into a target table based on whether any target rows satisfy a specified matching condition with the source row. MERGE replicates the UPSERT functionality, but over more than one row (i.e. Block Level). It also has fewer restrictions, making it more flexible then the UPSERT.

1. The update and insert portions of the query do not need to reference the same row of the same table. In addition, they both must reference the row's PI value to do their operations. The PI can be an Identity Column

2. For PPI tables, the insert can specify a different partition then the update. The update can modify any partitioning columns but not all the partitioning columns need be in the WHERE clause.

The general MERGE commands are as follows:

MERGE [INTO] *target-table-name*	In the ANSI SQL:2003 definition, this statement is named MERGE INTO, while in the Teradata definition, INTO is an unnecessary noise keyword.
USING	VALUES (*v1* [, ...]) AS *source-table-name* (*col1* [, ...]) *subquery* AS *source-table-name* (*col1* [, ...]) *source-table-name* [(COL1 [, ...])]
ON *match-condition*	*match-condition* must specify an equality constraint on the primary index of *target-table* to ensure that the candidate target row set can be hash-accessed on a single AMP. The specified primary index value must match the primary index value implied by the column values specified in the WHEN NOT MATCHED clause.

	WHEN MATCHED THEN UPDATE SET *update-column = update expression* [, ...] WHEN NOT MATCHED THEN INSERT [(*col1* [, ...])] VALUES (*val1* [, ...])
[LOGGING]	If logging is not specified, the system does no error handling. If an error occurs, an ANSI request rolls back, and a Teradata transaction aborts and rolls back.

Figure 12.8

LOGGING OPTIONS	
LOGGING [ALL] ERRORS	Log all data errors, reference index errors, and USI errors. If you do not specify a limit, the system defaults to a 10 error limit.
LOGGING ERRORS WITH NO LIMIT	There is no limit to the number of errors that can be logged in the error table associated with the target data table for this MERGE operation, other than the system-determined limit of 16,000,000 errors.
LOGGING ERRORS WITH LIMIT OF *error-limit*	The value you specify for *error_limit* can be anything in the range of 1 to 16,000,000, inclusive. If this limit is exceeded, the system aborts the transaction in Teradata session mode or the request in ANSI session mode, and rolls back all changes made to the target table, but does not roll back the logged error table rows.

Figure 12.9

Below is an MERGE INTO example:

```
MERGE INTO sales_table
USING sales_stage
ON sales_table.product_id = sales_stage.product_id
AND sales_table.sale_date = sales_stage.sale_date
WHEN MATCHED THEN UPDATE SET daily_sales =
sales_stage.daily_sales
WHEN NOT MATCHED THEN INSERT VALUES
(sales_stage.product_id, sales_stage.sale_date, sales_stage.daily_sales)
LOGGING ERRORS WITH LIMIT OF 100;
```

Figure 12.10

ERROR TABLE

The syntax to create an error table is:

CREATE ERROR TABLE *error-table-name* FOR *target-table-name*;

A syntax example is:

```
CREATE ERROR TABLE merge_errors FOR sales_table;
```

Figure 12.11

Chapter 12: Practice Questions

1. Which of the following statements about DELETE FROM t1 ALL; is true?
    a. It deletes data rows and index rows one at a time.
    b. It drops the table and then recreates the table's definition.
    c. It moves the data and index blocks to the Free Space list.
    d. The word ALL or a WHERE clause must be specified.

2. Which of the following statements about the update and insert portions of the Upsert is false?
    a. They must reference the same row in the same table.
    b. They must use the table's PI value.
    c. The PI can be an identity column.
    d. The update cannot modify partitioning columns.

3. Which of the following statements about update and insert portions of the Merge statement is false?
    a. They must reference the same row in the same table.
    b. They must use the table's PI value.
    c. The PI can be an identity column.
    d. The update cannot modify partitioning columns.

4. Given the following table definition, which Insert will fail?
CREATE TABLE t1(c1 INT NOT NULL, c2 INT NOT NULL, c3 INT, c4 INT NOT NULL, c5);
    a. INSERT INTO t1 VALUES(1, 2, 3, 4, 5);
    b. INSERT INTO t1 VALUES(1, 2, , 4);
    c. INSERT INTO t1 VALUES(1, 2, null, null, 5);
    d. INSERT INTO t1 VALUES(1, 2, , 4, null);

Chapter Notes

Utilize this space for notes, key points to remember, diagrams, areas of further study, etc.

Chapter 13: Data Interrogation

Certification Objectives

- ✓ Given a scenario, identify the result of the CASE expression.
- ✓ Given a scenario, identify the use of different forms (searched and valued) of the CASE expression.
- ✓ Given a scenario, identify the use of specialized functions (COALESCE, NULLIF) of the CASE expression.

Before You Begin

You should be familiar with the following terms and concepts.

Terms	Key Concepts
CASE	How to apply and understand the options (i.e. Horizontal, Nested, etc.)
COALESCE / NULLIF	Knowledge on how to apply

Data Interrogation is the ability to test column data. It brings conditional logic into the projection list portion of a query. The following functions specify alternate values for a conditional expression or expressions based on equality comparisons and conditions that evaluate to TRUE.

- CASE
- Special variations of the CASE expression:
    - NULLIF
    - COALESCE
- Two Teradata extensions
    - NULLIFZERO
    - ZEROIFNULL

CASE

- There are two forms of the CASE expression:
    - A valued CASE expression
    - A searched CASE expression
- CASE allows for conditional processing of returned rows.
- CASE returns a single result for each row processed.
- Each row is evaluated against each WHEN clause.
- First match returns a result for that row.
- If no match, the ELSE result is produced for that row.
- CASE is ANSI SQL-2003-compliant.
- WHEN clauses are processed sequentially.
- If no ELSE clause is defined, then the result defaults to NULL.
- The data type of value_expression must be comparable with the data types of all of the value_expression values.
- You can use a scalar subquery in the WHEN clause, THEN clause, and ELSE clause of a CASE expression. If you use a non-scalar subquery (a subquery that returns more than one row), a runtime error is returned.
- If you compare NULL to any value or to NULL, it is always FALSE. If you are testing for a NULL, it is recommended that you use a searched CASE expression with a IS NULL or IS NOT NULL option in the WHEN condition.

Valued CASE Format

```
CASE value-expr WHEN expr1 THEN result1
                WHEN expr2 THEN result2
            ELSE result
            END
```

The following is an example of a valued case.

```
SELECT   course_name
        ,CASE  credits
                WHEN 1  THEN '1 Credit'
                WHEN 2  THEN '2 Credits'
                WHEN 3  THEN '3 Credits'
                ELSE 'More than 3 Credits'
        END "Number of Credits"
FROM   course_table
ORDER BY credits, 1;

Result: 6 rows returned

Course_name                       Number of Credits
------------------------------    -------------------
TD12 SQL Features                 2 Credits
Advanced SQL                      3 Credits
Introduction to SQL               3 Credits
Teradata Basics                   3 Credits
Database Administration           More than 3 Credits
Physical Database Tuning          More than 3 Credits
```

Figure 13.1

Searched CASE Format

```
CASE   WHEN  condition1 THEN value-expr1
       WHEN  condition2 THEN value-expr2
       ELSE value-expr
       END
```

The following example gives the same result, but is coded as a searched case.

```
SELECT   course_name
           ,CASE
                WHEN credits=1  THEN '1 Credit'
                WHEN credits=2  THEN '2 Credits'
                WHEN credits=3  THEN '3 Credits'
               ELSE 'More than 3 Credits'
            END "Number of Credits"
FROM   course_table
ORDER BY credits, 1;

Result 6 rows returned

Course_name                     Number of Credits
------------------------------  -------------------
TD12 SQL Features               2 Credits
Advanced SQL                    3 Credits
Introduction to SQL             3 Credits
Teradata Basics                 3 Credits
Database Administration         More than 3 Credits
Physical Database Tuning        More than 3 Credits
```

Figure 13.2

The WHEN search condition expression has the following rules:

- Can take the form of any comparison operator, such as LIKE, =, or <>.
- Can be a quantified predicate, such as ALL or ANY.
- Can contain a scalar subquery.
- Can contain joins of two tables.
- Cannot contain SELECT statements.

- BLOB's can only be utilized in search_condition, scalar_expression, or scalar_expression when it is cast to BYTE or VARBYTE.
- CLOB's can only be utilized in search_condition, scalar_expression, or scalar_expression when it is cast to CHAR or VARCHAR.

Horizontal CASE Reporting

Typically, SQL row result sets are vertical. CASE allows for horizontal reporting, which displays the row result sets on one line instead of multiple row results.

```
SELECT  AVG(CASE class_code  WHEN 'FR' THEN grade_pt
              ELSE NULL  END) AS Freshman_GPA
       ,AVG(CASE class_code  WHEN 'SO' THEN grade_pt
              ELSE NULL  END) AS Sophomore_GPA
       ,AVG(CASE class_code  WHEN 'JR' THEN grade_pt
              ELSE NULL  END) AS Junior_GPA
       ,AVG(CASE class_code  WHEN 'SR' THEN grade_pt
              ELSE NULL  END) AS Senior_GPA
FROM student_table
WHERE class_code IS NOT NULL;

Result: 1 row returned

Freshman_GPA  Sophomore_GPA  Junior_GPA  Senior_GPA
------------  -------------  ----------  ----------
        2.29           2.90        2.92        3.18
```

Figure 13.3

Nested CASE Expressions

The CASE statement can be nested to check data in a second column from a second CASE statement before determining what value to return.

The following is an example of nested case statements.

```
SELECT last_name
  ,CASE class_code  WHEN 'JR'  THEN 'Junior ' ||
        (CASE WHEN grade_pt < 2  THEN 'Failing'
        WHEN grade_pt < 3.5  THEN 'Passing'  ELSE 'Exceeding'   END)
   ELSE  'Senior ' || (CASE WHEN grade_pt < 2  THEN 'Failing'
        WHEN grade_pt < 3.5  THEN 'Passing'  ELSE 'Exceeding'   END)
        END   AS  Current_Status
FROM student_table
WHERE class_code IN ('JR', 'SR')
ORDER BY class_code, last_name;

Result: 4 rows returned

Last_name              Current_Status
--------------------   ----------------
Bond                   Junior Exceeding
Rieter                 Junior Failing
Craig                  Senior Passing
Phillips               Senior Passing
```

Figure 13.4

COALESCE

COALESCE returns NULL if all of its arguments evaluate to null. Otherwise, it returns the value of the first non-null argument in the *expression* list.

COALESCE is ANSI SQL-2003-compliant and each COALESCE function must have at least two operands.

Syntax:

COALESCE (expression_1, expression_2 [, expression_n])

COALESCE is a shorthand expression for the following full CASE expression:

CASE
WHEN *expression_1* IS NOT NULL
THEN *expression_1*
...
WHEN *expression_n* IS NOT NULL
THEN *expression_n*
ELSE NULL
END

The next example demonstrates COALESCE by displaying a literal value if student does not have a class code.

```
SELECT  last_name
        ,COALESCE(class_code, 'Missing Class') AS Class_code
FROM    student_table
ORDER BY class_code;

Result: 10 rows returned

Last_name              Class_code
--------------------   -------------
Johnson                Missing Class
Garrett                FR
Kojack                 FR
Lamp                   FR
Rieter                 JR
Bond                   JR
McCann                 SO
McCormick              SO
Phillips               SR
Craig                  SR
```

Figure 13.5

The Teradata extension, ZEROIFNULL, can only test one argument and can only return a zero, or the argument.

ZEROIFNULL(*arg*)

It is the equivalent of the following CASE statement:

CASE WHEN *arg* IS NULL
    THEN 0
    ELSE *arg*
END

NULLIF

NULLIF returns NULL if its arguments are equal. Otherwise, it returns its first argument, *scalar_expression_1*.

NULLIF is a shorthand expression for the following full CASE expression:

CASE
WHEN *scalar_expression_1=scalar_expression_2*
THEN NULL
ELSE *scalar_expression_1*
END

The following figure is an example of the NULLIF.

```
SELECT student_id, grade_pt, NULLIF(grade_pt, 0)
FROM Student_Table ORDER BY grade_pt DESC;

*** Query completed. 10 rows found. 3 columns returned.
*** Total elapsed time was 1 second.

 Student_ID  Grade_Pt  <CASE  expression>
-----------  --------  ------------------
     234121      4.00                4.00
     322133      3.95                3.95
     231222      3.80                3.80
     324652      3.35                3.35
     123250      3.00                3.00
     125634      2.88                2.88
     333450      2.00                2.00
     280023      1.90                1.90
     423400       .00                   ?
     260000         ?                   ?
```

Figure 13.6

Chapter 13: Practice Questions

1. Which of the following is a Teradata extension?
   a. COALESCE
   b. NULLIFZERO
   c. CASE
   d. NULLIF

2. Which of the following statements about COALESCE is false?
   a. It returns the first non-null value.
   b. It returns the last non-null value.
   c. It returns NULL if all arguments evaluate to null.
   d. It is a shorthand for a CASE statement.

3. If (col2=33, 29, 490, 16, 8), what will NULLIF(col2, 17) return?
   a. 33, 29, 490, 16, 8
   b. 8, ?, 29, 33, 490
   c. 490, 33, 29, ?, 8
   d. ?, 16, 490, 29, 33

4. The two forms of the CASE expression are ____________________.
   a. constant and variable
   b. valued and cased
   c. valued and searched
   d. when and else

Chapter Notes

Utilize this space for notes, key points to remember, diagrams, areas of further study, etc.

Chapter 14: View and Macro Processing

Certification Objectives

- ✓ Describe the impact of using an access lock in a view or macro.
- ✓ Identify the benefits of using views and macros.
- ✓ Identify the restrictions of creating views and macros.
- ✓ Identify uses of simple and parameterized macros.

Before You Begin

You should be familiar with the following terms and concepts.

Terms	Key Concepts
Views	Reasons to use and considerations along with understanding CREATE, and DROP statements
Locking	Knowledge on how to apply with Views
Macros	Reason to use and considerations along with understanding CREATE, and DROP statements

Views

Views are an essential component to include when establishing or adding to your database schema. Here are some definitions, advantages, recommendations, and restrictions about views.

Definitions

- A view is a virtual table.
- A view may define a subset of rows of a table.
- A view may define a subset of columns of a table.
- Data is neither duplicated nor stored separately for a view.

- View definitions are stored in the Data Dictionary, not in the user's own space.
- Views can simplify the joins of multiple tables into a single virtual table
- Views can act as aggregated tables, where the aggregate data (sum, average etc.) is presented as the calculated results.
- Views can provide security by limiting the exposure of a table or tables to users accessing the data.

Advantages

- Provide an additional level of security/authorization.
- Can prevent the end user from missing join conditions
- Help control read and update privileges
- Are not affected if columns are added to a table.
- Are not affected if a column is dropped from a table unless the dropped column is referenced by the view
- Simplify end-user access

Recommendations

- Only utilities, such as FastLoad, MultiLoad, Tpump, and Teradata Parallel Transporter (TPT) should have direct access to the base tables. All other access should be done through views
- Create at least one view for each base table
- Create for commonly used business analytics.

Restrictions

- A view cannot contain an ORDER BY clause.
- Derived columns and aggregate columns must have an AS clause.
- A view cannot be used to UPDATE if it contains:

- Data from more than one table (JOIN VIEW)
- The same column twice
- Derived columns
- A DISTINCT clause
- A GROUP BY clause

Creating a View

The CREATE VIEW command defines a view. As discussed, a view is not physically created. Its definition is simply stored in the Data Dictionary. By design, Teradata will generate a query rewrite to support the retrieve operation of a view. To CREATE a full-table VIEW, do the following:

CREATE VIEW dept AS SELECT * FROM department_table;

To see a view definition, do the following:

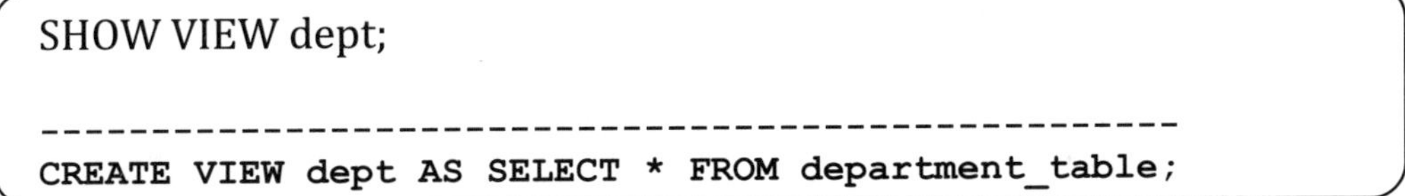

```
SHOW VIEW dept;

--------------------------------------------------
CREATE VIEW dept AS SELECT * FROM department_table;
```

Figure 14.1

The SHOW VIEW command only returns the original text. Therefore, it is recommended that all views be created with explicit column names in the SELECT statement.

When the view is created, the * will be expanded to the complete list of column names in the table. To see all of the columns in a view, do the following:

```
HELP VIEW dept;
```

Figure 14.2

Adding columns to a table does not affect or change any views referencing the table. Dropping a column from a table will render any view referencing the dropped column unusable. Views may not contain an ORDER BY unless they contain a TOP command the WITH TIES options.

The following is an example of the recommended way for creating a view by explicitly listing the columns. The users will see and use the column names supplied inside the parentheses.

```
CREATE VIEW  Employee_Dept_200_V
(Emp_Nbr, LAST_NM, Salary)
AS  SELECT  employee_no
            ,last_name
            ,salary
  FROM   employee_table
  WHERE  dept_no = 200;
```

Figure 14.3

Using a View

As stated above, the SHOW VIEW returns the CREATE VIEW text. Here is an example.

SHOW VIEW employee_dept_200_V ;

```
CREATE VIEW  Employee_Dept_200_V
(Emp_Nbr, LAST_NM, Salary)
AS  SELECT  employee_no
           ,last_name
           ,salary
    FROM   employee_table
    WHERE  dept_no = 200;
```

Figure 14.4

The name of a view is used in constructing SQL, just like using a table name. Here is the result of doing a query using the above view.

SELECT * FROM employee_dept_200_V ;

```
Result: 2 rows returned

    Emp_Nbr  LAST_NM                        Salary
-----------  --------------------  ----------
    1333454  Roberts                      48800.00
    1324657  Willis                       42788.88
```

Figure 14.5

LOCKING Request Modifier

When a view is defined with a LOCKING modifier, the specified lock is placed on the underlying base table set each time the view is referenced in an SQL statement.

A LOCKING modifier that specifies locking for ACCESS can be used in a CREATE VIEW statement to give concurrent access for end/business users and data integration processes that will modify the data. This is the recommended approach.

The default READ lock caused by the SELECT statement in a view can be overridden by placing a LOCKING FOR ACCESS modifier on the view. An ACCESS lock allows data to be retrieved during write activities. Be aware that a view defined with an ACCESS lock might display inconsistent results.

```
CREATE VIEW Read_to_Access AS
LOCKING sales_table FOR ACCESS
 SELECT * FROM sales_table;
```

Figure 14.6

Since this is an updatable view, the system will automatically upgrade the lock to a WRITE lock if the view is used to modify the sales_table.

Macro Processing

Macros are a Teradata extension. The following lists important attributes of macros.

Definitions

- Macros contain one or more prewritten SQL statements.
- Macros are a Teradata extension to ANSI SQL.
- Macros are stored in the Teradata Data Dictionary.

- Macros can be executed from any viable SQL front-end, including:
    - Teradadata SQL Assistant
    - BTEQ
    - CLI
    - LOGON Startup
    - Another macro

Advantages

- Users only need the EXEC privilege to run a macro.
- No underlying table or view privileges are required to EXECute a macro.
- Macros are executed as a single transaction. All SQL within a macro must successfully complete or any changes will be backed out.
- Macros can provide column-level security.
- Macros can be parameterized.
- Macros are a good method for encapsulating business logic
    - Reusability: Can be re-used (less repetitive code writing)
    - Single Set of Code: Ensures that a standardized set of logic is utilized (reduces likelihood of having "bad logic" or "stale" SQL, if everyone is using the same logic).

Restrictions

- The macro creator must have the necessary permissions to accomplish the SQL statements within a macro.
- The *macroname* must be a unique *objectname* within the database it resides.
- Every SQL statement in a macro must end with a semicolon.

- Nonqualified names in a macro definition are *not* resolved in DDL statements when the macro is created. They are resolved when the macro is executed.
- Nonqualified names in a macro definition are *fully* resolved in DML statements when the macro is created.
- There cannot be more than one DDL statement in a macro, and it must be the last statement.

The following chart lists the SQL commands associated with macros.

Macro-related Commands

COMMAND	DEFINITION
CREATE MACRO macroname AS (...);	Define a macro and store it the Data Dictionary.
REPLACE MACRO macroname AS (...);	Modify an existing macro. If the referenced macro does not exist, a new macro will be created.
EXECute macroname;	Execute the statements within the macro.
SHOW MACRO macroname;	Display a macro.
DROP MACRO macroname;	Remove a macro definition from the Data Dictionary
EXPLAIN EXEC macroname;	Display EXPLAIN text for the macro's execution.

Figure 14.7

Here is a macro to report employee job assignments:

```
CREATE MACRO EmpJob AS
( SELECT
  TRIM(last_name) || ', ' || TRIM(first_name) AS Employee
, TRIM(job_desc) AS JobTitle
FROM employee_table e
JOIN
emp_job_table  ej
ON e.employee_no = ej.emp_no
JOIN
job_table  j
ON ej.job_no = j.job_no
ORDER BY last_name;
);
```

Figure 14.8

Once a macros has been created, you run it by using the EXEC command, as shown below.

```
EXEC empjob;

Result: 8 rows returned

Employee                             JobTitle
-----------------------------------  ---------------------
Clooney, George                      Programmer
Ford, Harrison                       Manager
Gere, Richard                        Developer
Roberts, Julia                       Security Guard
Strickland, Stan                     Programmer
Student, Mandee                      Developer
Travolta, John                       Project Manager
Willis, Bruce                        Programmer
```

Figure 14.9

Here is another macro to show the students who are currently enrolled in classes:

```
CREATE MACRO enrollments AS
(SELECT
  last_name
 ,first_name
 ,sc.course_id
 ,course_name
FROM   student_table AS s
INNER JOIN
  Student_course_table AS sc
ON   s.student_id = sc.student_id
INNER JOIN
  Course_table c
ON   sc.course_id = c.course_id
ORDER BY sc.course_id, last_name;
);
```

Figure 14.10

Now, whenever anyone wants that report, all they have to do is EXEC the macro. The following is the example.

EXEC enrollments;

```
Result: 13 rows returned

Last_name            First_name   Course_ID Course_name
-------------------- ------------ --------- ------------------------------
Garrett              Wendy              100 Teradata Basics
Kojack               Henry              100 Teradata Basics
Phillips             Beth               100 Teradata Basics
Craig                Danny              200 Introduction to SQL
Kojack               Henry              200 Introduction to SQL
McCormick            Susie              210 Advanced SQL
Rieter               Richard            210 Advanced SQL
Bond                 Jimmy              220 TD12 SQL Features
Kojack               Henry              220 TD12 SQL Features
McCormick            Susie              220 TD12 SQL Features
Bond                 Jimmy              300 Physical Database Tuning
Johnson              Stephen            400 Database Administration
McCann               Andy               400 Database Administration
```

Figure 14.11

So, for canned reports like this, macros simplify life for the users.

Parameterized Macros

If you want to vary the results produced by a macro, Teradata macros can accept parameter values for data values. The syntax for creating a macro with parameters is:

```
CREATE | REPLACE MACRO macroname
(parametername  datatype [ , parametername  datatype . . . ]
AS
( <SQL statements> ) ;
```

To reference a parameter within an SQL statement, precede the parameter name with a colon (:). Here is an example of a parameterized macro to show which employees have a specific job code:

```
CREATE MACRO JobEmp (jobcode INT) AS
( SELECT
 TRIM(last_name) || ', ' || TRIM(first_name) AS Employee
, ej.Job_no AS JobCode
, TRIM(job_desc) AS JobTitle
FROM employee_table e
JOIN
emp_job_table ej
ON e.employee_no = ej.emp_no
JOIN
job_table j
ON ej.job_no = :jobcode
AND  ej.job_no = j.job_no
ORDER BY last_name;
);
```

Figure 14.12

The following shows running the macro and the result:

```
EXEC jobemp ( 20010 );


Result: 3 rows returned

Employee                                JobCode  JobTitle
---------------------------------  -----------  --------------------
Clooney, George                          20010  Programmer
Strickland, Stan                         20010  Programmer
Willis, Bruce                            20010  Programmer
```

Figure 14.13

Parameter Restrictions

When using parameters, you cannot pass the names of database objects in a macro as a parameter. Database objects refer to databases / tables / views and their columns. In addition, the following data attributes are never valid with macro parameters:

- CHECK constraints
- FROM statements cannot be parameterized
- COMPRESS phrase

Chapter 14: Practice Questions

1. Which of the following can have parameters?
    a. Tables
    b. Macros
    c. Indexes
    d. Views

2. Choose the correct view definition.
    a. CREATE VIEW v1 as sel c1, sum(c2), c3 from t1 group by 1,3 union sel c7, c8, c9 from t2;
    b. CREATE VIEW v1 as sel c1, c2, c3 from t1 union sel c7, sum(c8), c9 from t2;
    c. CREATE VIEW v1 as sel c1, c2, c3 from t1 union sel c7, sum(c8), c9 from t2 group by 1,3;
    d. CREATE VIEW v1 as sel c1, c2 from t1 union sel c7, sum(c8), c9 from t2 group by 1,3;

3. Given the following SQL, in what order will the queries execute?

    ```
    CREATE MACRO m1 as (sel 1; exec m4; sel 2;);
    CREATE MACRO m2 as (sel 3;);
    CREATE MACRO m3 as (sel 4; exec m1; sel 5;);
    CREATE MACRO m4 as (sel 6; exec m5; sel 7;);
    CREATE MACRO m5 as (sel 8; exec m2; sel 9;);
    EXECUTE m3;
    ```

    a. 4, 1, 6, 8, 3, 9, 7, 2, 5
    b. 4. 5, 1, 2, 6, 7, 8, 9, 3
    c. 4, 1, 3, 6, 8, 7, 9, 5, 2
    d. 4, 1, 2, 6, 7, 8, 9, 3, 2

Chapter Notes

Utilize this space for notes, key points to remember, diagrams, areas of further study, etc.

Chapter 15: Transaction Processing

Certification Objectives

- ✓ List the differences between ANSI and Teradata modes in the areas of transaction protocol, defaults, conversions, and table creation.

Before You Begin

You should be familiar with the following terms and concepts.

Terms	Key Concepts
Transaction Locking	Considerations and restrictions
BTET vs. ANSI	Knowledge on how to apply and the differences
ABORT	How does this work - Teradata vs. ANSI mode

Transactions

Transaction processing is designed to maintain a database in a known, consistent state by ensuring that any operations carried out are interdependent, which means that entire transactions are either completed successfully or canceled successfully.

Transaction processing allows for single or multiple operations. In addition, multiple transactions can be linked together to create a single transaction. In this case, the Teradata Transient Journal ensures that either all operations in a transaction are completed without error, or none of them are. This is accomplished through a series of row and table level locks. If some of the SQL statements are completed but errors occur when the others are attempted, the

Transient Journal will rollback all of the operations in the transaction, thereby erasing all traces of the transaction and restoring the system to the consistent, known state that it was in before processing of the transaction began.

If all SQL statements of a transaction are completed successfully, the transaction is committed by the system, and all changes to the database are made permanent; the transaction cannot be rolled back once this is done. Lastly, the Transient Journal will purge the before images upon successful completion of the transaction.

In addition, the Teradata database guards against hardware and software errors that might leave a transaction partially completed with the system left in an unknown, inconsistent state. For example, if the database crashes in the middle of a transaction, the transaction processing system guarantees that all operations in an *uncommitted* state are cancelled and their changes rolled back.

Transaction Locking

Any number of users and applications can simultaneously access data stored in a Teradata database.

The Teradata Database Lock Manager imposes concurrency control by locking the database object being accessed by each transaction and releasing those locks when the transaction either commits or rolls back its work. This control ensures that the data remains consistent for all users.

Locking Levels

Locking levels determine the type of object that is locked and the impact on other users, as follows:

LOCKING LEVEL	**Resource(s) unavailable to other users**
DATABASE	All tables, views, macros and triggers owned by the database/user.
VIEW	All tables referenced in the View.
TABLE	All rows in the base table and in any secondary index and fallback subtables associated with it.
ROW	The primary copy of rows sharing the same row hash value. A row hash lock permits other users to access other data in the table and is the least restrictive type of automatic lock. A row hash lock applies to a *set* of rows that shares the same hash code. It does not necessarily, nor even generally, lock only one row. • A row hash lock is applied whenever a table is accessed using a *primary index (PI)*. • For an update that uses a *unique secondary index (USI)*, the appropriate row of the secondary index subtable is also locked. • It is not necessary to lock the fallback copy of the row, nor any associated row, of a *nonunique secondary index* (NUSI) subtable.

Figure 15.1

Note: With the exception of pseudo-table locks, locks in the Teradata Database are not managed globally, but by each AMP individually.

Lock Types

The next chart lists the types of locks that can be placed on database objects.

LOCK TYPE	DESCRIPTION
ACCESS	• Permits selection of data from a base table that can be locked for write by other users. • Because the data selected using an ACCESS lock can be inconsistent because the data might be modified concurrently with the request, you should only use this lock for casual inspection of data. • Placing an ACCESS lock requires the SELECT privilege on the specified object.
READ	• Ensures data consistency during a read operation such as a SELECT request. • This is the default lock on SELECT statements. • Multiple users can concurrently hold a READ lock on a base table. As long as a READ lock is in place, no modification of the object is allowed. • Placing a READ lock requires the SELECT privilege on the specified object. • SHARE is a synonym for READ
WRITE	• Enables a single user to modify data. • This is the default for INSERT, UPDATE, and DELETE statements. • As long as the WRITE lock is in place, all other users are excluded from viewing or modifying the object except readers who are viewing data using an ACCESS lock. • Until a WRITE lock is released, no new READ locks are permitted on the locked object.

	• Placing a WRITE lock requires an UPDATE, INSERT, or DELETE privilege on the specified object.
EXCLUSIVE	• Excludes all other users. • This is the most restrictive lock. • EXCLUSIVE locks are rarely used except to make structural changes to a database. • This is the default on all DDL statements. • Placing an EXCLUSIVE lock on a database object requires the DROP privilege on that object.
CHECKSUM	• Used only with updatable cursors in embedded SQL and stored procedures.

Figure 15.2

Lock Queue

When a lock is requested, the system will either Grant the lock, or put the request into the lock Queue as follows.

	LOCK REQUESTED			
LOCK HELD	**ACCESS**	**READ**	**WRITE**	**EXCLUSIVE**
None	Grant	Grant	Grant	Grant
ACCESS	Grant	Grant	Grant	**Queue**
READ	Grant	Grant	**Queue**	**Queue**
WRITE	Grant	**Queue**	**Queue**	**Queue**
EXCLUSIVE	**Queue**	**Queue**	**Queue**	**Queue**

Figure 15.3

Notice in the chart above that ACCESS and WRITE locks are compatible.

Any lock can be upgraded, but only a READ lock can be downgraded to an ACCESS lock. Use the LOCKING modifier to change a lock.

Here are the syntax formats of the LOCKING Modifier:

LOCKING [<table-name>] FOR <desired-locking> [NOWAIT]
LOCKING ROW FOR <desired-locking> [NOWAIT]
LOCKING DATABASE <database-name> FOR <desired-locking> [NOWAIT]
LOCKING VIEW <view-name> FOR <desired-locking> [NOWAIT]
LOCKING TABLE <table-name> FOR <desired-locking> [NOWAIT]

NOWAIT instructs the system to abort the request if the lock cannot be granted immediately. Specify this option for situations in which it is not desirable to have a request wait for resources, and possibly tie up resources another request could use, while waiting.

Here is an example of the improper use of the LOCKING modifier.

```
LOCKING ROW FOR READ SELECT * FROM employee_table;
```

Figure 15.4

Though the request asks for a row hash Read lock, the query does not use either the Primary Index or a USI to access the table. Therefore, the system will ignore the row lock request and apply a full-table Read lock.

Transaction Modes

Here are some terms associated with transaction processing that you should understand:

TERM	**DEFINITION**
Statement	An SQL command that ends with a semicolon.
Request	One, or more, statements sent to the Parser for execution.
Transaction	One, or more, requests that take the database from one consistent state to another consistent state.

Figure 15.5

Teradata performs transaction processing in either of the following modes:

- ANSI
- Teradata

In ANSI mode, transaction processing adheres to the rules defined by the ANSI SQL specification. In Teradata mode, transaction processing follows the rules defined by Teradata. Below are a few comparisons between the two modes.

Comparison Chart

TERADATA Mode	**ANSI Mode**
Data comparison is **not case specific**. Character literal values can be coded in SQL as lower case or upper case. The search engine would view an 'A' the same as an 'a' and data would be returned.	Data comparison is **case specific**. Character literal values must be coded using the correct case in order for the search engine to determine a match. An 'A' is different than an 'a' and data would not be returned.

Allows truncation of displayed data. Certain SQL commands covered in earlier chapters allow the user to request less characters be returned than the number of characters stored in a column. This is perfectly acceptable.	**Forbids truncation** of display data. Any attempt to return less than all the data stored in a column will cause the SQL to fail with an error (3996).
A transaction is **implicit** by nature – each SQL statement is a stand-alone transaction and the work committed upon a successful completion. A transaction can also be **explicit** with a BEGIN TRANSACTION (BT) command and an END TRANSACTION (ET) command. The presence of the ET command will cause all successfully completed SQL work to be committed and make it permanent.	All transactions are **explicit only** and at the end of a transaction a COMMIT WORK command is required in order to commit all successfully completed work and make it permanent.
The **CREATE TABLE** will default to: **SET** table (no duplicate rows allowed). Non-case specific character data columns.	The **CREATE TABLE** will default to: **MULTISET** table (duplicate rows allowed). Case specific character data columns.

Figure 15.6

Setting the Transaction Mode

The default mode in Teradata is Teradata mode, which is set at the system level. To set the transaction processing mode, use the:

- SessionMode field of the DBS Control Record
- Preprocessor2 TRANSACT() option
- BTEQ command .SET SESSION TRANSACTION (shown below)

```
-- set transaction mode to Teradata
.SET SESSION TRANSACTION BTET;

or

-- set transaction mode to ANSI
.SET SESSION TRANSACTION ANSI;
```

Figure 15.7

Teradata Mode Transactions

Locks are acquired up front when users execute other requests using the same tables. These request types are also considered implicit transactions (or system-generated transactions). Therefore, the system holds locks for these request types until the requests complete.

- Multi-statement only DML requests
- Single statement DDL or DML requests
- Macro multi-statement or single statement requests

The table-level write locks needed in these requests are:

- Acquired in TableID order
- Held until done

This minimizes deadlocks at the table level when many users execute requests on the same tables.

Transaction Semantics - BTET Mode

The following discusses the difference between implicit and explicit transactions and how they are handled in BT/ET transaction mode.

Implicit transaction

- Each SQL request is an implicit transaction by default
- Each failed request is automatically rolled back.

Explicit transaction

- Launched with explicit BEGIN TRANSACTION (BT)

Ended explicitly by:

- END TRANSACTION (ET)—commit work done since BT
- ROLLBACK—rollback work done since BT

Ended implicitly by:

- Any request failure—rollback work done since BT

Here are examples for you to study.

Implicit Transaction	**Explicit Transaction**
.LOGON INSERT row1....; /*txn#1*/ INSERT row2....; /*txn#2*/ .LOGOFF	BT; /*txn#1*/ INSERT row1....; INSERT row2....; ET;
Two transactions. Failure of one doesn't affect the other.	One transaction. Failure of one will rollback to BT.

Figure 15.8

ANSI Mode Transactions

Apart from transaction semantics, you can write SQL code with explicit specifications to override defaults so that it performs identically in both ANSI and Teradata modes. The following rules are enforced in ANSI mode.

A transaction initiation is always *implicit*. A transaction is opened by the first SQL statement executed in a session or by the first statement executed following the close of a transaction. The COMMIT [WORK] or ROLLBACK [WORK] statements close a transaction.

In ANSI mode, the user must commit the work to disk in order to save the work. The COMMIT WORK; command must be used to successfully end an ANSI transaction (single or multi-step command):

To perform this statement in BTEQ - ANSI mode, the following can be used:

```
UPDATE Employee_Table
SET  Salary = Salary * 1.1
WHERE Employee_No = 1232578 ;
.if errorcode > 0  then .quit  ERRORCODE
UPDATE  Department_Table   FROM Employee_Table  AS  E
SET  Budget_Amount = Budget_Amount + (Salary * .01)
WHERE   E.Dept_No = Department_Table.Dept_no
AND      E.Employee_no = 1232578 ;
COMMIT WORK ;
```

Figure 15.9

Note: In Teradata (BTET) mode, the COMMIT WORK will cause an error.

Transaction Semantics - ANSI Mode

All transactions in ANSI mode are explicit. The following discusses ANSI explicit transactions and how they are handled.

Explicit transaction

- Transaction is launched with first SQL request.
- All transactions are explicitly ended.
- Transaction ended explicitly by:
    - COMMIT WORK—commit work done since launch
    - ROLLBACK—rollback work done since launch

The following chart summarizes this.

No Explicit Ending	Explicit Ending
.LOGON INSERT row1....; /*txn#1*/ INSERT row2....; .LOGOFF	.LOGON INSERT row1....; /*txn#1*/ INSERT row2....; COMMIT WORK; .LOGOFF
One transaction. LOGOFF without COMMIT – both INSERTs roll back.	One transaction. Failure of either has no effect on the other. COMMIT commits successful requests only.

Figure 15.10

Aborting Transactions

The other way to end a transaction besides either ET; or COMMIT WORK;, is to use either the ABORT or ROLLBACK statement. The syntax for the ABORT/ROLLBACK statement is:

ABORT | ROLLBACK ['abort_message'] [FROM_clause]
[WHERE_clause] ;

SYNTAX ELEMENT	DESCRIPTION
ABORT ROLLBACK	ABORT is a Teradata extension to the ANSI SQL-2003 standard.
'abort_message'	The text of the message to be returned when the transaction is terminated.
FROM_clause	Only required if the WHERE_clause includes a subquery.
WHERE_clause	• An optional clause that specifies an expression whose result must evaluate to TRUE if the transaction is to be rolled back. • If the result of the WHERE_clause evaluates to FALSE, then transaction processing continues. • If you do not specify a WHERE_clause, then rollback occurs unconditionally. • The abort condition described by the WHERE_clause can also specify an aggregate operation.

Figure 15.11

Note: In ANSI mode, if a user logs off without performing a COMMIT command, Teradata will consider this an aborted transaction and all work will be rolled back.

Chapter 15: Practice Questions

1. Which of the following can be downgraded to a Read lock?
   a. ACCESS
   b. READ
   c. WRITE
   d. EXCLUSIVE
   e. None of the above

2. Which of the following statements about COMMIT WORK is true?
   a. It commits only successful transactions.
   b. It commits all transactions.
   c. It can be used in both ANSI and BT/ET mode.
   d. It is a Teradata extension.

3. What access right is required in order to place each of the following locks (fill in the blank with DML statement)?

a. ACCESS	____________	INSERT or DELETE
b. READ	____________	DROP
c. WRITE	____________	SELECT
d. EXCLUSIVE	____________	

4. Given the following SQL executed in ANSI mode, circle the numbers below to indicate which c1-value rows will be returned?

```
CREATE TABLE o_words(c1 byteint, c2 char(4));
commit;

INSERT o_words values (1 ,'COok');
INSERT o_words values (2, 'woOD');
INSERT o_words values (3, 'coOl');
INSERT o_words values (4, 'bOOo');
INSERT o_words values (5, 'cOop');
INSERT o_words values (6, 'COOs');
INSERT o_words values (7, 'cooT');
INSERT o_words values (8, 'ZOoo');
INSERT o_words values (9, 'ToOo');
commit;

SELECT * from o_words where c2 like '%Oo'
order by 1;
```

a. 1 2 3 4 5 6 7 8 9

5. Given the following SQL, executed in BTET mode, circle the numbers below to indicate which rows will be returned.

```
CREATE TABLE o_words(c1 byteint, c2 char(4));

INSERT o_words values (1 ,'COok');
INSERT o_words values (2, 'woOD');
INSERT o_words values (3, 'coOl');
INSERT o_words values (4, 'bOOo');
INSERT o_words values (5, 'cOop');
INSERT o_words values (6, 'COOs');
INSERT o_words values (7, 'cooT');
INSERT o_words values (8, 'ZOoo');
INSERT o_words values (9, 'ToOo');

SELECT * from o_words where c2 like '%Oo'
order by 1;
```

a. 1 2 3 4 5 6 7 8 9

Chapter Notes

Utilize this space for notes, key points to remember, diagrams, areas of further study, etc.

Chapter 16: Data Definition Language

Certification Objectives

- ✓ Describe the attributes and constraints for a column in a table.
- ✓ Given a CREATE TABLE statement without a primary index declared, identify the column that Teradata will select as the primary index.
- ✓ Given a scenario, identify considerations using a CREATE TABLE AS definition.

Before You Begin

You should be familiar with the following terms and concepts.

Terms	Key Concepts
CREATE TABLE	Considerations, options, and restrictions
Table Attributes	Understand the types and how to utilize
PPI / MLPPI	Knowledge on how to apply and the differences

Data Definition Language (DDL) is used to create, modify, and remove object definitions. This chapter will discuss DDL in respect to Tables, Indexes, and Triggers.

CREATE TABLE

The CREATE TABLE statement can be broken down into four major areas as seen in the syntax example and chart below.

CREATE TABLE Syntax

```
CREATE [SET/MULTISET] [VOLATILE/GLOBAL TEMPORARY]
TABLE tablename
        <Create Table Options>
        <Column Definitions>
        <Table-level Constraints>
        <Index Definitions>
        <Row Retention>;
```

Where:

Create Table options	Specify physical attributes of table: Fallback, Journaling, Freespace, Datablocksize, BlockCompression
Column definitions	Define each column's data type, attributes, and any constraints: ○ PRIMARY KEY ○ UNIQUE ○ CHECK ○ REFERENCES or GENERATED
Table-level constraints	Define multi-column constraints: PRIMARY KEY FOREIGN KEY UNIQUE CHECK conditions
Index definitions	Specify indexes for physical access to data
Row retention	COMMIT options

Figure 16.1

SET/MULTISET - Duplicate row option

- SET – no duplicate rows allowed. This is the Teradata session default. If there is no UNIQUE declaration, the system will compare a new row to every table row having the same row hash. This is the Teradata session default.

- MULTISET - duplicate rows allowed. Multiset tables exist outside of the relational model, since relational tables must have a Primary Key. This is the ANSI session default.

Table type options

- Permanent – This is the default.
- VOLATILE – exists only for the duration of the user's session
- GLOBAL TEMPORARY– definition is permanent, but data exists only for the duration of the user's session

Table protection options

- [NO] FALLBACK PROTECTION
- [NO] LOG
- [NO|DUAL] BEFORE JOURNAL
- [NO|DUAL|LOCAL|[NOT] LOCAL] AFTER JOURNAL

Column names

Column names must be unique within the table.

Column data type

Refer to Chapter 4 for the list of data types.

Data Type Attributes

DEFAULT <value>	Specify a default value in place of a null
WITH DEFAULT	Specify the use of a system default value in place of a null
DEFAULT USER DEFAULT DATE DEFAULT TIME DEFAULT NULL	Insert username of the session Insert CURRENT_DATE Insert CURRENT_TIME Insert a null
FORMAT	Default display format
TITLE	Default column title
NAMED	Default name
UPPERCASE	Shift to uppercase for storage
CASESPECIFIC	Store as entered

Figure 16.2

Column-Level Constraints

Column-level constraints may be unnamed. If named, each name must be unique. Named constraint names must adhere to normal naming restrictions.

UNIQUE	The column must be NOT NULL and not allow duplicates
PRIMARY KEY	The column must be NOT NULL and not allow duplicates
CHECK (boolean condition)	Cannot reference other columns

REFERENCES [WITH [NO]] CHECK OPTION tablename (columnname)	The WITH CHECK OPTION will implement full referential integrity

Figure 16.3

Storage Attributes

COMPRESS	Nulls will be compressed to zero space.
COMPRESS NULL	Nulls will be compressed to zero space.
COMPRESS (<value_list>)	Nulls and the constant(s) will be compressed to zero space.

Figure 16.4

Table Naming Conventions

Names are 1 to 30 characters in length and may only include the following characters:

- Uppercase or lowercase letters (A to Z and a to z)
- Digits (0 through 9)
- The special characters DOLLAR SIGN ($), NUMBER SIGN (#), and LOW LINE (_) a.k.a. UNDERSCORE
- They must not begin with a digit.
- They must not be a reserved word.

Names that define databases and objects must observe the following rules.

- Databases, users, and profiles must have unique names within the system.
- Tables, views, stored procedures, join or hash indexes, triggers, user-defined functions, and macros must have unique names within a database or user.

- Table and view columns must have unique names within the table or view.
- Parameters defined for a macro or stored procedure must have unique names.
- Secondary indexes which are assigned names must have names that are unique to the table.
- Constraints on a table, which are assigned names, must have names that are unique to the table.
- CHECK constraints, REFERENCE constraints, and INDEX objects can also have *assigned* names. Names are optional for these objects.
- Names are not case-specific

ANSI standards state that indexes on a table are optional. However, Teradata requires a Primary Index for distributing rows across the AMPs. If no Primary Index is declared when a table is created, Teradata will make the first column a Non-Unique Primary Index (NUPI), if DefaultPrimaryIndex = D or P, as the illustrations below demonstrate. More on this in the section Default Primary Index, later in this chapter.

Note: If a Primary Key (PK) or UNIQUE constraints are defined, then they take precedence. Refer to Figure 16.12 for more information.

Teradata table creation syntax is illustrated below:

```
CREATE TABLE emp_data
        (employee_number  INTEGER        NOT NULL
        ,user_name        CHAR(25)       DEFAULT USER
        ,last_name        CHAR(20)       NOT NULL
                                         WITH DEFAULT
        ,street_address   VARCHAR(30) TITLE 'Address'
        ,city             CHAR(15)       DEFAULT 'Santa Clara'
        ,state            CHAR(2)        WITH DEFAULT
        ,birthdate        DATE           FORMAT 'mm/dd/yy'
        ,salary_amount    DEC(10,2)
        ,sex              CHAR(1)        UPPERCASE
                                         COMPRESS ('M', 'F') );
```

Figure 16.5

Teradata table implementation syntax shown in the next example:

```
CREATE SET TABLE CSQL_CLASS.emp_data ,NO FALLBACK ,
     NO BEFORE JOURNAL,
     NO AFTER JOURNAL,
     CHECKSUM = DEFAULT
     (employee_number INTEGER NOT NULL,
      user_name CHAR(25) CHARACTER SET LATIN
                         NOT CASESPECIFIC
                         DEFAULT USER,
      last_name CHAR(20) CHARACTER SET LATIN
                         NOT CASESPECIFIC
                         NOT NULL
                         DEFAULT '                    ',
      street_address VARCHAR(30) CHARACTER SET LATIN
                         NOT CASESPECIFIC
                         TITLE 'Address',
      city CHAR(15) CHARACTER SET LATIN
                         NOT CASESPECIFIC
                         DEFAULT 'Santa Clara    ',
      state CHAR(2) CHARACTER SET LATIN
                         NOT CASESPECIFIC
                         DEFAULT '  ',
      birthdate DATE FORMAT 'mm/dd/yy',
      salary_amount DECIMAL(10,2),
      sex CHAR(1) CHARACTER SET LATIN
                         UPPERCASE
                         NOT CASESPECIFIC
                         COMPRESS ('F','M'))
PRIMARY INDEX ( employee_number );
```

Figure 16.6

Note: More on this topic will be covered later in the chapter.

Referential Integrity

Referencing (Child) Table

The referencing table is referred to as the child table, and the specified child table columns are the referencing columns.

Referenced (Parent) Table

A child table must have a parent, and the referenced table is referred to as the parent table. The parent key columns in the parent table are the referenced columns. Because the referenced columns are always defined as unique, they must be implemented as one of the following unique indexes:

- A unique primary index (UPI), defined as NOT NULL
- A unique secondary index (USI), defined as NOT NULL

Rules for Assigning Columns as Foreign Keys

The FOREIGN KEY columns in the *referencing* table must be identical in definition with the keys in the *referenced* table. Corresponding columns must have the same data type and case sensitivity.

- The COMPRESS option is not permitted on either the referenced or referencing column(s).
- Column level constraints are not compared.
- A one-column FOREIGN KEY cannot reference a single column in a multicolumn primary or unique key—the foreign and primary/unique key must contain the same number of columns.

Circular References Are Allowed

References can be defined as circular in that TableA can reference TableB, which can reference TableA. In this case, at least one set of FOREIGN KEYS must be defined on nullable columns.

If the FOREIGN KEYS in TableA are on columns defined as nullable, then rows could be inserted into TableA with nulls for the FOREIGN KEY columns. Once the appropriate rows exist in TableB, the nulls of the FOREIGN KEY columns in TableA could then be updated to contain non-null values which match the TableB values.

References Can Be to the Table Itself

FOREIGN KEY references can also be to the same table that contains the FOREIGN KEY. The referenced columns must be different columns than the FOREIGN KEY, and both the referenced and referencing columns must subscribe to the referential integrity rules.

Maintaining Foreign Keys

Definition of a FOREIGN KEY requires that the Teradata Database maintain the integrity defined between the *referenced* and *referencing* table.

The Teradata Database maintains the integrity of foreign keys as explained in the following table.

For this data manipulation activity ...	The system verifies that ...
A row is inserted into a *referencing* table and foreign key columns are defined to be NOT NULL.	a row exists in the *referenced* table with the same values as those in the foreign key columns. If such a row does not exist, then

	an error is returned. If the foreign key contains multiple columns, and if any one column value of the foreign key is null, then none of the foreign key values are validated.
The values in foreign key columns are altered to be NOT NULL.	a row exists in the *referenced* table that contains values equal to the altered values of all of the foreign key columns. If such a row does not exist, then an error is returned.
A row is deleted from a *referenced* table.	no rows exist in *referencing* tables with foreign key values equal to those of the row to be deleted. If such rows exist, then an error is returned.
Before a *referenced* column in a *referenced* table is updated.	no rows exist in a referencing table with foreign key values equal to those of the referenced columns. If such rows exist, then an error is returned.
Before the structure of columns defined as foreign keys or referenced by foreign keys is altered.	the change would not violate the rules for definition of a foreign key constraint. An ALTER TABLE or DROP INDEX statement attempting to change such a columns structure returns an error.

A table *referenced* by another is dropped.	the referencing table has dropped its foreign key reference to the referenced table.
An ALTER TABLE statement adds a foreign key reference to a table.	all of the values in the foreign key columns are validated against columns in the referenced table. When the system parses ALTER TABLE, it defines an error table that: • Has the same columns and primary index as the target table of the ALTER TABLE statement. • Has a name that is the same as the target table name suffixed with the reference index number. A reference index number is assigned to each foreign key constraint for a table. To determine the number, use one of the following system views. ▪ RI_Child_Tables ▪ RI_Distinct_Children ▪ RI_Distinct_Parents ▪ RI_Parent_Tables • Is created under the same user or database as the table being altered. If a table already exists with the same name as that generated for the error table then an error is returned to the ALTER TABLE statement.

	Rows in the referencing table that contain values in the foreign key columns that cannot be found in any row of the referenced table are copied into the error table (the base data of the target table is not modified). It is your responsibility to: • Correct data values in the referenced or referencing tables so that full referential integrity exists between the two tables. Use the rows in the error table to define which corrections to make. • Maintain the error table.

Figure 16.7

Here is an example:

```
CREATE TABLE customer_table
(customer_number INTEGER NOT NULL PRIMARY KEY
,customer_name VARCHAR(20)
,phone_number CHAR(8)
)
INDEX (Customer_name)
INDEX (Phone_number);
```

Figure 16.8

Notice how the Primary Key has been implemented as a Unique Primary Index.

```
CREATE TABLE order_table
(order_number INTEGER NOT NULL
,customer_number INTEGER NOT NULL
 CONSTRAINT cust_fk REFERENCES WITH CHECK OPTION
customer_table (customer_number)
,order_date DATE FORMAT 'YY/MM/DD'
,order_total DECIMAL(10,2)
)
UNIQUE PRIMARY INDEX (Order_Number)
INDEX (Customer_number)
INDEX (Order_Date);
```

Figure 16.9

Multi-column constraints can only be declared as table-level constraints, after the final column declaration.

```
CREATE SET TABLE CSQL_CLASS.emp_job_table
   ( job_no INTEGER NOT NULL,
    emp_no INTEGER NOT NULL,
    PRIMARY KEY (job_no, emp_no))
PRIMARY INDEX ( job_no );

SHOW TABLE CSQL_CLASS.emp_job_table;
```

Figure 16.10

INDEX definitions

A CREATE TABLE may specify

- A Primary Index
- A Primary Key
- Both
- Neither

Primary Key vs. Primary Index

A Primary Index is different from a primary key in that its values can change, and that its purpose is not for row identification, but for data distribution.

The Primary Index is often, but not necessarily the same column(s) as the primary key. This is because the Primary Index is designed to be the best physical path to the data, whereas the primary key is intended to be the best logical path to the data. The Primary Index, by design, maximizes performance and accessibility. The following illustrates the key differences between the Primary Key and Primary Index.

Primary Key

- One or more columns used to uniquely identify the rows in a table
- Used in conjunction with foreign keys to define the important column relationships in a database
- Always unique and cannot be null
- Not known to the Teradata RDBMS as keys

Primary Index

- One or more columns used to distribute and locate the rows in a table.
- Choice of primary index will affect distribution, access, and thus, performance.
- Maybe used to enforce uniqueness.
- Maybe used to improve access.
- Maybe unique or non-unique.

Index Options

Depending on how you choose to count them, the Teradata Database supports between ten and twenty index types:

- Unique non-partitioned primary
- Non-unique non-partitioned primary
- Single-level unique partitioned primary
- Multilevel unique partitioned primary
- Single-level non-unique non-partitioned primary
- Multilevel non-unique partitioned primary
- Join
  A join index composed of virtual rows, with multiple fixed column sets appended to single repeating column set is said to be compressed.
  - Compressed
  - Non-compressed

  Whether compressed or non-compressed, a join index can be any of the following types:
  - Multi-table simple
  - Multi-table aggregate
  - Multi-table sparse
  - Single-table simple
  - Single-table aggregate
  - Single-table sparse
- Hash
- Unique secondary
- Non-unique secondary
  - Hash-ordered on all columns with ALL option
  - Hash-ordered on single column with ALL option
  - Value-ordered on single column with ALL option
  - Hash-ordered on all columns without ALL option
  - Hash-ordered on single column without ALL option
  - Value-ordered on single column without ALL option

The following chart shows the strengths and possible drawbacks of the various indexing methods provided by Teradata.

This access method ...	Has the following strengths ...	And the following possible drawbacks ...
Unique Primary Index (UPI)	• is the most efficient access method when the SQL statement contains the PI value • involves one AMP and one row • requires no spool file (for a simple SELECT) • can obtain the most granular locks	none, in the context of a SELECT statement specifying a PI value. However, a poorly chosen PI can cause poor overall performance in a large workload.
Non-Unique Primary Index (NUPI)	• provides efficient access when the SQL statement contains the PI value • involves one AMP • can obtain granular locks • may not require a spool file as long as the number of rows returned is small	• may slow down INSERTs for a SET table with no USIs. • may decrease the efficiency of SELECTs containing the PI value when some values are repeated in many rows.
Unique Secondary Index (USI)	• provides efficient access when the SQL statement contains the USI values, and you do not specify PI values • involves two AMPs and one row • requires no spool file (for a simple SELECT)	• requires additional overhead for INSERTs, UPDATEs, MERGEs, and DELETEs. • requires additional space for the subtable storage
Non-Unique Secondary Index	• provides efficient access when the number of rows per value in the table is	• requires additional overhead for INSERTs, UPDATEs, MERGEs, and

(NUSI)	relatively small • involves all AMPS and probably multiple rows • provides access using information that may be more readily available than a UPI value, such as employee last name, compared to an employee number • may require a spool file	DELETEs. • will not be used by the Optimizer if the number of data blocks accessed is a significant percentage of the data blocks in the table because the Optimizer will determine that a full table scan is cheaper. • requires additional space for the subtable storage
Full table scan	• accesses each row only once • provides access using any arbitrary set of column conditions	• examines every row. • usually requires a spool file possibly as large as the base table.
Multi-table Join Index (JI)	• can eliminate the need to perform certain joins and aggregates repetitively • may be able to satisfy a query without referencing the base tables • can have a different PI from that of the base table • can replace a NUSI or a USI	• requires additional overhead for INSERTs, UPDATEs, MERGEs, and DELETEs for any of the base tables that contribute to the multi-table JI. • usually is not suitable for data in tables subjected to a large number of daily INSERTs, UPDATEs, MERGEs, and DELETEs. • imposes some restrictions on operations performed on the base table. • requires additional space for the JI storage

Single-table join index (JI) or hash index	• Can be used for multiple purposes including: • Hash redistribution on non-index columns for join improvement • Sparse indexes • Aggregate indexes • Covered indexes	• requires additional overhead for INSERTs, UPDATEs, MERGEs, and DELETEs. • imposes some restrictions on operations performed on the base table. • requires additional space for the JI storage

Figure 16.11

Secondary and HASH indexes can be added to a table by using the CREATE INDEX and CREATE HASH INDEX commands.

No Primary Index (NoPI)

Except for unpartitioned NoPI tables, column-partitioned tables and join indexes, and global temporary trace tables, each Teradata Database table, hash, and join index must have a primary index.

The primary use of an unpartitioned NoPI table is as a staging table for FastLoad, and Teradata Parallel Data Pump Array INSERT data loading operations for both unpartitioned and column-partitioned tables.

Because there is no primary index for the rows of a NoPI table, its rows are not hashed to an AMP based on their primary index value. Instead, Teradata Database either hashes on the Query ID for a row, or it uses a different algorithm to assign the row to its home AMP.

Teradata Database then generates a RowID for each row in a NoPI table by using a hash bucket that an AMP owns and using it to generate a RowID. This strategy makes fallback and index maintenance very similar to their maintenance on a PI table.

Default Primary Index

When you issue a CREATE TABLE statement, the system examines the syntax and the DBS Control parameter DefaultPrimaryIndex to see if it's set to D, P, or N. The CREATE TABLE syntax, and the setting of that parameter, will control whether the table is created with a Primary Index. The following chart describes how the system decides.

IF . . .	**THEN . . .**
The table is a temporal table	Temporal tables must be Multiset and have a NUPI.
The table has an explicit NO PRIMARY INDEX clause	Create a Multiset table with NO PRIMARY INDEX.
The table has column partitioning	Create a Multiset table with NO PRIMARY INDEX.
The table has an explicit UPI or NUPI	Create the table with the defined index.
There is no Primary Index clause, but there is a PK defined	Then create the table with a UPI on the PK column set
There is no Primary Index clause, no PK, but there is a UNIQUE constraint	Then create the table with a UPI on the first UNQIUE constraint.
There is no Primary Index clause, no PK, no UNIQUE constraint, and the DefaultPrimaryIndex = D or P	Then create the table with a NUPI on the first column.
There is no Primary Index clause, no PK, no UNIQUE constraint, and the DefaultPrimaryIndex = N	Then create the table with NO PRIMARY INDEX.

Figure 16.12

CREATE TABLE AS

Use the CREATE TABLE AS command to create a new table from the results of a query. Syntax for the CREATE TABLE AS is:

CREATE [TEMPORARY | TEMP] TABLE <tablename>
[(<column_name> [, ...])]
AS <select_clause> [Primary Index (<column-list>)]
WITH [NO] DATA;

The example below illustrates a CREATE TABLE AS function:

```
CREATE TABLE order_table_new AS (SELECT * from order_table)
WITH DATA ;
```

Figure 16.13

Altering a Table

Through the ALTER TABLE [*databasename.*] *tablename* command, you can:

ADD/MODIFY	FALLBACK
ADD/MODIFY	BEFORE/AFTER journaling
ADD/MODIFY	CHECKSUM
ADD/MODIFY	FREESPACE
ADD/MODIFY	DATABLOCKSIZE
ADD/DROP/RENAME	Columns
ADD/DROP	FOREIGN KEY constraints
DROP	INCONSISTENT REFERENCES
ADD/DROP/MODIFY	CHECK constraints
DROP	Constraints
ADD	UNIQUE constraints
ADD	PRIMARY KEY constraints
MODIFY	Partitioned Primary Indexes
REVALIDATE	Partitioned Primary Indexes

Figure 16.14

Here are two examples:

ALTER TABLE emp_job_table, FALLBACK;
ALTER TABLE emp_job_table ADD PRIMARY KEY (job_no, emp_no);

BEFORE:

```
CREATE SET TABLE CSQL_CLASS.emp_job_table ,NO FALLBACK ,
     NO BEFORE JOURNAL,
     NO AFTER JOURNAL,
     CHECKSUM = DEFAULT
     (
      job_no INTEGER NOT NULL,
      emp_no INTEGER NOT NULL)
PRIMARY INDEX ( job_no );
```

AFTER:

```
CREATE SET TABLE CSQL_CLASS.emp_job_table ,FALLBACK ,
     NO BEFORE JOURNAL,
     NO AFTER JOURNAL,
     CHECKSUM = DEFAULT
     (
      job_no INTEGER NOT NULL,
      emp_no INTEGER NOT NULL)
PRIMARY INDEX ( job_no )
UNIQUE INDEX ( job_no ,emp_no );
```

Figure 16.15

When adding a constraint, no other options can be specified. Also notice how the PK became a USI.

Dropping Database Objects

To remove a table, view, or macro from a database, use the DROP command. The general syntax is:

DROP { TABLE | VIEW | MACRO } [*databasename.*] *objectname* ;

Example:

```
DROP TABLE names_table ;
```

Figure 16.16

Renaming Database Objects

To change the name of a database object, use the RENAME command. The general syntax is:

RENAME { TABLE | VIEW | MACRO } [databasename.] oldobjectname { TO | AS } [databasename.] newobjectname ;

Example:

```
RENAME TABLE csql_class.stats_table TO csql_class.mystats_table;
```

Figure 16.17

Partitioned Tables

Single-level PPI Table (SLPPI)

The previous examples have shown NPPI tables, which is the normal way of storing rows. The rows of NPPI table are hash-distributed across the AMPs and sorted by row hash.

When a table or join index is created with a PPI, its rows are hashed to the appropriate AMPs and then assigned to their computed internal partition number based on the value of a partitioning expression defined by the user when the table was created or altered. Once assigned to a partition, the rows are stored in row hash order.

PPI tables provide enhanced storing, deleting, and retrieval of rows when the Parser determines that the PPI can be used instead of a full-table scan.

The following is an example of an SLPPI table creation, based upon the current csql_class.sales_table:

```
CREATE TABLE ppi_sales_table
(product_id INTEGER
,sale_date DATE
,daily_sales DEC(9,2)
)
PRIMARY INDEX (product_id)
PARTITION BY RANGE_N (sale_date BETWEEN DATE '2007-09-01'
AND DATE '2007-10-30'
EACH INTERVAL '1' DAY);

INSERT INTO ppi_sales_table SELECT * FROM sales_table;

COLLECT STATISTICS COLUMN (product_id, sale_date) ON
ppi_sales_table;
```

Figure 16.18

EXPLAIN SELECT * FROM ppi_sales_table
WHERE sale_date = '2007-09-30';

```
Explanation
---------------------------------------------------------------
  1) First, we lock a distinct CSQL_CLASS."pseudo table"
     for read on a RowHash to prevent global deadlock for
     CSQL_CLASS.ppi_sales_table.
  2) Next, we lock CSQL_CLASS.ppi_sales_table for read.
  3) We do an all-AMPs RETRIEVE step from a single
     partition of CSQL_CLASS.ppi_sales_table with a
     condition of ("CSQL_CLASS.ppi_sales_table.sale_date =
     DATE '2007-09-30'") with a residual condition of
     ("CSQL_CLASS.ppi_sales_table.sale_date =
     DATE '2007-09-30'") into Spool 1 (group_amps), which
     is built locally on the AMPs.  The size of Spool 1 is
     estimated with no confidence to be 3 rows (159 bytes).
     The estimated time for this step is 0.02 seconds.
  4) Finally, we send out an END TRANSACTION step to all
     AMPs involved in processing the request.
  -> The contents of Spool 1 are sent back to the user as
     the result of statement 1.  The total estimated time
     is 0.02 seconds.
```

Figure 16.19

To delete the oldest month of rows and create a new partition for a new month, do the following:

```
ALTER TABLE ppi_sales_table
MODIFY PRIMARY INDEX (product_id)
DROP RANGE BETWEEN DATE '2007-09-01' AND DATE '2007-09-30'
EACH INTERVAL '1' DAY
ADD RANGE BETWEEN DATE '2007-11-01' AND DATE '2007-11-30'
EACH INTERVAL '1' DAY
WITH DELETE;
```

Figure 16.20

Note: Altering or dropping a partition can adversely affect performance of queries against the table. A full table scan may result once the partition has been removed, especially when performing range based queries.

Multilevel PPI Tables

Multilevel partitioning allows each partition at a given level to be further partitioned into sub-partitions. Each partition for a level is sub-partitioned the same per a partitioning expression defined for the next lower level. The system hash orders the rows within the lowest partition levels. Teradata combines multiple “where” predicates that result in partition elimination.

The following example shows how an insurance company's claims table could be partitioned by a range of claim dates and then sub-partitioned by a range of state identifiers using multilevel partitioning.

```
CREATE TABLE claims
(claim_id INTEGER NOT NULL
,claim_date DATE NOT NULL
,state_id BYTEINT NOT NULL
,claim_info VARCHAR(20000) NOT NULL
)
PRIMARY INDEX (claim_id)
PARTITION BY (RANGE_N(claim_date BETWEEN DATE '1999-01-01'
AND DATE '2005-12-31' EACH INTERVAL '1' MONTH)
,RANGE_N(state_id BETWEEN 1 AND 75 EACH 1))
UNIQUE INDEX (claim_id);
```

Figure 16.21

Eliminating all but one month out of their many years of claims history would facilitate scanning of less than 5 percent of the claims history for satisfying the following query:

```
SELECT *
FROM claims
WHERE claim_date BETWEEN DATE '2005-06-01'
AND DATE '2005-06-30';
```

Figure 16.22

Similarly, eliminating all but the Connecticut claims from the many states in which this insurance company does business would make it possible to scan less than 5 percent of the claims history to satisfy the following query:

```
SELECT *
FROM claims, states
WHERE claims.state_id = states.state_id
AND states.state = 'Connecticut';
```

Figure 16.23

Combining both of these predicates for partition elimination makes it possible to scan less than 0.5 percent of the claims history to satisfy the following query:

```
SELECT *
FROM claims, states
WHERE claims.state_id = states.state_id
AND states.state = 'Connecticut'
AND claim_date BETWEEN DATE '2005-06-01'
AND DATE '2005-06-30';
```

Figure 16.24

Clearly, combining both predicates for partition elimination has a significant performance advantage. Partition elimination by both of these columns, as described, provides higher performance, more space efficiency, and more maintenance efficiency than a composite NUSI or join index for most of the queries run at this insurance company.

Queue Tables

A queue table is a special database object: a persistent table used to handle queue-oriented data such as event processing, and asynchronous data loading applications. The properties of queue tables are similar to those of ordinary base tables, with the additional unique property of behaving like an asynchronous first-in-first-out (FIFO) queue.

You can think of a queue table as a regular table that also has a memory-resident cache associated with it that tracks the FIFO queue ordering of its rows. Additionally, consumed rows are retrieved and deleted from the database simultaneously, which ensures that no row can be processed more than once.

An ideal queue table has the following characteristics:

- Low cardinality (implying that its rows are consumed at roughly the same rate as they are inserted).
- Infrequent UPDATE operations to its rows.
- Infrequent DELETE operations on its rows.

A queue table might be used to process event alerts.

SYNTAX

```
CREATE [SET/MULTISET] TABLE tablename, QUEUE [ , <Create Table
Options> ]
        ( QITS_column_name TIMESTAMP(6) NOT NULL
           DEFAULT CURRENT_TIMESTAMP(6)
           [ <data_attributes> <constraints> ]
        [ , <Additional Column Definitions> ] )
        <Table-level Constraints>
        <Index Definitions>;
```

The first column defined for any queue table must be a Query Insertion Timestamp (QITS) column. The system uses the QITS column to maintain the FIFO ordering of rows in the queue table. Each queue table has only one QITS column, and it must be defined with the following attributes:

column_name TIMESTAMP(6) NOT NULL DEFAULT CURRENT_TIMESTAMP(6)

The following example illustrates the creation of a Queue table:

```
CREATE TABLE qtbl_5
,QUEUE
(qits TIMESTAMP(6) NOT NULL DEFAULT CURRENT_TIMESTAMP(6)
,qsn INTEGER GENERATED ALWAYS AS IDENTITY (NO CYCLE)
,col_3 INTEGER
)
UNIQUE PRIMARY INDEX (qsn)
INDEX (qits);
```

Figure 16.25

Trigger Processing

Triggers are associated with tables, and can be used to automate required steps whenever an INSERT, UPDATE, or DELETE is performed.

Some possible uses are:

- Business Rules
  - Update the inventory table when a sale is made.
  - Reorder an item when On Hand Quantity falls below a given point.
- Event Propagation
  - Send an email when a new customer is added.

- Summary Table Maintenance
    - Maintain a summary table if high value items are sold.
    - Can also use a Join Index to accomplish this.
- Audit Trail
    - Create a log of changes.
- Data Validation
    - Rollback bad changes.

TRIGGER Commands

CREATE TRIGGER	Creates a new trigger definition
REPLACE TRIGGER	Changes the definition for a trigger without having to drop and recreate it. If the named trigger does not exist, a new trigger will be created.
DROP TRIGGER	Removes a trigger from the system.
ALTER TRIGGER	This is a Teradata extension. It allows you to change the status of a trigger from DISABLED to ENABLED before/after loading.

Figure 16.26

CREATE / REPLACE TRIGGER Syntax

CREATE TRIGGER creates a new trigger definition.

REPLACE TRIGGER changes the definition for a trigger without having to drop and recreate it.

CREATE | REPLACE TRIGGER *trigger_name*
<trigger status> <trigger action time> <triggering event>
<trigger sequence> <referencing clauses> <trigger type>
<trigger firing condition> <triggered action>

TRIGGER COMPONENTS

<table>
<tr><td>Component</td><td>Purpose</td><td>Choices</td></tr>
<tr><td>Trigger Status</td><td>Can be changed using ALTER TRIGGER</td><td><u>ENABLED</u>
DISABLED</td></tr>
<tr><td>Trigger Action Time</td><td>When the trigger action should happen</td><td>BEFORE
or
AFTER
the triggering statement is executed</td></tr>
<tr><td>Triggering Event or Statement</td><td>Which action on the subject table causes the trigger to fire.</td><td><table>
<tr><td colspan="2">Triggering Event</td></tr>
<tr><td>INSERT</td><td>Is one of the following:<ul><li>INSERT</li><li>INSERT ... SELECT</li><li>Atomic Upsert</li><li>MERGE</li></ul></td></tr>
<tr><td>DELETE</td><td>Is a DELETE</td></tr>
<tr><td colspan="2">Triggering Statement</td></tr>
<tr><td>UPDATE</td><td>Is one of the following:<ul><li>UPDATE</li><li>Atomic Upsert</li><li>MERGE</li></ul>Any number of rows, including none, can be updated.</td></tr>
</table></td></tr>
</table>

Trigger Sequence	Allows you to control the order of trigger execution within a request when multiple triggers are defined on a subject table.	ORDER *<value>*
Referencing Clause	The references are to virtual variables and tables, which can include values from the subject table either before or after the data-changing statement.	OLD ROW or OLD TABLE NEW ROW or NEW TABLE
Trigger Type	Causes the triggered action to occur once per statement for a statement trigger and once per row for a row trigger.	STATEMENT ROW
Trigger Firing Condition	Defines the additional conditions that must be met for the triggered action to occur.	e.g. WHEN n.qoh < 5
Triggered Actions	Defines which SQL statement causes the triggered action to occur.	SET, INSERT, UPDATE, DELETE, CALL, ABORT, EXEC

Figure 16.27

Using Triggers Effectively

- Use EXPLAIN
  - Think about scalability
  - Try to limit all-AMP operations
- Use statement triggers when the statement that fires the trigger changes a lot of rows
- Consider alternatives to triggers
  - Use a Join Index to maintain a summary table
  - Use Referential Integrity to validate changes
  - May be able to use upsert (UPDATE … ELSE INSERT …)
- Be careful with loading
  - Triggers must be disabled to use MultiLoad
  - May have performance/locking issues with TPump
- Statement triggers use steps against a set of rows
- Row triggers re-execute steps for each row
- Typically, use row triggers for single-row changes

Using Roles

A role can be viewed as a pseudo-user with privileges on a number of database objects. Any user granted a role can take on the identity of the pseudo-user and access all of the objects it has rights to. A database administrator can create different roles for different job functions and responsibilities, grant specific privileges on database objects to these roles, and then grant these roles to users.

Advantages of roles include:

- Simplify access rights administration
- Reduce disk space usage
- Better performance
- Less dictionary contention during DDL operations because the commands use less time.

A database administrator can grant rights on database objects to a role and have these rights automatically applied to all users assigned to that role. When a user's function within his organization changes, it is easier to change his/her role than deleting old rights and granting new rights that go along with the new function.

Roles can improve performance and reduces dictionary contention for DDL if they are fully utilized on a Teradata system.

Implementing Roles

Roles define access privileges on database objects. When you assign a default role to a user, you give the user access to all the objects that the role has been granted privileges to. A default role that has a role as a member gives the user additional access to all the objects that the nested role has privileges to. A newly created role does not have any associated privileges until grants are made to it. To manage user access privileges with roles, you can do the following:

- Create different roles for different job functions and responsibilities.
- Grant specific privileges on database objects to the roles.
- Assign default roles to users.
- Add members to the role.
- Members of a role can be users or other roles.
- Roles can only be nested one level. Thus, a role that has a role member cannot also be a member of another role.

Use the CREATE USER / MODIFY USER command to assign a DEFAULT ROLE for a specific user as the following example demonstrates.

```
Create User CSQL01 AS DEFAULT ROLE = new_role;

Modify User CSQL01 AS DEFAULT ROLE = new_role;
```

Figure 16.28

Note: A user executing the CREATE USER / MODIFY USER command with the DEFAULT ROLE option must have ADMIN privileges on the specified role (i.e. new_role).

Chapter 16: Practice Questions

1. Which table definition is valid?
    a. CREATE PERMANENT VOLATILE TABLE . . .;
    b. CREATE PERMANENT GLOBAL TEMPORARY TABLE . . .;
    c. CREATE VOLATILE GLOBAL TEMPORARY TABLE . . .;
    d. CREATE MULTISET GLOBAL TEMPROARY TABLE . . .;

2. Given the following table definition, match each column to its index definition.

    CREATE TABLE t1 (c1 int not null primary key, c2 int not null, c3 int not null unique, c4 int not null, c5 int not null) unique primary index(c2), index(c5);

a.	____ c1	1. UPI
b.	____ c2	2. NUPI
c.	____ c3	3. USI
d.	____ c4	4. NUSI
e.	____ c5	5 No index

3. Which of the following table definitions is correct?
    a. CREATE SET TABLE t1(c1 PERIOD(DATE) AS VALIDTIME, c2 INT);
    b. CREATE SET TABLE t1(c1 PERIOD(DATE) AS VALIDTIME, c2 INT) PRIMARY INDEX(c2);
    c. CREATE MULTISET TABLE t1(c1 PERIOD(DATE) AS VALIDTIME, c2 INT) UNIQUE PRIMARY INDEX(c2);
    d. CREATE MULTISET TABLE t1(c1 PERIOD(DATE) AS VALIDTIME, c2 INT) PRIMARY INDEX(c2);
    e. CREATE MULTISET TABLE t1(c1 PERIOD(DATE) AS VALIDTIME, c2 INT);

4. Which of the following MLPPI definitions is correct?
    a. PRIMARY INDEX(c1) PARTITION BY RANGE_N(exp_1), PARTITION BY RANGE_N(exp_2);
    b. PRIMARY INDEX(c1)(PARTITION BY RANGE_N(exp_1), PARTITION BY RANGE_N(exp_2));
    c. (PRIMARY INDEX(c1) PARTITION BY RANGE_N(exp_1), PARTITION BY RANGE_N(exp_2));
    d. PRIMARY INDEX(c1) (PARTITION BY RANGE_N(exp_1) PARTITION BY RANGE_N(exp_2));

5. Which of the following statements is correct?
    a. CREATE SET QUEUE TABLE (c1 INT NOT NULL, c2 TIMESTAMP(6) NOT NULL DEFAULT CURRENT_TIMESTAMP(6), c3 INT) PRIMARY INDEX(C1);
    b. CREATE MULTISET QUEUE TABLE (c1 INT NOT NULL, c2 TIMESTAMP(6) NOT NULL DEFAULT CURRENT_TIMESTAMP(6), c3 INT) PRIMARY INDEX(C1);
    c. CREATE SET TABLE, QUEUE (c1 INT NOT NULL, c2 TIMESTAMP(6) NOT NULL DEFAULT CURRENT_TIMESTAMP(6), c3 INT) PRIMARY INDEX(C1);
    d. CREATE MULTISET TABLE, QUEUE (c1 INT NOT NULL, c2 TIMESTAMP(6) NOT NULL DEFAULT CURRENT_TIMESTAMP(6), c3 INT) PRIMARY INDEX(C1);
    e. CREATE SET TABLE, QUEUE (c1 TIMESTAMP(6) NOT NULL DEFAULT CURRENT_TIMESTAMP(6), c2 INT NOT NULL,c3 INT) PRIMARY INDEX(c2);

Chapter Notes

Utilize this space for notes, key points to remember, diagrams, areas of further study, etc.

Chapter 17: Temporary Tables

Certification Objectives

- ✓ Given a scenario, identify the use of a derived table using single or multiple WITH form.
- ✓ Given a scenario, identify the type of table that should be used (global temporary, volatile, and permanent).
- ✓ Given a scenario, identify the use of a derived table using a recursive WITH form.
- ✓ Given a scenario, identify the use of a derived table using the FROM clause form.

Before You Begin

You should be familiar with the following terms and concepts.

Terms	Key Concepts
Derived Tables	Non-Recursive and Recursive WITH Statements
Volatile Table	Knowledge on how to apply and options available
Global Temporary	Features vs. Volatile Tables
Uses	General Practices for using temporary tables

There are three types of temporary tables: Derived, Volatile, and Global Temporary tables. The following chart provides a quick overview of the differences between the types of temporary tables. We will discuss each type of temporary table in this chapter.

TEMPORARY TABLE TYPE	DEFINITION
Derived	• Exist only within a query. • Space comes from the user's Spool space.
VOLATILE	• Definition and data exist only within the user's session. • It is not recorded in the Data Dictionary. • Space comes from the user's Spool space.
GLOBAL TEMPORARY	• Definition is stored in the Data Dictionary, and can be used by other users. • Data exists only within the user's session. • Space comes from the user's Temporary space.

Figure 17.1

Derived Tables

Derived tables are created, used, and dropped as part of a query. They allow the use of aggregates in a WHERE clause. This query locates all employees whose salary is greater than the company average.

```
SELECT  last_name
        ,salary         (FORMAT '$,$$$,$99.99')
        ,avgsal         (FORMAT '$,$$$,$99.99')
 FROM
        /* Insert this data into the derived table */
        /* The subquery must be enclosed in parentheses */
 (SELECT AVG (salary) FROM employee_table)
        /* Derived tablename and column(s) */
my_temp (avgsal)
        /* Main query table */
,employee_table
WHERE salary > avgsal
ORDER BY 2 DESC;

Result: 5 rows returned

Last_name                    Salary        avgsal
--------------------   ------------  ------------
Gere                     $64,300.00    $46,879.93
Strickland               $54,590.00    $46,879.93
Ford                     $54,590.00    $46,879.93
Student                  $48,850.00    $46,879.93
Roberts                  $48,800.00    $46,879.93
```

Figure 17.2

The (SELECT AVG (salary) FROM employee_table) functions as an INSERT INTO followed by the declaration of the derived table's name and column name(s) *my_temp (avgsal).* There must be a one-for-one match between the projected columns in the SELECT and columns in the derived table. The derived table columns take their data type from the projected columns.

Non-Recursive WITH

The Non-Recursive WITH is another way to create and use Derived tables. The main difference is that they are no longer defined in the FROM statement. Instead, they are defined at the beginning of the query as seen in the following syntax:

WITH *named_query* (*columnnames*)
(*select expression(s)*
) <final query to show the results>;

The named query is similar to a derived table.

```
WITH query_name(dept, totalsal) AS
(SELECT dept_no, SUM(salary)
 FROM    employee_table
 GROUP BY dept_no
)
SELECT d.dept_no AS Dept
       , TRIM(department_name) AS DeptName
       , Budget   (FORMAT '$,$$$,$$$.99') AS BudgetAmt
       , TotalSal (FORMAT '$,$$$,$$$.99') AS TotalSalaries
FROM    department_table d
JOIN    query_name
ON      d.dept_no = dept
ORDER BY 1;

Result: 4 rows returned

  Dept  DeptName                   BudgetAmt  TotalSalaries
------  --------------------  ------------  -------------
   100  Marketing              $500,000.00     $48,850.00
   200  Research and Develop   $550,000.00     $91,588.88
   300  Sales                  $650,000.00     $40,200.00
   400  Customer Support       $500,000.00    $144,180.00
```

Figure 17.3

Just as a query can have multiple derived tables, it can have multiple non-recursive WITH statements.

Recursive WITH

The Recursive WITH is another variation of a Derived table. The major difference is that a set operator is used within the derived table. The recursive nature causes the table to be joined multiple times as long as there are matching rows recursively being generated. The general syntax of a Recursive WITH is:

WITH RECURSIVE *named_query* (*columnnames*)
(<seed select statement>
UNION ALL
<recursive select statement>
)
<final query to show the results>;

A Recursive WITH may have multiple seed statements, and the seed statement(s) may reference derived tables.

A WITH or WITH RECURSIVE request modifier cannot appear within a WITH or WITH RECURSIVE statement.

The following example uses the single-table recursion that exists in the employee_table. Employees have managers, and managers are also employees. Knowing that whoever is at the top of the hierarchy does not have a manager (currently) we start there and have the system work its way down.

```
WITH RECURSIVE query_name (employee_no, last_name, depth) AS
( SELECT root.employee_no, root.last_name, 0 AS depth
FROM employee_table root
WHERE root.mgr_employee_no IS NULL
UNION ALL
SELECT indirect.employee_no, indirect.last_name, seed.depth+1 AS
depth
FROM query_name seed, employee_table indirect
WHERE seed.employee_no = indirect.mgr_employee_no
AND depth <= 20
)
SELECT employee_no, last_name, depth FROM query_name
ORDER BY depth;
```

```
Result: 9 rows returned

employee_no  last_name             depth
-----------  --------------------  -----
    1121334  Strickland                0
    2000000  Travolta                  1
    1000234  Gere                      1
    1333454  Roberts                   1
    1324657  Willis                    2
    2312225  Mcfly                     2
    1256349  Ford                      2
    1232578  Student                   3
    2341218  Clooney                   3
```

Figure 17.4

Volatile and Global Temporary Tables

Temporary tables are ideal for holding intermediate data to be repeatedly used for queries by the user in their current session. This is a big advantage over derived tables.

Temporary tables are visible only to the user / session that create them. In addition, several users can create the same temporary tables and each user will see only their own version of the table. For example, suppose you need to run several complex queries on large tables during a session. An efficient strategy is to execute the complex query once, then store the result in a temporary table.

SYNTAX

CREATE [SET | MULTISET] [VOLATILE | GLOBAL TEMPORARY]
TABLE tablename
, [NO] LOG <other table definitions>
<column definitions>
<index definitions>
ON COMMIT [DELETE | PRESERVE] ROWS

OPTION	DEFINITION
[NO] LOG	The default is to record all INSERT, DELETE, and UPDATE operations. Though this is slower, it makes the table data recoverable in case of a restart. LOG is the default.
ON COMMIT	DELETE ROWS – In Teradata transaction mode, each statement is a transaction, unless it appears within a multi-statement request BT; . . . ET; Therefore, if you were to do an INSERT into a temporary table, the row would be deleted as soon as the INSERT completes. In ANSI transaction mode, the row would remain until a COMMIT is issued.

	DELETE is the default.
	PRESERVE ROWS – Rows will remain until deleted or End of Session.

Figure 17.5

Volatile Tables

Volatile tables do not have a persistent definition; they must be newly created each time you need to use them. The table definition is cached only for the duration of the session in which it is created.

If you frequently reuse particular volatile table definitions, consider writing a macro that contains the CREATE TABLE text for those volatile tables.

Because volatile tables are private to the session that creates them, the system does not check their creation, access, modification, or drop privileges.

The following list details the general characteristics of volatile tables:

- Both the contents and the definition of a volatile table are destroyed when a system reset occurs.
- Space usage is charged to the login user Spool space.
- A single session can materialize up to 1,000 volatile tables at one time.
- The primary index for a volatile table can be either an NPPI or a PPI.
- You cannot create secondary, hash, or join indexes on a volatile table.
- You can collect statistics on volatile table columns, including the PARTITION column of a PPI volatile table.

The following options are not permitted for volatile tables:

- Referential integrity constraints
- CHECK constraints
- Permanent journaling
- Compressed column values
- DEFAULT clause
- TITLE clause
- Named indexes

Otherwise, the options for volatile tables are identical to those for global temporary tables.

Below is a step-by-step example of building and utilizing a Temporary Table.

Step 1: Create the Temporary Table

```
CREATE VOLATILE  TABLE  dept_aggr_t
(dept_no        SMALLINT
,sum_salary     DECIMAL(10,2)
,avg_salary     DECIMAL(8,2)
,max_salary     DECIMAL(8,2)
,min_salary     DECIMAL(8,2)
,cnt_salary     INTEGER )
PRIMARY INDEX(dept_No)
ON COMMIT PRESERVE ROWS;
```

Figure 17.6

- You *cannot* collect statistics on a volatile table
- Even though a volatile table exists only within a user's current session, the HELP and SHOW TABLE commands can be used to view information about the table.
- ALTER TABLE cannot be used for VOLATILE tables.

Note: For TD12: Any time the Optimizer requires statistics for a volatile table, it requests an all-AMPs sample to get an estimate of the cardinality of the volatile table. This differs from the standard random AMP sample where the system samples rows from a single AMP only.

Global Temporary Tables

Global Temporary tables have a persistent definition but do not have persistent contents across sessions.

The following list details the general characteristics of global temporary tables:

- Space usage is charged against the temporary space of the user who owns the session.
- A single session can materialize up to 2,000 global temporary tables at one time.
- You materialize a Global Temporary table locally by referencing it in a data manipulation statement. To materialize a global temporary table, you must have the appropriate privilege on the base Global Temporary table or on the containing database or user as required by the statement that materializes the table.
- Any number of different sessions can materialize the same table definition, but the contents are different depending on the DML statements made against the individual materialized tables during the course of a session.
- The primary index for a Global Temporary table can be either an NPPI or a PPI.
- You cannot create a Global Temporary table with the ... AS ... WITH DATA. To use the ... AS ... feature to create a Global Temporary table, specify WITH NO DATA.

The following options are not permitted for global temporary tables:

- Referential integrity constraints

- Permanent journaling
- You cannot create secondary, hash, or join indexes on a Global Temporary table.
- You cannot collect the following types of statistics on Global Temporary tables:
  - Multicolumn statistics
  - PARTITION or PARTITION#L*n* statistics
  - Sampled statistics

Access checking is not done on the materialized instances of any Global Temporary tables because those tables exist only for the duration of the session in which they are materialized.

```
CREATE MULTISET GLOBAL TEMPORARY TABLE gtt_report_layout
,FALLBACK
(rpt_c01 INT NOT NULL
,rpt_c02 CHAR(12) NOT NULL
,rpt_c03 CHAR(20)
,rpt_c04 SMALLINT
,rpt_c06 CHAR(15)
,rpt_c07 VARCHAR(40)
) PRIMARY INDEX (rpt_c01);
```

Figure 17.7

To modify a temporary table, use the ALTER command. Keep in mind that the default for Volatile and Temporary table data is ON COMMIT DELETE ROWS. To change that, do the following:

```
ALTER TABLE gtt_report_layout, ON COMMIT PRESERVE ROWS;

SHOW TABLE gtt_report_layout;

CREATE MULTISET GLOBAL TEMPORARY TABLE
CSQL_CLASS.gtt_report_layout
,FALLBACK ,CHECKSUM = DEFAULT,LOG
     (
      rpt_c01 INTEGER NOT NULL,
      rpt_c02 CHAR(12) CHARACTER SET LATIN
              NOT CASESPECIFIC NOT NULL,
      rpt_c03 CHAR(20) CHARACTER SET LATIN
              NOT CASESPECIFIC,
      rpt_c04 SMALLINT,
      rpt_c06 CHAR(15) CHARACTER SET LATIN
              NOT CASESPECIFIC,
      rpt_c07 VARCHAR(40) CHARACTER SET LATIN
              NOT CASESPECIFIC)
PRIMARY INDEX ( rpt_c01 )
ON COMMIT PRESERVE ROWS;
```

Figure 17.8

Collecting Statistics on Global Temporary Tables

There are two aspects of collecting statistics on Global Temporary tables:

- Defining the statistics on the base Global Temporary table
- Collecting statistics on the data in a materialized instance

An example to define the statistics is as follows:

COLLECT STATISTICS ON CSQL_CLASS.gtt_report_layout index (rpt_c01);

Statistics are collected for an empty table. This is allowed so that when an instance is created, statistics can be re-collected by simply entering COLLECT STATISTICS on the materialized Global Temporary table without having to specify the desired columns and indexes.

To accomplish that, the user would enter:

```
COLLECT STATISTICS ON TEMPORARY gtt_report_layout;
```

Figure 17.9

General Comparisons and Practices

The following are comparison and guidelines to consider when determining which type of "temporary" table to use. Most of the criteria are based on the number of users needing access to the data along with the frequency of use.

Comparisons:

VOLATILE TABLE	GLOBAL TEMPORARY TABLE
• Logon • Create volatile table • Load private data into the volatile table • Use the data • Logoff	• Logon • Create Global temporary Table • Define collected statistics • Logoff • Now, authorized users can: • Logon • Load private data into their materialization of the global

	temporary table • Collect statistics on their data • Use their data • Logoff

Figure 17.10

TEMPORARY TABLE TYPE	**BENEFITS AND USE**
Derived	A special type of temporary table is the derived table. You can specify a derived table in an SQL SELECT statement. A derived table is obtained from one or more other tables as the result of a subquery. The scope of a derived table is only visible to the level of the SELECT statement calling the subquery. Using derived tables avoids having to use the CREATE and DROP TABLE statements for storing retrieved information and assists in coding more sophisticated, complex queries.
VOLATILE	If you need a temporary table for a single use only, you can define a volatile table. The definition of a volatile table resides in memory but does not survive across a system restart. Using volatile tables improves performance even more than using Global Temporary tables because the system does not store the definitions of volatile tables in the Data Dictionary. Privilege checking is not necessary because only the creator can access the volatile table.

GLOBAL TEMPORARY	Global Temporary tables are tables that exist only for the duration of the SQL session in which they are used. The contents of these tables are private to the session, and the system automatically drops the table at the end of the session. The data of a Global Temporary table resides in TEMP Space and the data in these tables do not survive a system restart. However, the system saves the Global Temporary table definition permanently in the Data Dictionary. The saved definition may be shared by multiple users and sessions with each session getting its own instance of the table.

Figure 17.11

Chapter 17: Practice Questions

1. Which of the following cannot have a PPI?
    a. Volatile tables
    b. Global Temporary tables
    c. Derived tables
    d. Multiset tables

2. Indicate, by number, which table type belongs to each definition.

DEFINITION	#	TABLE TYPE
a. DBA creates the table definition		1. Derived
b. Exists only within a query		2. Volatile
c. Definition and data are dropped at the end of the session		3. Global Temporary
d. Data is dropped but the definition persists at the end of session		
e. User creates and loads the table		

3. Indicate, by number, where space for the following objects comes from.

a. SET tables		1. Spool
b. Global Temporary		2. Perm
c. MULTISET tables		3. Temporary
d. Volatile tables		
e. Derived tables		

4. Which of the following queries will produce a hierarchical listing of all the databases and users in the system without overflowing?

   a.
   ```
   WITH RECURSIVE temp_table(databasename, ownername, depth) AS
   (SELECT root.databasename, root.ownername, 0 AS depth
    FROM dbc.databases root
    WHERE root.databasename = 'dbc'
    UNION ALL
    SELECT indirect.databasename, indirect.ownername,
    seed.depth + 1 AS depth
    FROM temp_table seed, dbc.databases indirect
    WHERE seed.databasename = indirect.ownername
    AND indirect.ownername <> indirect.databasename
    AND depth <= 10
   )
    SELECT ownername, databasename, depth
    FROM temp_table
    ORDER BY depth, ownername, databasename;
   ```

   b.
   ```
   WITH RECURSIVE temp_table(databasename, ownername, depth) AS
   (SELECT root.databasename, root.ownername, 0 AS depth
    FROM dbc.databases root
   ```

```
WHERE root.ownername = 'dbc'
UNION ALL
SELECT indirect.databasename, indirect.ownername,
seed.depth + 1 AS depth
FROM temp_table seed, dbc.databases indirect
WHERE seed.databasename = indirect.ownername
AND indirect.ownername <> indirect.databasename
AND depth <= 10
)
SELECT ownername, databasename, depth
FROM temp_table
ORDER BY depth, ownername, databasename;
```

c. WITH RECURSIVE temp_table(databasename, ownername, depth) AS

```
(SELECT root.databasename, root.ownername, 0 AS depth
FROM dbc.databases root
WHERE root.databasename = 'dbc'
UNION ALL
SELECT indirect.databasename, indirect.ownername,
seed.depth + 1 AS depth
FROM temp_table indirect, dbc.databases seed
WHERE seed.databasename = indirect.ownername
AND indirect.ownername <> indirect.databasename
AND depth <= 10
)
SELECT ownername, databasename, depth
FROM temp_table
ORDER BY depth, ownername, databasename;
```

d. WITH RECURSIVE temp_table(databasename, ownername, depth) AS

```
(SELECT root.databasename, root.ownername, 0 AS depth
FROM dbc.databases root
WHERE root.databasename = 'dbc'
```

```
UNION ALL
SELECT indirect.databasename, indirect.ownername,
seed.depth + 1 AS depth
FROM temp_table seed, dbc.databases indirect
WHERE seed.databasename = indirect.ownername
AND indirect.ownername = indirect.databasename
AND depth <= 10
)
SELECT ownername, databasename, depth
FROM temp_table
ORDER BY depth, ownername, databasename;
```

5. Which of the following are not allowed? (Choose two)
   a. CREATE SET VOLATILE TABLE . . .
   b. CREATE SET GLOBAL TEMPORARY TABLE . . .
   c. CREATE SET DERIVED TABLE . . .
   d. CREATE MULTISET VOLATILE TABLE . . .
   e. CREATE MULTISET DERIVED TABLE . . .

Chapter Notes

Utilize this space for notes, key points to remember, diagrams, areas of further study, etc.

Chapter 18: Temporal Tables

Certification Objectives

- ✓ Describe the functionality of the EXPAND ON keyword.
- ✓ Describe the effect of DELETES using Current, Sequenced or Non-sequenced qualifiers.
- ✓ Describe the effect of INSERTS using Current, Sequenced or Non-sequenced qualifiers.
- ✓ Describe the effect of the AS OF qualifier.
- ✓ Describe the effect of UPDATES using Current, Sequenced or Non-sequenced qualifiers.
- ✓ Describe the use of temporal data types and qualifiers.

Before You Begin

You should be familiar with the following terms and concepts.

Terms	Key Concepts
VALIDTIME	How to create, query, and maintain.
TRANSACTIONTIME	How to create, query, and maintain.
PERIOD Data Type	How to define and utilize.
UNTIL CHANGED	Defining an open-ended date/time period.
Bi-Temporal Tables	Tables containing both Valid Time and Transaction Time columns.
EXPAND ON	Create a regular time series of rows based on the period value in the input row.
AS OF	View a snapshot of temporal table rows.

Period Temporal Data Types

A Period is an anchored duration. It represents a set of contiguous time granules within that duration. It has a beginning bound (defined by the value of a beginning element) and an ending bound (defined by the value of an ending element). The representation of the period is inclusive-exclusive; that is, the period extends from the beginning bound up to but not including the ending bound. In the following example, the period begins on January 1st, and ends on January 9th.

PERIOD(DATE '2011-01-01', DATE '2011-01-10')

Feature	Description
Temporal data types	The PERIOD data type represents an anchored duration of time.
Kinds of time	The elements of a PERIOD may be DATE, TIME, TIME WITH TIME ZONE, TIMESTAMP, or TIMESTAMP WITH TIME ZONE.
Temporal functions	These include BEGIN, END, LAST, INTERVAL, PRIOR, NEXT, P_INTERSECT, LDIFF, RDIFF, and P_NORMALIZE.

Figure 18.1

DateTime Granule

A DateTime granule is the minimum interval that can be represented at a given precision. For example, if the element type of a period is DATE, the granule is one day; if the element type of a period is TIME(0), the granule is one second; if the element type of a period is TIMESTAMP(2), the granule is one hundredth of a second.

Therefore, the last value of a period is the greatest value of the element type that is less than the value of the ending element of the period. That is, the last value is the ending bound minus one granule of the element type.

Period Expressions

A Period definition takes the form:

PERIOD(<DateTime Expression> [, <DateTime Expression>])

If no ending bound is specified, then it is set to the beginning bound +1 granule, where the granule is derived from the data type.

A Period arithmetic expression takes the form:

<Period expression> +/- <Interval expression>
<Interval expression> +/- <Period expression>

A Period constant has the form of the PERIOD keyword followed by a quote string in a specific format. See the following examples.

Creating PERIOD Columns

The following is an example of creating and inserting a row into a period table.

```
CREATE TABLE period_table
(c1 INTEGER NOT NULL
,c2 PERIOD(DATE)
,c3 PERIOD(TIME(2))
,c4 PERIOD(TIME WITH TIME ZONE)
,c5 PERIOD(TIMESTAMP(4))
,c6 PERIOD(TIMESTAMP WITH TIME ZONE)
) PRIMARY INDEX(c1);
```

Figure 18.2

```
INSERT INTO period_table VALUES
(1
,PERIOD(DATE'2011-09-26', DATE'2011-10-01')
,PERIOD(TIME'11:22:33.44', TIME'11:33:33.44')
,PERIOD(TIME'09:09:09.000000+00:00',
TIME'10:10:10.000000+00:00')
,PERIOD(TIMESTAMP'2011-09-26 10:10:10.0000',
TIMESTAMP'2011-09-27 11:11:11.0000')
,PERIOD(TIMESTAMP'2011-09-26 12:34:56.123456+00:00',
TIMESTAMP'2011-09-27 01:01:01.654321+00:00')
);
```

Figure 18.3

The following query returns the row.

```
SET SESSION DATEFORM = ANSIDATE;
.SET FOLDLINE ON
.SET SIDETITLES ON
SELECT * FROM period_table;


 *** Query completed. One row found. 6 columns returned.
 *** Total elapsed time was 1 second.

c1             1
c2  ('2011/09/26', '2011/10/01')
c3  ('11:22:33.44', '11:33:33.44')
c4  ('09:09:09.000000+00:00', '10:10:10.000000+00:00')
c5  ('2011-09-26 10:10:10.0000', '2011-09-27
11:11:11.0000')
c6  ('2011-09-26 12:34:56.123456+00:00', '2011-09-27
01:01:01.654321+00:00')
```

Figure 18.4

UNTIL_CHANGED

UNTIL_CHANGED is used to represent the ending bound of periods for which the duration is indefinite, forever, or for which the end is an unspecified and unknown time in the future when the row will be changed. They are used in some circumstances when a new row is inserted into a temporal table:

The value of UNTIL_CHANGED depends on the data type and precision of the valid-time column. If the type is PERIOD(DATE), UNTIL_CHANGED is the value DATE '9999-12-31'. If the type is PERIOD(TIMESTAMP), UNTIL_CHANGED is the value of TIMESTAMP '9999-12-31 23:59:59.999999+00:00', with precision and time zone matching that specified for the valid-time data type.

UNTIL_CHANGED cannot be specified if the PERIOD is TIME.

Here's an example of inserting a row using UNTIL_CHANGED as the ending boundary.

```
INSERT INTO period_table VALUES
(2
,PERIOD(DATE'2011-09-26', UNTIL_CHANGED)
,PERIOD(TIME'11:22:33.44', TIME'11:33:33.44')
,PERIOD(TIME'09:09:09.000000+00:00',
TIME'10:10:10.000000+00:00')
,PERIOD(TIMESTAMP'2011-09-26 10:10:10.0000', UNTIL_CHANGED)
,PERIOD(TIMESTAMP'2011-09-26 12:34:56.123456+00:00',
UNTIL_CHANGED)
);
```

Figure 18.5

```
SELECT * FROM period_table WHERE c1 = 2;


 *** Query completed. One row found. 6 columns returned.
 *** Total elapsed time was 1 second.

c1            2
c2   ('2011/09/26', '1999/12/31')
c3   ('11:22:33.44', '11:33:33.44')
c4   ('09:09:09.000000+00:00', '10:10:10.000000+00:00')
c5   ('2011-09-26 10:10:10.0000', '9999-12-31
23:59:59.9999')
c6   ('2011-09-26 12:34:56.123456+00:00', '9999-12-31
23:59:59.999999+00:00')
```

Figure 18.6

Additional Attributes

The following attributes may be applied to PERIOD data types.

	DATE	TIME	TIMESTAMP
[NOT] NULL	X	X	X
FORMAT	X	X	X
TITLE	X	X	X
NAMED	X	X	X
DEFAULT NULL	X	X	X
DEFAULT value	X	X	X
WITH DEFAULT	X	na	X

X = Allowed, na = Not Allowed

Figure 18.7

Data Conversion

Implicit and explicit data conversions are allowed on Period data types. Implicit conversion is allowed only from PERIOD to CHAR/VARCHAR.

The following are the data types appearing in the following table.

- CH/VCH   CHARACTER/VARCHAR
- DT   DATE
- TIM[WZ]   TIME[(n)] [WITH TIME ZONE]
- TS[WZ]   TIMESTAMP[(n)] [WITH TIME ZONE]
- PD(DT)   PERIOD(DATE)
- PD(TIM[WZ])   PERIOD(TIME[(n)] [WITH TIME ZONE])
- PD(TS[WZ])   PERIOD(TIMESTAMP[(n)] [WITH TIME ZONE])

	TARGET						
SOURCE	CH/VCH	DT	TIM[WZ]	TS[WZ]	PD(DT)	PD(TIM[WZ])	PD(TS[WZ])
CH/VCH	X	X	X	X	X	X	X
DT	X	X	na	X	X	na	X
TIM[WZ]	X	na	X	X	na	X	X
TS[WZ]	X	X	X	X	X	X	X
PD(DT)	X	X	na	X	X	na	X
PD(TIM[WZ])	X	na	X	X	na	X	X
PD(TS[WZ])	X	X	X	X	X	X	X

X = Allowed, na = Not Allowed

Figure 18.8

As the chart shows, the only conversions which are not allowed involve TIME and DATE since they do not share any common elements.

User Interface

Besides being used in CREATE/ALTER table statements, an argument of a Period data type can be passed to UDFs and UDTs.

IN and INOUT parameters may have Period data types in Stored Procedures and External Stored Procedures.

Period data type arguments cannot be passed to or returned from UDFs or external stored procedures that are written in Java.

Period data types can also be used in Macros, Views, and Triggers.

Example Table and Data

The examples which follow are based upon the following tables and data rows.

```
CREATE MULTISET TABLE emp_dept_hist
(emp_no INTEGER NOT NULL
,dept_no SMALLINT NOT NULL
,dept_assignment PERIOD(DATE)NOT NULL
)PRIMARY INDEX(emp_no);
```

Figure 18.9

```
INSERT INTO emp_dept_hist VALUES
(1, 200, PERIOD(DATE '1995-01-03', UNTIL_CHANGED));
INSERT INTO emp_dept_hist VALUES
(2, 10, PERIOD(DATE '2000-04-20', DATE '2011-07-18'));
INSERT INTO emp_dept_hist VALUES
(2, 200, PERIOD(DATE '2011-07-18', UNTIL_CHANGED));
INSERT INTO emp_dept_hist VALUES
(3, 400, PERIOD(DATE '1997-07-06', UNTIL_CHANGED));
INSERT INTO emp_dept_hist VALUES
(4, 100, PERIOD(DATE '2004-03-01', UNTIL_CHANGED));
INSERT INTO emp_dept_hist VALUES
(5, 400, PERIOD(DATE '2003-10-22', UNTIL_CHANGED));
INSERT INTO emp_dept_hist VALUES
(6, 400, PERIOD(DATE '1999-04-01', UNTIL_CHANGED));
INSERT INTO emp_dept_hist VALUES
(7, 200, PERIOD(DATE '2002-02-02', DATE '2005-05-05'));
INSERT INTO emp_dept_hist VALUES
(7, 10, PERIOD(DATE '2005-05-05', UNTIL_CHANGED));
INSERT INTO emp_dept_hist VALUES
(8, 300, PERIOD(DATE '2009-06-28', DATE '2011-03-03'));
INSERT INTO emp_dept_hist VALUES
(8, 10, PERIOD(DATE '2011-03-03', DATE '2013-03-03'));
INSERT INTO emp_dept_hist VALUES
(8, 400, PERIOD(DATE '2014-03-03', UNTIL_CHANGED));
```

Figure 18.10

SELECT * FROM emp_dept_hist ORDER BY emp_no, dept_assignment;

```
     emp_no  dept_no  dept_assignment
-----------  -------  ------------------------
          1      200  ('95/01/03', '99/12/31')
          2       10  ('00/04/20', '11/07/18')
          2      200  ('11/07/18', '99/12/31')
          3      400  ('97/07/06', '99/12/31')
          4      100  ('04/03/01', '99/12/31')
          5      400  ('03/10/22', '99/12/31')
          6      400  ('99/04/01', '99/12/31')
          7      200  ('02/02/02', '05/05/05')
          7       10  ('05/05/05', '99/12/31')
          8      300  ('09/06/28', '11/03/03')
          8       10  ('11/03/03', '13/03/03')
          8      400  ('14/03/03', '99/12/31')
```

Figure 18.11

Notice that employee #8 has a future history row. The change to department 400 is scheduled for next year.

Period Operators

BEGIN (<Period expression>)

Returns the beginning bound value.

PRIOR (<Period expression>)

Returns the DateTime value one granule less that the input argument.

Here's an example. Notice the BEGIN is used as an argument to the PRIOR function.

```
SELECT dept_no, emp_no,  BEGIN(dept_assignment) AS start_date,
PRIOR(BEGIN(dept_assignment)) AS prior_date
FROM emp_dept_hist
ORDER BY dept_no, start_date;

dept_no        emp_no  start_date  prior_date
-------   -----------  ----------  ----------
     10             2  2000-04-20  2000-04-19
     10             7  2005-05-05  2005-05-04
     10             8  2011-03-03  2011-03-02
    100             4  2004-03-01  2004-02-29
    200             1  1995-01-03  1995-01-02
    200             7  2002-02-02  2002-02-01
    200             2  2011-07-18  2011-07-17
    300             8  2009-06-28  2009-06-27
    400             3  1997-07-06  1997-07-05
    400             6  1999-04-01  1999-03-31
    400             5  2003-10-22  2003-10-21
    400             8  2013-03-03  2043-03-02
```

Figure 18.12

LAST (<Period expression>)

Returns a DateTime one granule less than the ending bound of the period.

Here's an example.

```
SELECT dept_no, emp_no, LAST(dept_assignment) AS last_date
FROM emp_dept_hist
ORDER BY dept_no, last_date;


dept_no        emp_no   last_date
-------   -----------  ----------
     10             2  2011-07-17
     10             8  2013-03-02
     10             7  9999-12-31
    100             4  9999-12-31
    200             7  2005-05-04
    200             1  9999-12-31
    200             2  9999-12-31
    300             8  2011-03-02
    400             5  9999-12-31
    400             6  9999-12-31
    400             8  9999-12-31
    400             3  9999-12-31
```

Figure 18.13

NEXT (<Period expression>)

Returns a DateTime value one granule greater than the input argument. The query would error out if an input argument = the UNTIL_CHANGED value.

```
SELECT dept_no, emp_no, NEXT(LAST(dept_assignment)) AS
next_date
FROM emp_dept_hist
WHERE LAST(dept_assignment) < DATE'9999-12-31'
ORDER BY dept_no, next_date;

dept_no        emp_no   next_date
-------  -----------  ----------
     10             2  2011-07-18
     10             8  2013-03-03
    200             7  2005-05-05
    300             8  2011-03-03
```

Figure 18.14

END (<Period expression>)

Returns the ending bound of a period.

Here's an example. It shows the difference between the END and LAST functions.

```
SELECT dept_no, emp_no, LAST(dept_assignment) AS last_date,
END(dept_assignment) AS end_date
FROM emp_dept_hist
ORDER BY dept_no, last_date;

dept_no       emp_no  last_date   end_date
-------  -----------  ----------  ----------
     10            2  2011-07-17  2011-07-18
     10            8  2013-03-02  2013-03-03
     10            7  9999-12-31  9999-12-31
    100            4  9999-12-31  9999-12-31
    200            7  2005-05-04  2005-05-05
    200            1  9999-12-31  9999-12-31
    200            2  9999-12-31  9999-12-31
    300            8  2011-03-02  2011-03-03
    400            5  9999-12-31  9999-12-31
    400            6  9999-12-31  9999-12-31
    400            8  9999-12-31  9999-12-31
    400            3  9999-12-31  9999-12-31
```

Figure 18.15

INTERVAL (<Period expression>) Interval Qualifier

It returns the difference between the beginning and ending bounds in terms of a specified interval qualifier.

The interval qualifier must be appropriate for the argument's element type.

The interval qualifiers are as follows:

- Year-Month intervals:
    - YEAR
    - YEAR TO MONTH

    - MONTH
- Day-Time Intervals:
    - DAY
    - DAY TO HOUR, MINUTE or SECOND
    - HOUR
    - HOUR TO MINUTE or SECOND
    - MINUTE
    - MINUTE to SECOND
    - SECOND

In this next query, IS NOT UNTIL_CHANGED is the equivalent of the earlier < date '9999-12-31', and eliminates internal overflow.

```
SELECT dept_no, emp_no, INTERVAL(dept_assignment) YEAR(4) TO
MONTH AS duration
FROM emp_dept_hist WHERE END(dept_assignment) IS NOT
UNTIL_CHANGED
ORDER BY dept_no, BEGIN(dept_assignment);

dept_no       emp_no  duration
-------  -----------  --------
     10            2     11-03
     10            8      2-00
    200            7      3-03
    300            8      1-09
```

Figure 18.16

<Period expression> P_INTERSECT <Period expression>

Returns the common period of the periods overlap, or nulls if they don't overlap.

The following is an example.

```
SELECT a.dept_no
       , CAST( a.emp_no AS BYTEINT) AS emp_no
       , a.dept_assignment
         P_INTERSECT
         b.dept_assignment AS intersects_with
       , CAST(b.emp_no AS BYTEINT) AS emp_no
FROM emp_dept_hist a JOIN emp_dept_hist b
ON a.dept_no = b.dept_no
AND a.emp_no <> b.emp_no
ORDER BY 1, 2;
```

```
dept_no  emp_no  intersects_with                emp_no
-------  ------  ----------------------------   ------
     10       2  ('2005-05-05', '2011-07-18')        7
     10       2  ('2011-03-03', '2011-07-18')        8
     10       7  ('2011-03-03', '2013-03-03')        8
     10       7  ('2005-05-05', '2011-07-18')        2
     10       8  ('2011-03-03', '2011-07-18')        2
     10       8  ('2011-03-03', '2013-03-03')        7
    200       1  ('2011-07-18', '9999-12-31')        2
    200       1  ('2002-02-02', '2005-05-05')        7
    200       2  ?                                   7
    200       2  ('2011-07-18', '9999-12-31')        1
    200       7  ?                                   2
    200       7  ('2002-02-02', '2005-05-05')        1
    400       3  ('2013-03-03', '9999-12-31')        8
    400       3  ('1999-04-01', '9999-12-31')        6
    400       3  ('2003-10-22', '9999-12-31')        5
    400       5  ('2013-03-03', '9999-12-31')        8
    400       5  ('2003-10-22', '9999-12-31')        3
    400       5  ('2003-10-22', '9999-12-31')        6
    400       6  ('2013-03-03', '9999-12-31')        8
    400       6  ('1999-04-01', '9999-12-31')        3
    400       6  ('2003-10-22', '9999-12-31')        5
    400       8  ('2013-03-03', '9999-12-31')        3
    400       8  ('2013-03-03', '9999-12-31')        5
    400       8  ('2013-03-03', '9999-12-31')        6
```

Figure 18.17

<Period expression> LDIFF <Period expression>

Returns the portion of the first period that exists before the begin of the second period if the periods overlap. It returns nulls if they don't.

Here's an example.

```
SELECT a.dept_no, CAST(a.emp_no AS CHAR(2)), a.dept_assignment
LDIFF b.dept_assignment AS left_difference, CAST(b.emp_no AS
CHAR(2))
FROM emp_dept_hist a JOIN emp_dept_hist b
ON a.dept_no = b.dept_no AND a.emp_no <> b.emp_no
ORDER BY 1, 2;
```

Figure 18.18

The output appears in Figure 18.19 on the next page.

```
dept_no  emp_no  left_difference               emp_no
-------  ------  ----------------------------  ------
     10  2       ('2000-04-20', '2005-05-05')  7
     10  2       ('2000-04-20', '2011-03-03')  8
     10  7       ('2005-05-05', '2011-03-03')  8
     10  7       ?                             2
     10  8       ?                             2
     10  8       ?                             7
    200  1       ('1995-01-03', '2011-07-18')  2
    200  1       ('1995-01-03', '2002-02-02')  7
    200  2       ?                             7
    200  2       ?                             1
    200  7       ?                             2
    200  7       ?                             1
    400  3       ('1997-07-06', '2013-03-03')  8
    400  3       ('1997-07-06', '1999-04-01')  6
    400  3       ('1997-07-06', '2003-10-22')  5
    400  5       ('2003-10-22', '2013-03-03')  8
    400  5       ?                             3
    400  5       ?                             6
    400  6       ('1999-04-01', '2013-03-03')  8
    400  6       ?                             3
    400  6       ('1999-04-01', '2003-10-22')  5
    400  8       ?                             3
    400  8       ?                             5
    400  8       ?                             6
```

Figure 18.19

<Period expression> RDIFF <Period expression>

Returns the portion of the first period that exists after the end of the second period if the periods overlap, or nulls.

Here's an example.

```
SELECT a.dept_no, CAST(a.emp_no AS CHAR(2)), a.dept_assignment
RDIFF b.dept_assignment AS right_difference, CAST(b.emp_no AS
CHAR(2))
FROM emp_dept_hist a JOIN emp_dept_hist b
ON a.dept_no = b.dept_no AND a.emp_no <> b.emp_no
ORDER BY 1, 2;

dept_no  emp_no  right_difference              emp_no
-------  ------  ----------------------------  ------
     10  2       ?                             7
     10  2       ?                             8
     10  7       ('2013-03-03', '9999-12-31')  8
     10  7       ('2011-07-18', '9999-12-31')  2
     10  8       ('2011-07-18', '2013-03-03')  2
     10  8       ?                             7
    200  1       ?                             2
    200  1       ('2005-05-05', '9999-12-31')  7
    200  2       ?                             7
    200  2       ?                             1
    200  7       ?                             2
    200  7       ?                             1
    400  3       ?                             8
    400  3       ?                             6
    400  3       ?                             5
    400  5       ?                             8
    400  5       ?                             3
    400  5       ?                             6
    400  6       ?                             8
    400  6       ?                             3
    400  6       ?                             5
    400  8       ?                             3
    400  8       ?                             5
    400  8       ?                             6
```

Figure 18.20

<Period expression> P_NORMALIZE <Period expression>

Returns a period that is a combination of two periods if the periods overlap or meet.

Here's an example.

```
SELECT a.dept_no, CAST(a.emp_no AS CHAR(2)), a.dept_assignment
P_NORMALIZE b.dept_assignment AS normalized, CAST(b.emp_no AS
CHAR(2))
FROM emp_dept_hist a JOIN emp_dept_hist b
ON a.dept_no = b.dept_no AND a.emp_no <> b.emp_no
ORDER BY 1, 2;
```

Figure 18.21

The output appears in Figure 18.22 on the next page.

```
dept_no  emp_no  normalized                    emp_no
-------  ------  ----------------------------  ------
     10  2       ('2000-04-20', '9999-12-31')  7
     10  2       ('2000-04-20', '2013-03-03')  8
     10  7       ('2005-05-05', '9999-12-31')  8
     10  7       ('2000-04-20', '9999-12-31')  2
     10  8       ('2000-04-20', '2013-03-03')  2
     10  8       ('2005-05-05', '9999-12-31')  7
    200  1       ('1995-01-03', '9999-12-31')  2
    200  1       ('1995-01-03', '9999-12-31')  7
    200  2       ?                             7
    200  2       ('1995-01-03', '9999-12-31')  1
    200  7       ?                             2
    200  7       ('1995-01-03', '9999-12-31')  1
    400  3       ('1997-07-06', '9999-12-31')  8
    400  3       ('1997-07-06', '9999-12-31')  6
    400  3       ('1997-07-06', '9999-12-31')  5
    400  5       ('2003-10-22', '9999-12-31')  8
    400  5       ('1997-07-06', '9999-12-31')  3
    400  5       ('1999-04-01', '9999-12-31')  6
    400  6       ('1999-04-01', '9999-12-31')  8
    400  6       ('1997-07-06', '9999-12-31')  3
    400  6       ('1999-04-01', '9999-12-31')  5
    400  8       ('1997-07-06', '9999-12-31')  3
    400  8       ('2003-10-22', '9999-12-31')  5
    400  8       ('1999-04-01', '9999-12-31')  6
```

Figure 18.22

EXPAND ON

The EXPAND ON clause expands a column having a PERIOD data type, creating a regular time series of rows based on the period value in the input row.

The expansion of a PERIOD column produces one value-equivalent row for each of the time granules in the epoch or timestamp representation of the specified time granule.

You can perform time series expansions only on PERIOD expressions.

The EXPAND ON clause enables several different forms of time series expansion on a PERIOD column value of an input row by producing a set of value-equivalent rows, one for each granule in the specified time period. The number of granules is defined by the anchor name you specify for the clause.

This makes it possible to expand sparse PERIOD representations of relational data into a dense representation of the same data. After the data has been converted to a dense form, it can be more easily manipulated by complex analyses such as moving average calculations.

This minimizes the need to write complex SQL requests to respond to business questions made against sparse relational data.

The available forms of time series expansion for the EXPAND ON clause are the following.

- Interval expansion, where rows are expanded by user-specified intervals.
- Anchor point expansion, where rows are expanded by user-specified anchored points.
- Anchor PERIOD expansion, where rows are expanded by user-specified anchored periods.

The following example includes the use of the LAST( ) function to limit the output.

```
SELECT emp_no, dept_no, dept_assignment, yearly
FROM emp_dept_hist
WHERE  LAST(dept_assignment) < DATE'9999-12-31'
EXPAND ON dept_assignment AS yearly
BY ANCHOR YEAR_END
ORDER BY emp_no, yearly;
```

emp_no	dept_no	dept_assignment	Yearly
2	10	('00/04/20', '11/07/18')	('00/12/31', '01/12/31')
2	10	('00/04/20', '11/07/18')	('01/12/31', '02/12/31')
2	10	('00/04/20', '11/07/18')	('02/12/31', '03/12/31')
2	10	('00/04/20', '11/07/18')	('03/12/31', '04/12/31')
2	10	('00/04/20', '11/07/18')	('04/12/31', '05/12/31')
2	10	('00/04/20', '11/07/18')	('05/12/31', '06/12/31')
2	10	('00/04/20', '11/07/18')	('06/12/31', '07/12/31')
2	10	('00/04/20', '11/07/18')	('07/12/31', '08/12/31')
2	10	('00/04/20', '11/07/18')	('08/12/31', '09/12/31')
2	10	('00/04/20', '11/07/18')	('09/12/31', '10/12/31')
2	10	('00/04/20', '11/07/18')	('10/12/31', '11/12/31')
7	200	('02/02/02', '05/05/05')	('02/12/31', '03/12/31')
7	200	('02/02/02', '05/05/05')	('03/12/31', '04/12/31')
7	200	('02/02/02', '05/05/05')	('04/12/31', '05/12/31')
8	300	('09/06/28', '11/03/03')	('09/12/31', '10/12/31')
8	300	('09/06/28', '11/03/03')	('10/12/31', '11/12/31')
8	10	('11/03/03', '13/03/03')	('11/12/31', '12/12/31')
8	10	('11/03/03', '13/03/03')	('12/12/31', '13/12/31')

Figure 18.23

Restrictions

- UDFs or external stored procedures that are written in Java do not support arguments or return values that have a Period data type.
- A primary index column or partitioning column cannot be a column that has a Period data type.

Temporal Tables

As mentioned earlier, Teradata supports different ways of representing time in a conventional table column.

- DATE
- TIME
- TIME WITH TIME ZONE
- TIMESTAMP
- TIMESTAMP WITH TIME ZONE

The addition of the PERIOD data type allows for a single column to represent an anchored beginning and ending pair of time values.

- PERIOD(DATE)
- PERIOD(TIME)
- PERIOD(TIME WITH TIME ZONE)
- PERIOD(TIMESTAMP)
- PERIOD(TIMESTAMP WITH TIME ZONE)

Once set, the values for a period column remain fixed until changed through an UPDATE statement.

Starting with Teradata 13.10, you can now create temporal (time aware) tables using the PERIOD data type. Temporal tables must be defined as Multiset tables.

The difference between a temporal table and a conventional table is that a temporal table maintains data with respect to time and allows time-based reasoning, whereas a conventional table captures only a current snapshot of reality.

For example, a conventional table cannot directly support historical queries about past status and cannot represent inherently retroactive or proactive changes. Without built-in temporal table support from the DBMS, applications are forced to use complex and often manual methods to manage and maintain temporal information.

Transaction Time and Valid Time

Teradata supports two built-in time dimensions that can be used to create temporal tables: transaction time and valid time.

Each of these time dimensions are represented by a column with a period data type. The column stores a pair of DATE or TIMESTAMP values that define the beginning and end of the transaction- or valid-time period for a row. Transaction time and valid time are independent time dimensions. A table can have either type of column, both, or neither:

- A table with a transaction-time column is called a transaction-time table.
- A table with a valid-time column is called a valid-time table.
- A table with both a transaction-time and a valid-time column is called a bitemporal table.
- A table with neither a transaction-time nor a valid-time column is a regular, nontemporal table.

Transaction-Time

Transaction time is the time period during which a fact, represented by all the information in a row, is or was known to be in effect in the database. It models the database reality, recording when rows added, modified, and changed in the database. The transaction-time period is stored in a transaction-time column:

colname PERIOD(TIMESTAMP(6) WITH TIME ZONE) AS TRANSACTIONTIME NOT NULL

- The beginning of the transaction-time period is the time when the database became aware of a row, when the row was first recorded in the database. This is when the row was added to a table.

- The end of a transaction time period reflects when the fact was superseded by an update to the row, or when the row was deleted from the database. Rows containing information that is currently in effect have transaction-time periods with indefinite ending bounds, represented as UNTIL_CLOSED.

You cannot normally set or modify the value of a transaction-time column. Teradata Database maintains these values automatically. (However, for database maintenance and troubleshooting, closed rows can be modified or deleted by administrators who have been granted the NONTEMPORAL privilege.)

Every change to a table that has a transaction-time column is tracked by the database. In a sense, physical rows are never deleted nor modified in tables that have a transaction-time column:

- When a row is "deleted" from the table, the row is not physically deleted from the table. Instead, the transaction-time column is automatically modified to have an ending bound that specifies the time of the deletion, which marks the row as "closed," and no longer available.

- When a row is "modified" in the table, the original row with the original values is marked as closed, and a copy of the row having the modified values is automatically inserted into the table.

The resulting snapshots of deleted and modified rows, which are retained in the table, provide a complete internal history of the table. Any prior state of a table having a transaction-time column can be reproduced. However, closed rows are unavailable to most DML modifications or deletions.

Add transaction-time columns to tables for which historical changes should be automatically tracked and maintained in the database. For example, transaction-time tables can be used for information that must retain a history of all changes, such as for tables used for regulatory compliance reporting.

Valid-Time

Valid time models the real world, and denotes the time period during which a fact, represented by all the information in a row, is in effect or true. The valid-time period is stored in a valid-time column. Valid-time columns store information such as the time an insurance policy or contract is valid, the length of employment of an employee, or other information that is important to track and manipulate in a time-aware fashion. The valid-time period is also known as the period of validity (PV) of the row.

Valid-time columns are defined by specifying AS VALIDTIME in the column definition, and have a period data type with an element type of DATE or TIMESTAMP:

colname PERIOD(DATE) AS VALIDTIME
colname PERIOD(TIMESTAMP) AS VALIDTIME

You specify the value of the valid-time column when a new row is inserted into the table.

Teradata Database automatically maintains the valid-time column for rows that are changed or deleted, according to how the time period specified for the change or deletion relates to the original PV (period of validity) of the row.

For example, assume a row in a valid-time table represents the terms of a contract that is valid for two years. If the terms (row) must be modified during the contract period:

- A copy of the row is automatically created and modified to show the new terms. The PV of the row begins at the time of the change, to show when the new terms started. The PV of the row retains the original ending bound for the valid-time column, to retain the original contract end date.

- The original row, storing the original terms of the contract is marked as a history row. The PV is set to end at the time of the modification, because that is when the old terms ceased to be valid.

Such a modification changes the row information starting at the current time of the modification, and the change is valid throughout the remaining PV of the row.

Modifications to tables that have valid-time columns can also apply to specified time periods, even periods that do not overlap the current time, such as times that have passed or that are in the future. The changes will affect only those rows with PVs that overlap the specified time period, and only for the period during which the change is applicable. Other kinds of modifications to these tables can affect rows for their entire PVs, much like changes to nontemporal tables.

For example, if the terms of the contract in the example above were changed for only six weeks during the middle of the two-year contract period, the change would automatically yield three rows in the table:

- A copy of the row is automatically created and modified to show the new terms. The PV of the row reflects the six weeks for which the new terms are in effect.

- The original row, storing the original terms of the contract, is marked as a history row. The PV is set to end at the time the new terms begin.

- A new row is inserted to reflect the conditions after the six-week change in terms has ended, when the contract reverts to the original terms. The PV for the new row begins when the new terms expire, and ends at the original end time for the original row.

In this way, valid-time tables also keep an automatic history of all changes. Unlike transaction-time, however, history rows in tables with valid-time remain accessible to temporal SQL queries and DML. Because they model the real world, valid-time tables can have rows with a PV in the future, because things like contracts and policies may not begin until a future date.

Add valid-time columns to tables for which the information in a row is delimited by time, and for which row information should be maintained, tracked, and manipulated in a time-aware fashion. A valid time column is most appropriate when changes to rows occur relatively infrequently. To represent attributes that change very frequently, such as a point of sale table, an event table is preferable to a valid-time table. Temporal semantics do not apply to event tables.

Bitemporal Tables

Transaction time and valid time are independent time dimensions that are used for different purposes. Bitemporal tables have both a transaction-time column and a valid-time column. Changes to bitemporal tables that happen automatically as a result of row modifications are independent for the transaction-time and valid-time dimensions. These dimensions must be considered separately when determining what will happen to a row as a result of a modification.

For example, if a row in a bitemporal table is deleted, the ending bound of the transactiontime period is automatically changed to reflect the time of the deletion, and the row is closed to further modifications. The database reality, reflected by the modified ending bound of the transaction-time period, is that the row was deleted.

The valid-time period of the row remains unchanged. Because the deletion does not affect the ending bound of the valid-time period, the row information retains its character in the validtime dimension as historical, current, or future information. However, because the row was deleted, the row does not participate in further DML operations for the table, even though it remains in the table as a closed row in transaction time.

Because of the transaction-time column, all modifications to rows in bitemporal tables automatically create closed rows in the transaction time dimension, just as they do for transaction-time tables. This is in addition to rows that might be created to account for changes in the valid-time dimension.

For example, assume the terms of a contract are stored in a row of a bitemporal table. If the terms are changed during the period when the contract is valid, the row must be modified, as with an UPDATE statement. Because this is a temporal table, Teradata Database automatically inserts a copy of the row to store the new terms. The period of validity of the new row is automatically set to begin at the time of the change, and end at the original end date of the contract. The beginning bound of the transaction-time period of the new row reflects when the new row was created.

The original row is automatically modified to have the end of the period of validity reflect the time of the change, when the old terms become no longer valid. This row becomes a history row in the valid-time dimension. Note that both rows remain open rows in transaction time, and as such, are still available to all types of DML queries and modifications. These changes are purely a result of the valid-time dimension of the table.

Because the table also includes a transaction-time dimension, another copy is made of the original row, reflecting the original period of validity, but the row is closed in transaction time at the time the terms changed. No further changes can be made to this row, because it is closed in transaction time. It provides a permanent "before" snapshot of the row as it existed in the database before it was changed.

Note that the actions, which are performed automatically by Teradata Database on the row, include independent actions that result from the table having both a valid-time column and a transaction-time column.

The following diagram shows the relationship of temporal rows to current time.

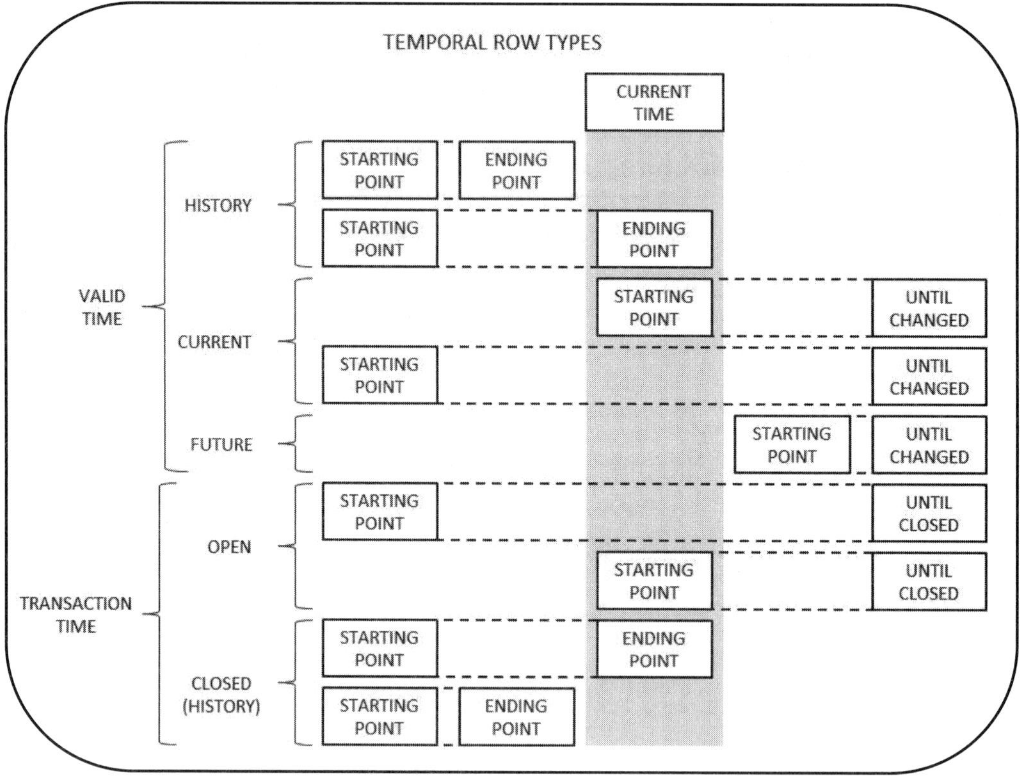

Figure 18.24

To illustrate the features of temporal tables, we will be using the following bitemporal table.

```
CREATE MULTISET TABLE BiTemporal
(emp_no INTEGER NOT NULL
,dept_no SMALLINT
,dept_assign PERIOD(DATE) NOT NULL VALIDTIME
,tracking PERIOD(TIMESTAMP(6) WITH TIME ZONE) NOT NULL
TRANSACTIONTIME
) PRIMARY INDEX (emp_no);
```

Figure 18.25

The following query returns the rows that are open in Transaction-Time, and current in Valid-Time.

```
SELECT * FROM BITEMPORAL ORDER BY 1;


*** Query completed. 7 rows found. 2 columns returned.
*** Total elapsed time was 1 second.

     emp_no  dept_no
-----------  -------
    1000234       10
    1256349      400
    1324657      200
    1333454      200
    2000000        ?
    2312225      300
    2341218      400
```

Figure 18.26

Notice that the settings for the dept_assign and tracking columns are not returned. The normal Select, Insert, Update, and Delete commands only operate on rows meeting the above criteria.

The following query returns the dept_assign column, without a minor sort on the beginning time.

```
NONSEQUENCED VALIDTIME SELECT * FROM BiTemporal
ORDER BY 1;


*** Query completed. 11 rows found. 3 columns returned.
*** Total elapsed time was 1 second.

     emp_no  dept_no  dept_assign
-----------  -------  ----------------------------
    1000234       10  ('1995-06-28', '9999-12-31')
    1121334      400  ('1994-03-13', '2011-09-15')
    1232578      100  ('2013-01-17', '9999-12-31')
    1256349      400  ('2003-10-07', '9999-12-31')
    1324657      200  ('2005-05-05', '9999-12-31')
    1333454      200  ('2006-12-15', '9999-12-31')
    2000000      200  ('2013-01-15', '9999-12-31')
    2000000      200  ('1983-07-07', '2001-01-15')
    2000000        ?  ('2001-01-15', '2013-01-15')
    2312225      300  ('1999-03-15', '9999-12-31')
    2341218      400  ('2007-07-17', '9999-12-31')
```

Figure 18.27

This query returns the same rows but includes the additional sort.

SEQUENCED VALIDTIME SELECT * FROM BiTemporal ORDER BY 1;

```
*** Query completed. 11 rows found. 3 columns returned.
*** Total elapsed time was 1 second.


     emp_no  dept_no  VALIDTIME
-----------  -------  ----------------------------
    1000234       10  ('1995-06-28', '9999-12-31')
    1121334      400  ('1994-03-13', '2011-09-15')
    1232578      100  ('2013-01-17', '9999-12-31')
    1256349      400  ('2003-10-07', '9999-12-31')
    1324657      200  ('2005-05-05', '9999-12-31')
    1333454      200  ('2006-12-15', '9999-12-31')
    2000000      200  ('1983-07-07', '2001-01-15')
    2000000        ?  ('2001-01-15', '2013-01-15')
    2000000      200  ('2013-01-15', '9999-12-31')
    2312225      300  ('1999-03-15', '9999-12-31')
    2341218      400  ('2007-07-17', '9999-12-31')
```

Figure 18.28

By examining the dates, we can determine each row's position within Valid-Time

```
    emp_no  dept_no  VALIDTIME
----------- -------  ----------------------------
   1000234       10  ('1995-06-28', '9999-12-31')  <-Current
   1121334      400  ('1994-03-13', '2011-09-15')  <-History
   1232578      100  ('2013-01-17', '9999-12-31')  <-Future
   1256349      400  ('2003-10-07', '9999-12-31')  <-Current
   1324657      200  ('2005-05-05', '9999-12-31')  <-Current
   2000000      200  ('1983-07-07', '2001-01-15')  <-History
   2000000        ?  ('2001-01-15', '2013-01-15')  <-Current
   2000000      200  ('2013-01-15', '9999-12-31')  <-Future
   2312225      300  ('1999-03-15', '9999-12-31')  <-Current
   2341218      400  ('2007-07-17', '9999-12-31')  <-Current
```

Figure 18.29

The following query returns the values for the tracking column.

```
NONSEQUENCED TRANSACTIONTIME SELECT * FROM BiTemporal
ORDER BY 1;

*** Query completed. 7 rows found. 3 columns returned.
*** Total elapsed time was 1 second.

  emp_no dept_no tracking
-------- ------- ----------------------------------------
   1000234      10    ('2012-02-25 14:16:35.850000-08:00', '9999-12-31 23:59:
   1256349     400    ('2012-02-25 14:16:35.940000-08:00', '9999-12-31 23:59:
   1324657     200    ('2012-02-25 14:16:36.040000-08:00', '9999-12-31 23:59:
   1333454     200    ('2012-02-25 14:16:36.070000-08:00', '9999-12-31 23:59:
   2000000       ?    ('2012-02-25 14:16:36.100000-08:00', '9999-12-31 23:59:
   2312225     300    ('2012-02-25 14:16:36.130000-08:00', '9999-12-31 23:59:
   2341218     400    ('2012-02-25 14:16:36.270000-08:00', '9999-12-31 23:59:
```

Figure 18.30

Notice that only seven rows were returned by this query, whereas nine rows were returned by the previous query.

For Nontemporal tables, the system has CURRENT_DATE, CURRENT_TIME, and CURRENT_TIMESTAMP.

For Temporal tables, the system has TEMPORAL_DATE and TEMPORAL_TIMESTAMP. The next query returns the value for TEMPORAL_DATE and TEMPORAL_TIMESTAMP.

```
SELECT TEMPORAL_DATE, TEMPORAL_TIMESTAMP;

Temporal Date                   Temporal TimeStamp(6)
-------------  ---------------------------------
     12/02/27  2012-02-27 08:42:44.680000-08:00
```

Figure 18.31

In the next statement, the Personnel Department has notified us that employee 2000000 has returned from sabbatical and should be assigned to department 300.

```
UPDATE BiTemporal SET dept_no = 300
WHERE emp_no = 2000000;

 *** Update completed. One row changed.
 *** Total elapsed time was 1 second.
```

Figure 18.32

Here are the current rows.

```
SELECT * FROM BITEMPORAL ORDER BY 1;

 *** Query completed. 7 rows found. 2 columns returned.
 *** Total elapsed time was 1 second.

     emp_no  dept_no
-----------  -------
    1000234       10
    1256349      400
    1324657      200
    1333454      200
    2000000      300
    2312225      300
    2341218      400
```

Figure 18.33

The following figure shows the current Valid-Time rows. Notice how the original row has been closed and a new row has been inserted to reflect the change.

SEQUENCED VALIDTIME SELECT * FROM BiTemporal
ORDER BY 1;

```
 *** Query completed. 12 rows found. 3 columns returned.
 *** Total elapsed time was 1 second.

     emp_no  dept_no  VALIDTIME
-----------  -------  ------------------------
    1000234       10  ('95/06/28', '99/12/31')
    1121334      400  ('94/03/13', '11/09/15')
    1232578      100  ('13/01/17', '99/12/31')
    1256349      400  ('03/10/07', '99/12/31')
    1324657      200  ('05/05/05', '99/12/31')
    1333454      200  ('06/12/15', '99/12/31')
    2000000      200  ('83/07/07', '01/01/15')
    2000000        ?  ('01/01/15', '12/02/27')
    2000000      300  ('12/02/27', '13/01/15')
    2000000      200  ('13/01/15', '99/12/31')
    2312225      300  ('99/03/15', '99/12/31')
    2341218      400  ('07/07/17', '99/12/31')
```

Figure 18.34

And here are the rows that are "open" in Transaction-Time.

```
CURRENT TRANSACTIONTIME SELECT * FROM BiTemporal
ORDER BY 1;

 *** Query completed. 7 rows found. 2 columns returned.
 *** Total elapsed time was 1 second.

     emp_no  dept_no
-----------  -------
    1000234       10
    1256349      400
    1324657      200
    1333454      200
    2000000      300
    2312225      300
    2341218      400
```

Figure 18.35

Here are all of the Transaction-Time rows. Notice how the changed row has been closed and a new row inserted.

```
NONSEQUENCED TRANSACTIONTIME SELECT * FROM BiTemporal
ORDER BY 1;

  emp_no   dept_no   tracking
 --------  --------  ----------------------------------------
 1000234        10   ('2012-02-27 08:35:01.380000-08:00', '9999-12-31 23:59:59.999999+00:00')
 1256349       400   ('2012-02-27 08:35:01.510000-08:00', '9999-12-31 23:59:59.999999+00:00')
 1324657       200   ('2012-02-27 08:35:01.540000-08:00', '9999-12-31 23:59:59.999999+00:00')
 1333454       200   ('2012-02-27 08:35:01.570000-08:00', '9999-12-31 23:59:59.999999+00:00')
 2000000         ?   ('2012-02-27 08:35:01.640000-08:00', '2012-02-27 08:39:05.000000-08:00')
 2000000       300   ('2012-02-27 08:39:05.000000-08:00', '9999-12-31 23:59:59.999999+00:00')
 2312225       300   ('2012-02-27 08:35:01.700000-08:00', '9999-12-31 23:59:59.999999+00:00')
 2341218       400   ('2012-02-27 08:35:01.730000-08:00', '9999-12-31 23:59:59.999999+00:00')
```

Figure 18.36

The Personnel department has notified us that employee 1121334 is rejoining the company and is to be assigned to department 300. Looking back at the Valid-Time rows, there is a history row for the employee, but the employee also isn't known within Transaction-Time. Therefore, the following Update won't make any changes since the employee isn't known in Current-Time.

```
UPDATE BiTemporal SET dept_no = 300 WHERE emp_no =
1121334;

 *** Update completed. No rows changed.
 *** Total elapsed time was 1 second.
```

Figure 18.37

```
INSERT INTO BiTemporal VALUES(1121334, 300);

 *** Insert completed. One row added.
 *** Total elapsed time was 1 second.
```

Figure 18.38

The following is the result of the Insert on Valid-Time and Transaction-Time.

```
SEQUENCED VALIDTIME SELECT * FROM BiTemporal
ORDER BY 1;

 *** Query completed. 13 rows found. 3 columns returned.
 *** Total elapsed time was 1 second.

     emp_no  dept_no  VALIDTIME
-----------  -------  ------------------------
    1000234       10  ('95/06/28', '99/12/31')
    1121334      400  ('94/03/13', '11/09/15')
    1121334      300  ('12/02/27', '99/12/31')
    1232578      100  ('13/01/17', '99/12/31')
    1256349      400  ('03/10/07', '99/12/31')
    1324657      200  ('05/05/05', '99/12/31')
    1333454      200  ('06/12/15', '99/12/31')
    2000000      200  ('83/07/07', '01/01/15')
    2000000        ?  ('01/01/15', '12/02/27')
    2000000      300  ('12/02/27', '13/01/15')
    2000000      200  ('13/01/15', '99/12/31')
    2312225      300  ('99/03/15', '99/12/31')
    2341218      400  ('07/07/17', '99/12/31')
```

Figure 18.39

```
NONSEQUENCED TRANSACTIONTIME SELECT *
FROM BiTemporal ORDER BY 1;

 *** Query completed. 9 rows found. 3 columns returned.
 *** Total elapsed time was 1 second.

  emp_no  dept_no  tracking
--------  -------  ----------------------------------------
 1000234       10  ('2012-02-27 08:35:01.380000-08:00', '9999-12-31 23:59:59.999999+00:00')
 1121334      300  ('2012-02-27 09:40:31.730000-08:00', '9999-12-31 23:59:59.999999+00:00')
 1256349      400  ('2012-02-27 08:35:01.510000-08:00', '9999-12-31 23:59:59.999999+00:00')
 1324657      200  ('2012-02-27 08:35:01.540000-08:00', '9999-12-31 23:59:59.999999+00:00')
 1333454      200  ('2012-02-27 08:35:01.570000-08:00', '9999-12-31 23:59:59.999999+00:00')
 2000000        ?  ('2012-02-27 08:35:01.640000-08:00', '2012-02-27 08:39:05.000000-08:00')
 2000000      300  ('2012-02-27 08:39:05.000000-08:00', '9999-12-31 23:59:59.999999+00:00')
 2312225      300  ('2012-02-27 08:35:01.700000-08:00', '9999-12-31 23:59:59.999999+00:00')
 2341218      400  ('2012-02-27 08:35:01.730000-08:00', '9999-12-31 23:59:59.999999+00:00')
```

Figure 18.40

The Personnel department has notified us that employee 2312225 has decided to leave the company. Here is the statement to remove the employee's row from the table.

```
DELETE FROM BiTemporal WHERE emp_no = 2312225;

 *** Delete completed. One row removed.
 *** Total elapsed time was 1 second.
```

Figure 18.41

The following queries show the resulting effect on the Valid-Time and Transaction-Time rows.

```
SELECT * FROM BITEMPORAL ORDER BY 1;


 *** Query completed. 7 rows found. 2 columns returned.
 *** Total elapsed time was 1 second.

     emp_no  dept_no
-----------  -------
    1000234       10
    1121334      300
    1256349      400
    1324657      200
    1333454      200
    2000000      300
    2341218      400
```

Figure 18.42

SEQUENCED VALIDTIME SELECT * FROM BiTemporal
ORDER BY 1;

```
 *** Query completed. 13 rows found. 3 columns returned.
 *** Total elapsed time was 1 second.

     emp_no  dept_no  VALIDTIME
-----------  -------  ------------------------
    1000234       10  ('95/06/28', '99/12/31')
    1121334      400  ('94/03/13', '11/09/15')
    1121334      300  ('12/02/27', '99/12/31')
    1232578      100  ('13/01/17', '99/12/31')
    1256349      400  ('03/10/07', '99/12/31')
    1324657      200  ('05/05/05', '99/12/31')
    1333454      200  ('06/12/15', '99/12/31')
    2000000      200  ('83/07/07', '01/01/15')
    2000000        ?  ('01/01/15', '12/02/27')
    2000000      300  ('12/02/27', '13/01/15')
    2000000      200  ('13/01/15', '99/12/31')
    2312225      300  ('99/03/15', '12/02/27')
    2341218      400  ('07/07/17', '99/12/31')
```

Figure 18.43

```
NONSEQUENCED TRANSACTIONTIME SELECT *
FROM BiTemporal ORDER BY 1;

 *** Query completed. 9 rows found. 3 columns returned.
 *** Total elapsed time was 1 second.

   emp_no  dept_no  tracking
---------  -------  ------------------------------------
  1000234       10  ('2012-02-27 08:35:01.380000-08:00', '9999-12-31 23:59:59.999999+00:00')
  1121334      300  ('2012-02-27 09:40:31.730000-08:00', '9999-12-31 23:59:59.999999+00:00')
  1256349      400  ('2012-02-27 08:35:01.510000-08:00', '9999-12-31 23:59:59.999999+00:00')
  1324657      200  ('2012-02-27 08:35:01.540000-08:00', '9999-12-31 23:59:59.999999+00:00')
  1333454      200  ('2012-02-27 08:35:01.570000-08:00', '9999-12-31 23:59:59.999999+00:00')
  2000000        ?  ('2012-02-27 08:35:01.640000-08:00', '2012-02-27 08:39:05.000000-08:00')
  2000000      300  ('2012-02-27 08:39:05.000000-08:00', '9999-12-31 23:59:59.999999+00:00')
  2312225      300  ('2012-02-27 08:35:01.700000-08:00', '2012-02-27 09:53:22.880000-08:00')
  2341218      400  ('2012-02-27 08:35:01.730000-08:00', '9999-12-31 23:59:59.999999+00:00')
```

Figure 18.44

You cannot normally set or modify the value of a transaction-time column. Teradata Database maintains these values automatically. (However, for database maintenance and troubleshooting, closed rows can be modified or deleted by administrators who have been granted the NONTEMPORAL privilege.)

Unlike transaction-time, however, history rows in tables with valid-time remain accessible to temporal SQL queries and DML.

Remember, even though temporal tables are multiset tables, no more than one row for any PI value can be Current in a validtime table, Open in a transactiontime table, or both in a bitemporal table.

AS OF Queries

An as of query is a SELECT statement that extracts and operates on rows in temporal tables with valid-time and transaction-time periods that overlap an AS OF date or time specified in the query. As of queries operate on the data as a snapshot at any point in time. Typically, as of queries are used for querying historical data.

The AS OF clause can be applied to the valid-time and transaction-time dimensions together or independently. When applied to the valid-time dimension, it retrieves rows where the PV overlaps the specified AS OF time. When applied to the transaction-time dimension, it retrieves rows with transaction-time periods that overlap the specified AS OF time.

An as of query is similar in semantics to a current query; an AS OF extracts the information based on the specified time and a current query extract the information as of the current time or date of the query being executed. However, a current query operates on only open rows in the transaction-time dimension. An AS OF query can read rows as of a particular point in time in the transaction-time dimension regardless of whether the rows are closed or open.

An as of query produces a nontemporal table as a result set.

Here's an Explain of an AS OF query.

EXPLAIN
AS OF CURRENT_DATE SELECT * FROM bitemporal ORDER BY 1;

```
Explanation
---------------------------------------------------------
  1) First, we lock a distinct CSQL_CLASS."pseudo table"
for read on a RowHash to prevent global deadlock for
CSQL_CLASS.bitemporal.
  2) Next, we lock CSQL_CLASS.bitemporal for read.
  3) We do an all-AMPs RETRIEVE step from
CSQL_CLASS.bitemporal (with temporal qualifier as
"VALIDTIME AS OF DATE '2013-04-03' AND TRANSACTIONTIME AS
OF DATE '2013-04-03'") by way of an all-rows scan with a
condition of ("((BEGIN(CSQL_CLASS.bitemporal.tracking
))<= TIMESTAMP '2013-04-03 00:00:00.000000+00:00') AND
(((END(CSQL_CLASS.bitemporal.dept_assign ))> DATE '2013-04-
03')AND (((BEGIN(CSQL_CLASS.bitemporal.dept_assign ))<=
DATE '2013-04-03') AND ((END(CSQL_CLASS.bitemporal.tracking
))> TIMESTAMP '2013-04-03 00:00:00.000000+00:00')))") into
Spool 1 (group_amps), which is built locally on the AMPs.
Then we do a SORT to order Spool 1 by the sort key in spool
field1.  The size of Spool 1 is estimated with no
confidence to be 7 rows (266 bytes). The estimated time for
this step is 0.03 seconds.
  4) Finally, we send out an END TRANSACTION step to all
AMPs involved in processing the request.
  -> The contents of Spool 1 are sent back to the user as
the result of statement 1.  The total estimated time is
0.03 seconds.
```

Figure 18.45

Chapter 18: Practice Questions

1. Which of the following is correct?
    a. PERIOD DATE'2011-01-01', UNTILCHANGED
    b. PERIOD (DATE'2011-01-01', UNTIL CHANGED)
    c. (PERIOD DATE 2011-01-01, UNTIL_CHANGED)
    d. PERIOD(DATE'2011-01-01', UNTIL_CHANGED)

2. Given the following column definition:

    Col2 PERIOD(DATE)

    and the following insert:

    INSERT INTO pt VALUES(1, PERIOD(DATE'2000-01-01', UNTIL_CHANGED));

    what will the following query return?

    SELECT NEXT(LAST(c2));

    a. Error
    b. 2001-12-31
    c. 2000-12-31
    d. 2001-01-01

3. Given the following table:

```
CREATE TABLE granule_test
(c1 INTEGER NOT NULL
,c2 PERIOD(DATE)
,c3 PERIOD(TIME(2))
,c4 PERIOD(TIME WITH TIME ZONE)
,c5 PERIOD(TIMESTAMP(4))
,c6 PERIOD(TIMESTAMP WITH TIME ZONE)
) PRIMARY INDEX(c1);
```

and the following insert:

```
INSERT INTO granule_test VALUES
(1
,PERIOD(DATE'2011-09-26')
,PERIOD(TIME'11:22:33.44')
,PERIOD(TIME'09:09:09.000000+00:00')
,PERIOD(TIMESTAMP'2011-09-26 10:10:10.0000')
,PERIOD(TIMESTAMP'2011-09-26
12:34:56.123456+00:00')
);
```

what will the ending value for column c2 be?

a. 2011-09-27
b. 2012-09-27
c. 2011-10-26
d. 2012-10-27

4. Given the following table:

```
CREATE TABLE granule_test
(c1 INTEGER NOT NULL
,c2 PERIOD(DATE)
,c3 PERIOD(TIME(2))
,c4 PERIOD(TIME WITH TIME ZONE)
,c5 PERIOD(TIMESTAMP(4))
,c6 PERIOD(TIMESTAMP WITH TIME ZONE)
) PRIMARY INDEX(c1);
```

and the following insert:

```
INSERT INTO granule_test VALUES
(1
,PERIOD(DATE'2011-09-26')
,PERIOD(TIME'11:22:33.44')
,PERIOD(TIME'09:09:09.000000+00:00')
,PERIOD(TIMESTAMP'2011-09-26 10:10:10.0000')
,PERIOD(TIMESTAMP'2011-09-26
12:34:56.123456+00:00')
);
```

What will the ending value for column c6 be?

a. 2011-09-26 12:34:56.123456+00:00
b. 2011-09-26 12:34:56.123457+00:00
c. 2011-09-26 12:34:57.123456+00:00
d. 2011-09-26 12:34:56.123456+00:01

5. The use of the AS OF modifier requires a table containing _____.

a. TRANSACTIONTIME columns.
b. VALID_TIME and TRANSACTION_TIME columns.
c. VALID_TIME columns.
d. VALIDTIME and TRANSACTIONTIME columns.

6. In order to modify or set a value in a transactiontime column, an administrator must have which permission?
    a. Modify Timestamp
    b. Modify Transactiontime
    c. Non Temporal
    d. Override Delete

7. Use the word list below to fill in the following sentence correctly.

    Even though temporal tables are ___ tables, no more the one row for any ____ can be ____ in a _____ table, ____ in a _____ table, or ____ in a _____ table.

    a. bitemporal
    b. both
    c. Current
    d. multiset
    e. open
    f. PI value
    g. transactiontime
    h. validtime

Chapter Notes

Utilize this space for notes, key points to remember, diagrams, areas of further study, etc.

Chapter 19: Stored Procedures

Certification Objectives

- ✓ Identify the functionality of Stored Procedures.
- ✓ Identify conditions when Stored Procedures may be used.
- ✓ Describe the types and uses of Stored Procedure parameters and variables.
- ✓ Describe methods to debug Stored Procedures.

Before You Begin

You should be familiar with the following terms and concepts.

Terms	Key Concepts
SPL	Knowledge of SPL statements such as those used for logic flow control, variable and cursor declaration and exception handling.
External Stored Procedures	Understanding of how they are different than SQL Stored Procedures (SPs).
DML / DDL	Knowledge of these statements and which ones are available for use in Stored Procedures.

An SQL Stored Procedure is a combination of SQL statements and procedural statements called Stored Procedure Language (SPL) statements. It is not necessary for SQL statements to be present – it may consist solely of SPL statements. An External Stored Procedure is written in C, C++ or Java language. It also may contain SQL however it is submitted using the CLIv2, ODBC or JDBC interfaces. The majority of the information in this section concerns SQL Stored Procedures.

A stored procedure is a database object executed on the Teradata Database. Typically, a stored procedure consists of a procedure name, input and output parameters, and a procedure body.

For each stored procedure, the database stores the SPs consisting of the procedure body you write and the corresponding compiled object code. The Data Dictionary tables contain stored procedure parameters and attributes.

A stored procedure provides control and condition handling statements, in addition to input and output parameters and local variables, which make SQL a computationally complete programming language.

Applications based on stored procedures provide the following benefits over equivalent embedded SQL applications:

- Better performance because of greatly reduced network traffic between the client and server.
- Better application maintenance because business rules are encapsulated and enforced on the server.
- Better transaction control.
- Better application security by restricting user access to procedures rather than requiring them to access data tables directly.
- Better application execution because all SQL language statements are embedded in a stored procedure to be executed on the server through one CALL statement.

Nested CALL statements extend performance by combining all transactions and complex queries in the nested procedures into one explicit transaction, and by handling errors internally in the nested procedures.

Stored Procedures allow the combination of both SPL (Stored Procedures Language) and SQL control statements to manage the delivery and execution of the procedure.

CREATE PROCEDURE

A stored procedure is created like all Teradata objects using a CREATE statement. However, it is stored as an executable piece of code. In order for a stored procedure to be executable, it must be compiled as part of the CREATE request. A stored procedure can be created from the following:

- BTEQ utility using the .COMPILE command
- CLIv2 applications, ODBC, JDBC, and Teradata SQL Assistant using the SQL CREATE PROCEDURE or REPLACE PROCEDURE statement.

Once compiled, the Stored Procedure is stored in a user database as an object, and seen as a "P" when using a HELP USER or HELP DATABASE command.

The following is the basic syntax to CREATE a procedure:

```
CREATE PROCEDURE  [<database-name>.]<procedure-name>
( [ <parameter-list> ] )  <procedure-body>;
```

Elements in a Procedure Body

A procedure body can contain the following elements:

Stored procedure body of this type ...	Can contain the following ...
Single statement	one SQL statement or control statement, including dynamic SQL. Note: The following elements are not allowed: • Any declaration (local variable, cursor, or condition handler) statement • A cursor statement (OPEN, FETCH, or CLOSE)
Compound statement	• Local variable declarations • Cursor declarations • Condition handler declaration statements • Control statements • DDL, DCL, and DML statements supported by stored procedures, including dynamic SQL

Figure 19.1

Stored Procedural Language (SPL) Statements

The <procedure-body> may contain any or all of the following SPL commands:

- BEGIN / END – Defines scope and functionality of the procedure body
- CALL – Executes a procedure from a procedure

- CASE/ END CASE – Provides simplified IF/THEN/ELSE logic when processing multiple rows from an open cursor
- DECLARE – Optional, establishes local variables or handler routines for use within the procedure
- FOR / END FOR – Executes a statement for each row fetched from a table by the implied cursor
- IF / END IF - Provides for a conditional test of a variable
- ITERATE - Permits logic branching to defined labels within the stored procedure. Functions like a GO TO statement
- LEAVE – Allows for an exit from a loop
- LOOP / END LOOP – Defines the processing logic to repeat unconditionally
- REPEAT / END REPEAT - Repeats the execution of one or more statements until the specified condition evaluates to true
- SET – Assigns a value to a variable or parameter
- WHILE / END WHILE – Repeats the execution of a statement or statement list while a specified condition evaluates to true

BEGIN / END Statements

The BEGIN and END specifications are both required and they define the body of the procedure. All other SPL commands will be contained within the boundaries delineated by these two statements. Again, they are both required and because of the dependency on each other, they are referred to as a compound statement.

The following demonstrates a simple procedure with a single section used to INSERT a row with all null values into the Customer table:

```
CREATE PROCEDURE First_Procedure ( )
BEGIN
   INSERT INTO Customer_table DEFAULT VALUES;
END;
```

Figure 19.2

To execute the procedure:

```
CALL first_procedure( );
```

Figure 19.3

After the execution of the above procedure, the next SELECT returns:

```
SELECT * FROM customer_table;

Result: 6 rows returned

Customer_Number  Customer_name          Phone_number
---------------  ---------------------  ------------
       31313131  Acme Designs           555-5564
              ?  ?                      ?
       31323134  ABC Consulting         555-1010
       57896883  XYZ Landscapers        447-7954
       11111111  Best Electronics       559-9987
       87323456  Database Pros          622-1012
```

Figure 19.4

Establishing Variables and Data Values

A stored procedure can be written to provide additional functionality by naming local variables to store and manipulate values. The variables receive their values either by being explicitly assigned internally or passed from the client that calls the procedure. This can be accomplished by doing the following:

- A DECLARE statement is used to establish the variable.
- A SET statement is used to assign a value to a variable within a procedure.

The value may be a literal or an equation. However, before using a variable name, the name and the data type must be defined.

DECLARE Statement to Define Variables

The DECLARE is primarily used to establish a local variable name for use within the stored procedure. The variable is called 'local' because it is local to the compound statement in which it is defined.

Variable Declaration Rules

Variables within the same procedure need to follow the below rules:

- You can only declare local variables within a BEGIN ... END compound statement.
- You can specify any number of local variable declarations in each BEGIN ... END compound statement. Each declaration must end with a semicolon character.
- Within each declaration, you can specify any number of local variables, separated by commas in a list.
- The scope of a local variable is the BEGIN ... END compound statement in which it is declared and all nested compound statements.
- No two variables declared in a compound statement can have the same name.
- A variable name can, however, be reused in any nested compound statement.
- Each local variable declaration consists of the following elements:
  - Local variable name (mandatory)
  - Variable data type (mandatory)
  - Default value for the local variable (optional)

Variable declaration syntax is:

DECLARE *var1* [, *var2* ...] <data_type> [DEFAULT {*literal* | <u>NULL</u> }] ;

An example is:

DECLARE v01, v02, v03 CHAR(5) DEFAULT 'xxxxx' ;

If the three variables have different data types or default values, then declare them individually:

DECLARE v01 INT;
DECLARE v02 SMALLINT DEFAULT 0;
DECLARE v03 CHAR(20) DEFAULT 'No errors';

Additionally, a variable name cannot be any of these reserved Status variable names:

Status Variable	Description
SQLCODE	Its use has been largely superseded by the use of the ANSI variable SQLSTATE. It is implicitly declared within a stored procedure application as SMALLINT.
SQLSTATE	SQLSTATE is a CHAR(5) value divided logically into a two-character class and a three-character subclass. Subclass values can be any numeric or simple uppercase Latin character string. This is declared implicitly within a stored procedure application.

ACTIVITY_COUNT	The ACTIVITY_COUNT status variable returns the number of rows affected by an SQL DML statement in an embedded SQL or stored procedure application. It is declared implicitly within a stored procedure application as DEC(18,0). ACTIVITY_COUNT is a Teradata extension to the ANSI SQL-2003 standard.

Figure 19.5

A successful completion will assign the value of zero to the SQLSTATE and SQLCODE variables. Since SQLSTATE is a CHAR field, it will be '00000' for comparison purposes.

The next procedure defines var1 as a local variable and assigns an initial value using a DEFAULT and then substitutes the value into the WHERE clause of a DELETE:

```
CREATE PROCEDURE Second_Procedure ( )
 BEGIN
   DECLARE var1   INTEGER  DEFAULT  11111111;
        DELETE FROM Customer_table
        WHERE Customer_number = :var1;
 END;
```

Figure 19.6

SET to Assign a Data Value as a Variable

The SET statement is an assignment statement. Once the variable name and data type have been defined, a value needs to be assigned. As seen above, the DEFAULT can establish an initial value. It may retain the initial value throughout the life of the procedure, or may be modified at any time using a SET command.

The following is an alternate Second_Procedure used to SET the value instead of using DEFAULT:

```
CREATE PROCEDURE Second_Procedure ( )
 BEGIN
  DECLARE var1   INTEGER ;
  SET var1 = 11111111 ;
       DELETE FROM Customer_table
WHERE customer_number = :var1;
 END;
```

Figure 19.7

Assigning a Data Value as a Parameter

Like macros, stored procedures may receive information passed from the client software. This ability provides much more flexibility and enhances the power of stored procedures. When using parameters in a stored procedure, the syntax for a parameter list is comprised of three elements: <parameter-usage> <parameter-name> <data-type>

- <parameter-usage> can be one of these:
    - IN only provides input from the caller (default)
    - OUT only provides output to the caller
    - INOUT allows both input and output for the caller
- <parameter-name> is any valid Teradata SQL name
- <data-type> is any valid Teradata data type

The following is an alternative to and a better version of Second_Procedure that receives the value from the CALLer and passes the value for var1 instead of using a DECLARE or SET:

```
CREATE PROCEDURE Second_Procedure (IN  var1 INTEGER )
 BEGIN
        DELETE FROM  Customer_table
WHERE Customer_number = :var1;
 END;
```

Figure 19.8

CALL Statement

The CALL is used to execute a stored procedure. The CALL statement is normally executed either by a client program or interactively by a user. Additionally, a stored procedure is allowed to call another stored procedure.

The following CALL executes the first procedure shown above:

```
CALL First_Procedure ( );
```

Figure 19.9

Since the First_Procedure does not define any parameters, none are passed to it. However, Second_Procedure has evolved to the point of expecting a parameter value at run time to identify the row to delete. The next CALL executes the Second_Procedure and passes the value of 11111111:

```
CALL Second_Procedure(11111111);
```

Figure 19.10

Now, the procedure can be called again and a different row can be deleted using:

```
CALL Second_Procedure(31313131);
```

Figure 19.11

Exception Handling

At times, things may happen within stored procedures that are unexpected. The status variables can be a major help in determining what happened. However, at times, the same error handling logic might be needed multiple times within the same procedure. When this is the case, a Handler routine may be written to "handle" the condition. This is an alternative to coding the same IF statements multiple times.

DECLARE HANDLER Statement

The DECLARE is also used to establish a Handler as well as a variable. A Handler is a section of logic that executes automatically based on error conditions that may occur during the execution of a stored procedure. The syntax for DECLARE HANDLER:

DECLARE <handler-type> HANDLER
FOR { *<sqlstate-code-list>* | *<generic-condition-list>* }
<handler-action>;

Syntax element ...	Specifies ...
CONTINUE	executes the handler action and passes control to the next statement following the statement that invoked it.
EXIT	Executes the handler action and then implicitly exits the BEGN...END compound statement in

	which the handler is declared. If the procedure contains no other compound statement, the procedure terminates or returns to its caller.
sqlstate-code	the five-character literal SQLSTATE code to be handled. You can specify any number of valid SQLSTATE values in a comma-separated list, but '00000' which represents successful completion of statements, is not allowed. You can specify either a list of SQLSTATE values or a list of generic conditions, but not both.
SQLEXCEPTION SQLWARNING NOT FOUND	generic condition to be handled. You can specify one of these or any combination of the generic conditions in a comma-separated list in a handler declaration. These can be specified in any order, but you cannot repeat any generic condition in the same compound statement.
handler-action	either a single statement or multiple statements enclosed in a compound statement that defines the handler action. The handler action is executed when a particular exception or completion condition is returned to the application. The statement(s) can be any of the following: • SQL DML, DDL, or DCL statements supported by stored procedures. • Control statements, including nested compound statements.

	Declaration (local variable, cursor, or handler) statements are not allowed as a single statement for handler action. These can be submitted from within a compound statement.

Figure 19.12

The next procedure contains two handler routines, the first one is a CONTINUE type and the second is an EXIT:

```
CREATE PROCEDURE Samp_Hdlr ( )
BEGIN
   DECLARE CONTINUE HANDLER
       FOR SQLSTATE '41020', SQLSTATE '52100'
      INSERT INTO My_Err_Tbl
      VALUES (:SQLSTATE, 'Error Handled');
DECLARE EXIT HANDLER
      FOR SQLEXCEPTION
      INSERT INTO My_Err_Tbl (:SQLSTATE, 'Unknown Error');
END;
```

Figure 19.13

DML Statements

These DML statements are allowed in a stored procedure:

INSERT (using UPI or USI)
UPDATE (using UPI or USI)
DELETE (using UPI or USI)
SELECT-INTO (using UPI or USI)
DELETE using cursor (for multiple rows in FOR statement)
UPDATE using cursor (for multiple rows in FOR statement)
SELECT using cursor (for multiple rows in FOR statement)
Nested CALL statements

Figure 19.14

The syntax for the SELECT-INTO is:

```
{ SELECT | SEL } <column-list> INTO <assignment-target-list>
FROM <table-name>
WHERE  <comparison>
[ <other-clauses> ];
```

Here's an example:

```
CREATE PROCEDURE NewProc
(IN name CHAR(12),
IN number INTEGER,
IN dept INTEGER,
IN salary DECIMAL(10,2),
OUT dname CHAR(10))
        BEGIN
        INSERT INTO Employee_Table
                (EmpName, EmpNo, DeptNo, Salary_Amount)
                VALUES (:name, :number, :dept, :salary);
        SELECT DeptName INTO dname FROM Department
        WHERE DeptNo = dept;
END;
```

Figure 19.15

DDL Statements

The following DDL statements in a stored procedure are allowed when the creator is also the owner of the procedure. That is, a stored procedure can contain DDL statements only if it is created in the database of the user.

ALTER FUNCTION	CREATE TRIGGER	DROP USER
ALTER TABLE	CREATE USER	DROP VIEW
ALTER TRIGGER	CREATE VIEW	END LOGGING
BEGIN LOGGING	DELETE DATABASE	MODIFY DATABASE
COLLECT STATISTICS (Optimizer Form)	DELETE USER	LOGGING ONLINE ARCHIVE OFF
COLLECT STATISTICS (QCD Form)	DROP CAST	SET QUERY BAND ... FOR TRANSACTION
COMMENT	DROP DATABASE	MODIFY PROFILE
CREATE CAST	DROP ERROR TABLE	MODIFY USER
CREATE DATABASE	DROP HASH INDEX	RENAME MACRO
CREATE ERROR TABLE	DROP INDEX	RENAME PROCEDURE

CREATE FUNCTION	DROP JOIN INDEX	RENAME TABLE
CREATE HASH INDEX	DROP MACRO	RENAME TRIGGER
CREATE INDEX	DROP ORDERING	RENAME VIEW
CREATE JOIN INDEX	DROP PROCEDURE	REPLACE CAST
CREATE MACRO	DROP PROFILE	REPLACE FUNCTION
CREATE ORDERING	DROP ROLE	REPLACE MACRO
CREATE PROFILE	DROP STATISTICS	REPLACE ORDERING
CREATE ROLE	DROP TABLE	REPLACE TRANSFORM
CREATE TABLE	DROP TRANSFORM	REPLACE TRIGGER
CREATE TRANSFORM	DROP TRIGGER	REPLACE VIEW

Figure 19.16

External Stored Procedures

External stored procedures are written in the C, C++, or Java programming language. In addition, they are installed on the database, and are executed similarly to stored procedures.

Usage

Below is a synopsis of the steps you need to follow in order to develop, compile, install, and use external stored procedures:

- When using Java, place the class or classes for the external stored procedure in a JAR file and call the SQLJ.INSTALL_JAR external stored procedure to register the JAR file and its classes with the database.
- Use CREATE PROCEDURE or REPLACE PROCEDURE for external stored procedures to create a database object for the external stored procedure.
- Use GRANT option to grant privileges to users who are authorized to use the external stored procedure.
- Invoke the procedure using the CALL statement.

Executing SQL from External Stored Procedures

To execute SQL within an External Stored Procedure, use the following guidelines:

- C or C++ external stored procedure use CLIv2
- Java external stored procedure use JDBC

Differences between Stored Procedures and External Stored Procedures

Using external stored procedures is very similar to in-database stored procedures, except for the following:

- Invoking an external stored procedure from a client application does not count against nesting limit.
- To install an external stored procedure on a database, you must have the CREATE EXTERNAL PROCEDURE privilege on the database.
- The CREATE PROCEDURE statement for external stored procedures is different from the CREATE PROCEDURE statement for stored procedures.
- In addition to syntax differences, you do not have to use the .COMPILE command as with BTEQ.

Macros or Stored Procedures for Tactical Queries

Macros were once a better choice than stored procedures for simple requests, multi-statement requests (statements executed in parallel), and statements returning multiple rows because performance was almost always better. Stored procedures now support multi-statement requests and result sets, and with their conditional logic, are a better choice than macros for running tactical queries.

Simple Requests

Stored procedures may perform better than macros for simple requests. You can use either macros or stored procedures to run simple requests.

Multi-statement Requests

Both macros and stored procedures support multi-statement requests. Multi-statement request performance for stored procedures is the same, if not better than, macro performance.

Statements Returning Multiple Rows

Stored procedures now support result sets, which means that a stored procedure can now return multiple rows. Macros have no advantage over stored procedures in returning multiple rows.

Differences between Macros and Stored Procedures

The following table summarizes the differences between macros and stored procedures:

MACRO	STORED PROCEDURE
Limited procedural logic.	Sophisticated procedural logic.
Can return multi-row result sets for the same request.	DYNAMIC RESULT SETS allows the stored procedure to return up to 15 result sets.

Multi-statement request parallelizes multiple single row statements.	Multi-statement request using the BEGIN REQUEST – END REQUEST statements parallelizes multiple single row DML statements.
Macro text stored in dictionary.	Stored procedure text stored in user database.
Can EXPLAIN a macro.	Cannot EXPLAIN a stored procedure. Instead must EXPLAIN each individual stored procedure SQL statement individually.
Can be invoked by a trigger.	Can be invoked by a trigger.

Figure 19.17

Chapter 19: Practice Questions

1. Which of the following is the correct way to declare multiple variables, in a Stored Procedure, that have different characteristics?
   a. DECLARE v1 int, v2 CHAR(20), v3 SMALLINT
   b. DECLARE v1 int, v2 CHAR(20), v3 SMALLINT;
   c. DECLARE v1 int; v2 CHAR(20); v3 SMALLINT;
   d. DECLARE v1 int; DECLARE v2 CHAR(20); DECLARE v3 SMALLINT;

2. Which of the following variables has been deprecated by ANSI?
   a. SQLSTATE
   b. SQLCODE
   c. SQL_STATE
   d. SQL_CODE

3. Which statement about Stored Procedures is true?
   a. They are stored in a user database.
   b. They are stored in the Data Dictionary.
   c. They cannot be invoked by a trigger.
   d. You can EXPLAIN a Stored Procedure.

4. Which of the following are not part of the Store Procedure Language? (Choose two)
   a. END FOR
   b. END REPEAT
   c. END DO
   d. END LOOP
   e. END DELACRE

Chapter Notes

Utilize this space for notes, key points to remember, diagrams, areas of further study, etc.

Appendix

Answers to the Chapter Practice Questions

CHAPTER 2	CHAPTER 3	CHAPTER 4
1. a=2 b=4 c=1 d=3 2. c 3. d 4. d 5. c 6. d	1. d 2. a 3. d 4. d 5. b 6. d	1. a 2. c 3. d 4. e 5. c 6. d
CHAPTER 5	**CHAPTER 6**	**CHAPTER 7**
1. a 2. d 3. d 4. b 5. a 6. b 7. d	1. b 2. c 3. a 4. c	1. b 2. c 3. e 4. a 5. d
CHAPTER 8	**CHAPTER 9**	**CHAPTER 10**
1. d 2. c 3. b 4. a	1. b 2. a 3. c 4. c	1. b 2. b 3. b 4. e

<table>
<tr>
<td>CHAPTER 11
1. c
2. a
3. d
4. a</td>
<td>CHAPTER 12
1. c
2. c
3. a
4. c</td>
<td>CHAPTER 13
1. b
2. b
3. a
4. c</td>
</tr>
<tr>
<td>CHAPTER 14
1. b
2. c
3. a</td>
<td>CHAPTER 15
1. e
2. a
3. a=SELECT
b=SELECT
c= INSERT or DELETE
d=DROP
4. 4 9
5. 4 8 9</td>
<td>CHAPTER 16
1. d
2. a=3
b=1
c=3
d=5
e=4
3. d
4. b
5. e</td>
</tr>
<tr>
<td>CHAPTER 17
1. c
2. a=3
b=1
c=2
d=3
e=2
3. a=2
b=3
c=2
d=1
e=1
4. a
5. c, e</td>
<td>CHAPTER 18
1. d
2. a
3. a
4. b
5. d
6. c
7. d, f, c, h, e, g, b, a</td>
<td>CHAPTER 19
1. d
2. b
3. a
4. c, e</td>
</tr>
</table>

Index

A

Aborting, 262
Active Data Warehousing, 9, 39, 59, 85, 103, 115, 133, 153, 172, 199, 211, 223, 235, 251, 269, 311, 385
Aggregation, 85, 89
Altering, 290, 295
ANSI, 33, 34, 39, 60, 62, 65, 66, 69, 75, 76, 77, 91, 133, 134, 136, 141, 142, 153, 158, 161, 162, 173, 174, 177, 178, 179, 183, 212, 217, 218, 224, 229, 240, 251, 257, 259, 261, 262, 263, 271, 274, 317, 392, 393, 405

B

BEGIN / END, 388, 389
BTET, 34, 141, 142, 251, 259, 260, 261
BYNET, ii

C

CALL, 47, 302, 386, 388, 390, 395, 396, 399, 401
CASE, 47, 223, 224, 225, 226, 227, 228, 229, 230, 389
CAST, 47, 66, 69, 70, 72, 81, 118, 137, 138, 141, 142, 143, 147, 400, 401
Certification, 1, 2, 3, 6, 7, 8, 9, 39, 59, 85, 103, 115, 133, 153, 171, 199, 211, 223, 235, 251, 269, 311, 331, 385
Certification Objectives, 9, 39, 59, 85, 103, 115, 133, 153, 171, 199, 211, 223, 235, 251, 269, 311, 331, 385
Certified Professional, 1, 3, 8
CHARACTER_LENGTH, 154, 158
COALESCE, 223, 229, 230, 232
Compound Comparisons, 20
Correlated Subquery, 103, 107
CREATE PROCEDURE, 387, 389, 393, 394, 395, 398, 400, 401, 402
CREATE TABLE, 48, 49, 154, 213, 215, 258, 269, 270, 275, 281, 282, 289, 293, 296, 299, 318, 401
Cross Join, 127, 128
CUBE, 95, 96, 99, 100

D

Data Conversions, 59, 66
Data Definition Language, 269
Data Interrogation, 223
Data Layers, 9, 39, 59, 85, 103, 115, 133, 153, 172, 199, 211, 223, 235, 251, 269, 311, 385
Data Manipulation, 211
Data Types, 59, 65, 133
Data Warehouse, 1
Date, 62, 66, 75, 92, 93, 94, 96, 98, 99, 133, 134, 137, 138, 141, 143, 144, 145, 177, 178, 180, 181, 182, 183, 184, 185, 191, 192, 282
Date Arithmetic, 137
DATEFORM, 136, 137
DDL, 242, 255, 259, 269, 303, 304, 385, 388, 397, 400
DELETE, 10, 211, 212, 254, 295, 298, 299, 301, 302, 317, 322, 393, 394, 395, 399, 400
Derived Tables, 311, 312
DESC, 179, 181, 182, 183
DISTINCT, 17, 18, 19, 53, 199, 237
DML, 211, 242, 259, 320, 385, 388, 393, 397, 399, 404

E

Evaluation Order, 125
Exam, 1, 2, 5, 6, 7
EXCEPT/MINUS, 205
Exception Handling, 396

EXPLAIN, 39, 51, 52, 53, 55, 242, 294, 303, 404
External Stored Procedures, 385, 401, 402
EXTRACT, 76, 77, 135, 139, 140, 141, 184, 185

F

FORMAT, 72, 73, 74, 75, 76, 77, 79, 110, 142, 143, 154, 272, 275, 276, 282, 313, 314

G

Global, 311, 317, 320, 321, 322, 323, 324, 325
GROUP BY, 89, 90, 91, 92, 93, 94, 95, 96, 98, 99, 100, 110, 140, 178, 181, 200, 215, 237, 314
GROUPING SETS, 93, 94, 98, 99, 100

H

HELP, 39, 40, 42, 43, 44, 47, 48, 49, 137, 237, 319, 387

I

IN, 9, 19, 28, 30, 104, 160, 163, 164, 228, 394, 395, 400
INDEX, 42, 49, 154, 161, 215, 274, 276, 279, 281, 282, 287, 291, 293, 295, 296, 299, 319, 321, 322, 400, 401
INNER JOIN, 115, 116, 117, 118, 126, 204, 244
INSERT, 10, 211, 213, 214, 215, 216, 217, 219, 254, 260, 262, 293, 299, 301, 302, 303, 313, 317, 389, 398, 399, 400
INSERT/SELECT, 211, 214
INTERSECT, 53, 199, 204, 206, 207
INTERVAL, 63, 64, 80, 144, 145, 146, 147, 148, 293, 295, 296

J

Join Processing, 115, 116

L

LIKE operator, 31
Linux, ii
Locking, 235, 251, 252

M

Macro, 43, 235, 240, 242, 259, 404
MERGE, 217, 218, 219, 301

N

NOT IN, 9, 28, 29, 104, 105, 106
NPPI, 129
Nulls, 13, 14, 26, 273

O

OCTET Function, 159
OLAP, 171, 172, 173, 174, 176, 183
ORDER BY, 10, 13, 14, 15, 16, 17, 18, 74, 77, 91, 92, 93, 94, 96, 98, 99, 100, 108, 110, 117, 118, 120, 121, 122, 123, 126, 140, 157, 158, 159, 160, 161, 162, 163, 164, 175, 176, 177, 178, 179, 180, 181, 182, 183, 184, 185, 191, 192, 194, 200, 201, 202, 203, 204, 225, 226, 228, 230, 236, 238, 243, 244, 246, 313, 314, 316
OUTER JOIN, 115, 119, 120, 121, 122, 123, 124, 200
OVERLAPS, 136, 147, 148

P

Parameterized Macros, 245
PARTITION BY, 179, 182, 183, 185
Partitioned, 290, 292

performance, 129
POSITION, 154, 159, 160, 161, 163, 164
PPI, 115, 128, 129, 131, 216, 217, 269, 292, 293, 295, 318, 320
Practice Questions, 36, 55, 81, 97, 111, 130, 149, 168, 195, 208, 220, 232, 248, 264, 306, 326, 380, 405
Primary Index, 129, 256, 274, 281, 282, 283, 285, 289, 290
Primary Key, 44, 271, 281, 282, 283

Q

QUALIFY, 181, 182, 183
Queue Tables, 298

R

Rank, 172
RANK, 179, 180, 181, 182, 183
RANK / OVER, 174, 179, 182
RDBMS, 1
Referential Integrity, 277, 303
Residual Conditions, 123
Roles, 303, 304
ROLLUP, 91, 92, 99, 100
Rounding, 59, 70
ROW_NUMBER / OVER, 183, 185

S

SAMPLE, 188, 191, 192, 194
SAMPLEID, 188, 191, 192
SELECT, 9, 10, 11, 12, 13, 14, 15, 16, 17, 18, 19, 20, 21, 22, 23, 24, 25, 27, 28, 29, 30, 33, 34, 51, 52, 69, 70, 72, 73, 74, 77, 85, 86, 88, 89, 90, 91, 92, 93, 94, 96, 98, 99, 100, 104, 105, 106, 108, 110, 115, 116, 117, 118, 120, 121, 122, 123, 126, 127, 128, 137, 138, 139, 140, 141, 142, 143, 144, 145, 146, 147, 148, 154, 155, 156, 157, 158, 159, 160, 161, 162, 163, 164, 177, 178, 180, 181, 182, 183, 184, 185, 188, 191, 192, 193, 194, 199, 201, 202, 203, 204, 205, 206, 207, 214, 215, 225, 226, 227, 228, 230, 237, 238, 239, 240, 243, 244, 246, 254, 256, 285, 289, 293, 294, 296, 297, 301, 313, 314, 316, 324, 390, 399, 400
Self-Join, 126
Set Operators, 199, 206
SHOW, 39, 48, 49, 50, 51, 237, 239, 242, 282, 319, 322
SPL, 385, 386, 388, 389
Stored Procedures, 385, 386, 402, 403
Subquery, 103, 104, 110
SUBSTR, 154, 159, 162
SUBSTRING, 154, 159, 162, 163, 164
SUM / OVER, 174, 177, 178

T

Table Aliasing, 115
Tactical Queries, 403
Technology, iv
Temporal, 133, 134, 354
Temporary Tables, 311, 317, 320, 322
Teradata, ii, iv, 77, 78
Teradata Administrator, ii
Time, 62, 133, 134, 141, 147, 301
TOP, 193, 194, 238
Transaction, 53, 141, 142, 251, 252, 257, 259, 260, 262
Trigger, 299, 301, 302
TRIM, 154, 155, 156, 157, 158, 243, 246, 314

U

UDFs, 77, 78
UDTs, 78
UNION, 53, 199, 200, 201, 202, 203, 206, 207, 315, 316
UNION ALL, 199, 202, 315, 316
Upgrade, 2
UPSERT, 211, 216, 217
User Defined Functions, 77

User Defined Types, 78
Utilities, 4, 5

V

View, 43, 235, 236, 237, 239, 253
Volatile, 311, 317, 318, 322

W

WHERE, 10, 19, 20, 21, 22, 23, 24, 25, 27, 28, 29, 30, 33, 34, 73, 74, 90, 104, 105, 106, 108, 110, 123, 124, 127, 128, 143, 144, 145, 146, 147, 148, 177, 178, 184, 185, 203, 207, 212, 216, 217, 227, 228, 238, 239, 261, 262, 263, 294, 296, 297, 312, 313, 316, 393, 394, 395, 399, 400